Living with Mild Cognitive Impairment

Living with Mild Cognitive Impairment

A Guide to Maximizing Brain Health and Reducing Risk of Dementia

NICOLE D. ANDERSON
Rotman Research Institute, Baycrest, Toronto, Canada
Departments of Psychiatry (Medicine) and Psychology, University of Toronto, Canada

KELLY J. MURPHY
Neuropsychology and Cognitive Health, Baycrest, Toronto, Canada
Department of Psychology, University of Toronto, Canada

ANGELA K. TROYER
Neuropsychology and Cognitive Health, Baycrest, Toronto, Canada
Department of Psychology, University of Toronto, Canada

OXFORD
UNIVERSITY PRESS

OXFORD
UNIVERSITY PRESS

Oxford University Press is a department of the University of Oxford.
It furthers the University's objective of excellence in research,
scholarship, and education by publishing worldwide.

Oxford   New York
Auckland   Cape Town   Dar es Salaam   Hong Kong   Karachi
Kuala Lumpur   Madrid   Melbourne   Mexico City   Nairobi
New Delhi   Shanghai   Taipei   Toronto

With offices in
Argentina   Austria   Brazil   Chile   Czech Republic   France   Greece
Guatemala   Hungary   Italy   Japan   Poland   Portugal   Singapore
South Korea   Switzerland   Thailand   Turkey   Ukraine   Vietnam

Oxford is a registered trademark of Oxford University Press in the
UK and certain other countries.

Published in the United States of America by
Oxford University Press
198 Madison Avenue, New York, NY 10016

Library of Congress Cataloging-in-Publication Data
Anderson, Nicole D.
Living with Mild Cognitive Impairment: a guide to maximizing
brain health and reducing risk of dementia / Nicole D. Anderson,
Kelly J. Murphy, Angela K. Troyer.
p. cm.
Includes bibliographical references and index.
ISBN-13: 978–0–19–976482–2 (pbk.)
1. Cognition disorders in old age—Diagnosis.   2. Cognition disorders in
old age—Treatment.   3. Cognition disorders—Nutritional aspects.
I. Murphy, Kelly J.   II. Troyer, Angela K.   III. Title.
RC553.C64A53 2012
618.97'8—dc23
2012006119

5 7 9 8 6 4
Printed in the United States of America on acid-free paper

For my family, Paul, Zoë, and Ben Fletcher, for giving me the best of both worlds. For my parents, Ron and Charlotte Anderson, for your unwavering support, this book is for you.

—*NDA*

For Rick, Roan, and Mary Russo, and my parents Paul and Sharron Murphy. Yes, I finally finished my 'book report' Mary.

—*KJM*

Dedicated to my parents, Dick and Kathy Troyer, who embody an active and engaged lifestyle post-retirement, and to the memory of my grandparents, John and Gertrude Powell and Ora and Freda Troyer. For Shawn, Graham, and Ellen, who keep my life interesting and full of adventure.

—*AKT*

Contents

Foreword

Ronald C. Petersen, PhD, MD
Professor of Neurology
Director, Mayo Clinic Study of Aging
Mayo Clinic College of Medicine
Rochester, Minnesota
Cora Kanow Professor of Alzheimer's Disease Research

Formerly, the field of aging and dementia involved two stages: normal cognition and dementia. Most of the research that had been done and the rating scales developed characterized a person as being normal or abnormal. More recently, however, it has become apparent that, with many types of dementia, including Alzheimer's disease, there is likely a gradual progression of clinical symptoms between the cognitive changes of normal aging and those that constitute a dementia. The term *mild cognitive impairment* (abbreviated MCI) was coined to address this gradual progression. I have been involved in research in this area since the early 1990s and have watched it blossom. Our group at the Mayo Clinic has been at the forefront of characterizing MCI and has contributed to the revision of new criteria for the condition.

Although the construct was somewhat foreign at its introduction, it has come to be accepted by practicing clinicians. There have been literally thousands of research articles written on MCI, and recent surveys of practicing clinicians have indicated that the term is used in clinical practice. In addition, several groups have incorporated the criteria into their overall diagnostic scheme. For example, recently, the National Institute on Aging and the Alzheimer's Association assembled panels to establish new criteria for the Alzheimer's disease spectrum. In this effort, MCI is defined as a state of minimal cognitive impairment with preservation of functional abilities, and the dementia is defined as the stage at which the person has cognitive and functional impairments due to the underlying biological process of Alzheimer's disease. These criteria were published in 2011 and are now being validated in the research community.

However, in spite of its acceptance in the medical community, relatively little is known about how to care for persons with MCI. Often people are concerned about their own memories as they age. Is this a part of normal aging or when should I become concerned? These answers are not readily available to patients and families. When the diagnosis is made, the patients need educational material about the nature of the condition and what to expect. There is a great deal of practical information, expectations, family implications, financial and retirement issues, among others that are not easily obtained. Currently, there are no medications for MCI, but lifestyle recommendations are becoming increasingly important. *Living with Mild Cognitive Impairment* fills this void. It provides basic background and diagnostic criteria for patients and families, but more importantly, it provides useful information for the treatment and expectations of the condition. I have seen many patients over the years who could have benefited from this type of resource, but none existed until now.

Living with Mild Cognitive Impairment constitutes an important addition to the field to help translate the construct of MCI to patients, families, and professionals. This work defines the essence of the clinical characterization of persons with MCI and describes how the diagnosis is made. The strengths and weaknesses of the condition are well articulated and the experienced authors discuss the nuances of making the diagnosis. In addition, the work describes expected outcomes and uncertainties for individuals with this diagnosis. Most important, this book provides practical information to patients, families and care providers on how to deal with individuals who experience this clinical condition. Because most patients are, by definition, quite mildly impaired at this point, they are often able to benefit from a variety of behavioral techniques designed to improve their overall function. Recent data indicate that these approaches may be quite beneficial at promoting stabilization of the condition over years. As such, this volume fills an important void.

Drs. Anderson, Murphy, and Troyer have done a superb job at translating the subtle complexities of these clinical conditions to the reader. There often can be issues involving jargon that make these constructs more obscure than they need to be, but these expert authors have avoided this trap. *Living with Mild Cognitive Impairment* is an excellent compendium on this condition and should be very useful for the field as well as for lay readers.

Preface

This book was inspired by our clients, our research participants, and by those close to us, many of whom have asked us to recommend a book on mild cognitive impairment (MCI). There are a handful of exceptional academic books on MCI written by our esteemed colleagues, but none written for a lay audience. Until now. We wrote this book for individuals with MCI, for their loved ones, and for the health-care professionals with whom they navigate their journey with MCI. Our aim is to provide you with knowledge about what MCI is, how it may affect you, and what you can do about it so that you can be proactive with your health and well-being as a person living with mild cognitive impairment.

The book is organized into three sections: What Is Mild Cognitive Impairment?, How Is Mild Cognitive Impairment Identified and Managed? and What Can Be Done To Improve Prognosis? Each section contains five chapters. Although we hope that you read the book cover to cover, each chapter was written so that it could be read and understood on its own.

The 15 chapters are book-ended by a case study, a story of a gentleman living with MCI. When we first meet him, he does not fully understand his diagnosis and is frustrated by his symptoms. By the end of the book, however, he is equipped with a variety of tools to effectively manage living with MCI. Each chapter also includes case vignettes, shorter stories of individuals illustrating points we are making in the book. These case vignettes, like the more extended case study in the prologue and epilogue, do not represent any real-life individual client, but rather each one is an amalgamation of many clients we have worked with over the years. We use these examples to demonstrate recurrent symptoms we have observed, concerns clients have expressed, and strategies that they have implemented. Many of the chapters also include "Questions to ask your doctor," and most chapters provide links to useful Web sites. The third section of the book contains worksheets to help guide you through healthy, proactive changes in your everyday living that will make MCI more manageable. These worksheets also can be downloaded from www. baycrest.org/livingwithMCI.

The three of us equally contributed to the writing and editing of this book. As clinical neuropsychologists and active researchers in the field of aging, we believe firmly in evidence-based clinical practice. Our goal with this book is to share scientifically substantiated information about all the important topics related to living with MCI. We cover a wide range of topics. For those who want further information, academic references are included at the end of the book, and each chapter includes recommended readings of books you can find in your local bookstore or library or Web sites you can visit. The Web site addresses in this book were valid at the time of publication; any updates to these addresses will be listed at www.baycrest. org/livingwithMCI.

We aimed to provide information on a variety of topics that would be useful to most people with MCI and their loved ones. Nevertheless, this book is not meant to substitute for current, personalized, professional advice from your doctors and other health care providers or from legal counsel.

The information provided in this book represents the current state of knowledge derived from scientific journals and books as of the time of publication. The number of research studies on MCI grows exponentially year over year. Indeed, it is our hope that new findings will rapidly emerge about the effectiveness of current prevention and treatment options for MCI.

This book would not be possible without the support and assistance of a number of individuals. We would like to thank the Hy & Bertha Shore and Harry & Sarah Gorman families for their support of our ambitions, Preeyam Parikh for her research support throughout the process, Sandra Priselac and Vinay Kansal for helping with literature reviews, and Kelly Connelly for her unwavering support of all of our projects. We are grateful to the following individuals for reading chapters and providing critical and helpful editorial advice: Dr. Michael Gordon, Sheila Bacher, Dr. Jill Rich, Dr. Morris Moscovitch, Dr. Sandra Black, Dr. Morris Freedman, Dr. Larry Leach, Dr. John Fisk, Dr. Alex Henri-Barghava, Renee Climans, Dr. Dmytro Rewilak, Janet Murchison, Dr. Carol Greenwood, Cheli Barokas-Agate, Dr. Louis Bherer, Dr. Fergus Craik, Dr. Gordon Winocur, Dr. Alison Chasteen, and our parents. Dr. Guy Proulx, former Chief of Psychology at Baycrest, was instrumental in providing the vision, leadership, and resources needed to develop the MCI program at Baycrest, without which this book would never have happened. We are also grateful to the clients and research participants with MCI and their family members who shared their experiences with us over the years and inspired us to write this book.

Prologue

"What time are we meeting the Reiners for dinner?" Joe could see it in Ruth's face as soon as he asked the question. It was that look of annoyance and concern rolled into one. Those expressions were like real-life sticky notes reminding him that something wasn't right. *I've done it again.* But Joe was certain this was the first time he had asked this question. He quickly reviewed the day. Ruth was out getting her hair done when he woke, so he couldn't have asked her then. He was paying the bills when she got back, then they had lunch, and then she ran to the store. No, he was sure he hadn't asked her this yet. Maybe it was something else. "Ruth, is something bothering you?" Joe asked.

It was the second time Joe had asked about the meeting time for dinner that day. Ruth felt equally annoyed and afraid. *Here he goes again! Why doesn't he pay attention? But . . . what if it isn't a problem of attention?* It wasn't that long ago that she and Joe looked after his mother and her dementia. That was a difficult experience for both of them. Ruth can't imagine her husband following that same path. "No, dear, we're meeting them at 6:30," Ruth replied. She thought, *It can't be that. Just yesterday he reminded me of something. We all forget. What do you expect when you're in your early 70s? I'm sure he's fine.*

"Can you please sign that birthday card for Bev? I want to give it to her tonight," Ruth asked. Joe started searching the kitchen counters, the desk, and the table where they kept the mail until it got sorted. Finally, when he started to go through some of her things she asked, "What are you looking for?"

Joe answered, somewhat hastily, "I'm looking for that card. I signed it earlier." *Where did that thing go? Why does she keep moving things?* The card wasn't by the phone where Ruth had left it for him to sign. It took them 20 minutes until they finally found the card mixed in with some bills that had been paid.

"I think I'm going to stay home tonight. You go, though. I'm just not up to it. I'm tired," said Joe. *It's just too much work. Things seem to wear me out way more than they used to. Maybe I need the doctor to check my heart medication.*

"But we have had this planned for weeks. It's Bev's birthday. We can't cancel on them now," Ruth replied in disbelief.

"We don't have to cancel. You go. I wouldn't add much to the evening anyway," Joe responded.

Ruth knew there would be no changing his mind at this point. Joe would just get angry if she tried to push him into going. She thought it was strange, though, as the Reiners have been their good friends for over 30 years. *This is happening more and more. He just doesn't seem interested in doing things anymore. First it was his golf games with his former co-workers, then the bridge club. He doesn't even read like he used to. I've bought him a ton of books and they just sit there unread.*

Ruth thought that maybe having Joe stay home tonight was for the better. Joe had always been a great driver, and Ruth was still completely confident in his ability to drive safely, but she had noticed that he has started asking which way to turn or when to turn, even in places that they had driven frequently. It often leads to arguments, because it is hard not to snap at him when he seems not to be able to remember things that he used to know like the back of his hand.

"What time are you supposed to meet the Reiners?" Joe asked.

Ruth looked at her husband with that face again, but this time Joe noticed her eyes welling up. "Joe, we need to talk."

Ruth didn't make it out that night either. Instead they had a long talk sharing their concerns about Joe's memory. Joe acknowledged that his memory was worse than it used to be, but he thought he could chalk it up to normal aging. In the end, he agreed with Ruth that it would be best to get his memory checked out, and they made an appointment with his family doctor. After a couple of referrals, Joe had seen a neurologist and a neuropsychologist, and they found themselves waiting outside Dr. Wong's office waiting for the results of his cognitive testing.

"Mr. and Mrs. Thornton? Please come in," Dr. Wong said as he led Ruth and Joe into his office. "It is good to see you again." Two weeks earlier, he had spoken with Joe and Ruth before starting the testing session. "As you know, we examined your cognitive, or thinking, abilities, Joe. The tests we used were standardized, which means that they have been given to hundreds of people of different ages, and what we did was compare your results to other people your age. What the results showed was that you are a very bright man; based on your vocabulary and reasoning abilities, we estimate your intelligence to be above average. You also performed above average on tests of attention, and on speeded tests that tell us about how quickly you can think and do simple tasks. Your problem solving skills are also in great shape, in the superior range for your age. This was true too for what we call your executive abilities, which includes things like being able to multitask and avoid interference. Compared to these results, your performance on tests of memory was below average, in the borderline range."

Ruth's grip on Joe's hand tightened. *Here we go.*

"I see in my referral letter from your neurologist that you have high blood pressure, but that this is well controlled by your medication," Dr. Wong continued. "All the other medical tests and assessments that have been done haven't found anything, either, which is great news. And you and your wife have told me that you are still driving, paying the bills, and other tasks like that. But the tests that we gave you did identify that you are having a problem with memory. This profile of poor memory but intact abilities in other cognitive areas is consistent with what we call mild cognitive impairment, specifically amnestic mild cognitive impairment. What that describes is people whose memory—that's where the word *amnestic* comes from—is worse than we would expect for their age, but everything else is fine."

"Are you saying I have Alzheimer's?" Joe asked.

"I can't say for certain what underlies your cognitive problems," Dr. Wong replied. "Mild cognitive impairment describes something in between normal aging and dementias, including dementia due to Alzheimer's disease."

"What does this mean in terms of the future?" Ruth asked.

Dr. Wong explained that having mild cognitive impairment put Joe at a greater risk for developing dementia, and that, given his results showing a problem with memory, Dr. Wong thought that the biggest risk was for Joe developing Alzheimer's type dementia, especially since his mother had Alzheimer's disease. However, he was careful to point out that for many people, their cognitive symptoms stay stable for many years, they may slowly worsen or they may get better.

"Only time will tell." Dr. Wong said, "I would like to see you again in 18 months so that we can get a better idea of what mild cognitive impairment means for you. In the meantime, however, what you need to know is that you can do things to help. Research shows that staying physically healthy by engaging in exercise and eating well, and also keeping mentally and socially active can help maintain cognitive health and reduce dementia risk." Dr. Wong gave Joe and Ruth some specific ideas about community centers and other informal ways to stay active. "Do you have any questions for me?" Dr. Wong asked. Ruth and Joe felt that their heads were spinning too much to think of any other questions.

Joe was very quiet on the drive home. *It's not normal, it's not dementia. It could get worse, it could get better, or it could stay the same. Exercise, doing mentally challenging activities, staying social…what's the point of any of that if the doctors don't know what's going on?*

Ruth was quiet, too. She was concerned about her husband and their future, but she was determined to fight this. *I'll start with the library tomorrow.* "We'll be okay, Joe," Ruth said, as she took her husband's hand again.

WHAT IS MILD COGNITIVE IMPAIRMENT?

1

Defining Mild Cognitive Impairment

With age, you may have noticed changes in your thinking abilities, such as how easily you can focus your attention, how well you remember new information, or how quickly you come up with words in conversation. The scientific term for "thinking abilities" is *cognition*, which refers to various processes of thought like intelligence, reasoning, judgment, learning, remembering, and other mental abilities. Although some degree of cognitive change is normal with age, more significant cognitive changes may herald the beginning of a memory disorder like Alzheimer's disease. This book focuses on mild cognitive impairment (MCI), which is a transition stage or border zone between the mild cognitive changes associated with normal aging and the more substantial problems caused by a dementia such as Alzheimer's disease. Joe, who you met in the prologue of this book, is one example of how MCI may present and develop over time.

A CONTINUUM OF AGING

Cognitive changes associated with aging can range from subtle to severe. At one end of the spectrum, the cognitive changes that everyone experiences with normal aging are generally mild and do not interfere with the ability to participate in normal daily activities.

At the other end of the spectrum, dementia is associated with multiple, significant cognitive changes that affect a person's ability to live independently. MCI falls between these extremes. In MCI, cognitive changes are more substantial than those seen in normal aging, but not severe enough to cause major lifestyle changes. Both MCI and dementia are *pathological* conditions, meaning that they are caused by underlying brain disorders or conditions that are not a part of the normal aging process. You'll learn more about how MCI differs from normal aging and dementia in chapters 2 and 3 of this book.

Although we can identify three different categories of cognitive aging, it is more accurate to think of them as part of a continuum, as shown in the figure in Box 1.1. Cognitive changes associated with dementia don't appear overnight. They may take months or years to develop to the point where they are noticeable, and one phase can gradually progress into another over time. So, although it is sometimes clear that a particular person fits into one or another of these categories, there can be quite a bit of overlap. For example, when a person expresses concern about his or her memory, it may be difficult

---

Box 1.1 Differences between Normal Aging (solid line), MCI (dashed line), and Dementia (dotted line)

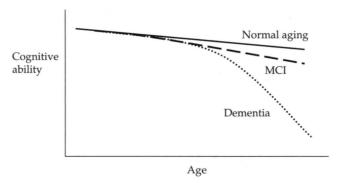

Note that MCI departs from normal aging, and dementia departs from MCI. Normal aging does not necessarily lead to MCI, and MCI does not necessarily lead to dementia, but dementia is preceded by MCI and normal aging.

for even an experienced clinician to tell with certainty whether the memory changes are related to very early MCI or simply normal aging.

It is important to know that, although there *can* be progression along the continuum from normal aging to MCI to dementia, this does not always occur. We know this because of studies that have measured the *prevalence* (the number of people with a particular disorder in the general population) and *incidence* (the number of new cases of the disorder that develop within a particular period of time) of MCI and dementia. Although findings vary somewhat from one study to another, a general estimate of the prevalence of MCI is between 10 and 15% of adults over the age of 65. What this tells us is that only a minority of older adults have cognitive problems that are greater than expected for their age, and the large majority do not have MCI. Likewise, as we discuss in chapter 4, not everyone who has MCI will develop dementia. In some studies, up to 40% of individuals who initially meet criteria for MCI return to normal within a year. In these cases, temporary or fluctuating problems such as mood or side effects of medications may have produced the mild cognitive problems. On the other hand, 10–15% of individuals with MCI will progress to dementia within the first year, and about 50% will develop dementia within 5 years. This is a higher incidence rate than seen for individuals without MCI, but it is certainly clear that MCI doesn't always progress to dementia. For this reason, MCI is sometimes referred to as a *risk factor* for dementia. In other words, if you have MCI, you have an increased risk of developing dementia over the next several years, but your cognitive abilities may also remain stable over that time or even return to normal.

DIAGNOSING AND CLASSIFYING MCI

Subtypes of MCI

A wide range of cognitive abilities can potentially be impaired in MCI. As such, the term MCI is general, and can include people that are very different from each other. To provide more specificity, several MCI subtypes have been identified. These subtypes differ in the *type* and in the *number* of cognitive abilities that are impaired.

Box 1.2 Classifying Subtypes of MCI According to the Type and Number of Cognitive Impairments

		Type of impairment:	
		Memory impairment	Non-memory impairment
Number of impairments:	1 impairment	**Amnestic MCI single domain**	**Nonamnestic MCI single domain**
	2 or more impairments	**Amnestic MCI multiple domains**	**Nonamnestic MCI multiple domains**

For most people who have MCI, the cognitive ability that is affected is memory. For this reason, MCI is often classified according to whether memory is involved. If there are memory problems, we use the term *amnestic MCI*. If memory is not involved, we use the term *nonamnestic MCI*. Similarly, if only one cognitive ability is impaired (that is, memory or any other single ability), the term *single-domain MCI* is used. In contrast, if more than one ability is impaired, the term *multiple-domain MCI* is used. As you can see in Box 1.2, when you take into account both the type and number of abilities that are impaired, four different MCI subtypes are possible: amnestic single-domain, amnestic multiple-domain, nonamnestic single-domain, and nonamnestic multiple-domain. The reason that it can be useful to be so specific in classification is that the various subtypes are generally caused by different disease processes. For example, individuals with Alzheimer's disease are likely to have met criteria for amnestic single-domain MCI sometime before they were diagnosed with Alzheimer's. You will learn more about the causes of different MCI subtypes in Chapter 4.

The Mayo Clinic Criteria for Amnestic MCI

MCI is diagnosed in the same way that other cognitive or medical disorders are diagnosed. There are specific *criteria*, or standards, that have been agreed on by clinicians and scientists based on extensive research and experience with the disorder. These criteria are documented in a way that allows a clinician to diagnose MCI or to rule it out for an individual person. As you will see, like other cognitive disorders, MCI is currently a *clinical* diagnosis. This means that its presence or absence is determined by evaluating a person's behavioral and cognitive changes, not physical changes. Although MCI does involve physical changes in the brain, as we'll discuss later, these vary widely from one person to another. Although this may change with advances in scientific research, at present, an evaluation that is based on physical changes alone would not be a reliable way to diagnose MCI and, thus, it is not the norm among health professionals.

The most common form of MCI is the amnestic subtype, and a majority of the research on MCI overall has involved amnestic MCI. Dr. Robert Petersen and his colleagues at the Mayo Clinic have developed criteria for diagnosing amnestic MCI that are widely used in clinical and research settings. These are listed in Box 1.3 and described in more detail in this section. To be diagnosed with MCI, a person will usually meet all five of the criteria listed in the box. (There are some exceptions, however, as we mention later.) In addition, because MCI is sometimes used to detect the earliest stages of a possible dementia, MCI is not diagnosed if there are other medical, neurological, or psychiatric problems that could account for the mild memory changes. So, for example, if a person experiences memory problems that can be attributed to a brain tumor or the

---

Box 1.3 Mayo Clinic Criteria for Diagnosing Amnestic MCI

1. Subjective memory complaint.
2. Objective memory impairment for age.
3. No generalized cognitive impairment.
4. Largely intact functional activities.
5. No dementia.

Reprinted from Peterson, R.C., Mild Cognitive Impairment as a Diagnostic Entity, Journal of Internal Medicine, 256, 183–184, 2004, adapted with permission of John Wiley and Sons.

side effects of a medication, he or she wouldn't normally be diagnosed with MCI.

1. Subjective memory complaint. If you have MCI, you may have a subjective sense that your memory is not as good as it used to be. This criterion is used as an indication that there has been a *change* in memory. If you have always had a poor memory, for example because of a learning disability that you have had since you were a child, and if there has been no further change in your memory, then this criterion would not be met. The term MCI is used only for memory problems that have appeared later in life.

To determine whether there has been a subjective change in your memory, your physician or other health-care clinician would simply ask you whether you have noticed a change. In other words, this is a self-report measure. The clinician may also ask someone who knows you well whether he or she has noticed a change in your memory. This type of corroboration can be useful to provide increased certainty that there has, indeed, been a change.

It is possible that someone with MCI does not have a memory complaint. This is an exception to the usual rule that individuals with MCI meet all five criteria. As memory problems become worse, sometimes it is difficult for a person to remember all their memory mistakes. As a result, someone with quite significant memory problems may feel they do not have memory problems at all. This loss of insight is common in dementia, and occasionally may also be present in MCI.

2. Objective memory loss. It is not enough for you to have a subjective sense that your memory is worse than it used to be. Some degree of memory loss is associated with normal aging. As such, you may not be able to judge whether or not your memory changes are normal for your age. For this reason, in order to be diagnosed with MCI, there has to be objective evidence of memory loss that supports the (usually present) subjective memory complaint.

Objective memory impairments in MCI are detected through a process of administering and scoring clinical memory tests. If you have been diagnosed with MCI, there is a good chance that at some point in time, your doctor or perhaps a neuropsychologist tested your memory formally. This may have been a fairly simple affair in which you were told three words and asked to say them back a few minutes later. On the other hand, if you had neuropsychological testing, this process would have been more extensive. You may have listened to a short story or a long list of words, or you might have been shown a geometric design or a series of shapes to remember. Some time after hearing or seeing the information, you would have been asked to recall it as well as you could, by telling the story, saying the words, drawing the design, or pointing out the shapes you saw from a larger display of shapes. A more detailed description of formal cognitive testing is provided in chapter 6.

In order to tell whether your current memory ability represents a change, your clinician has to know what your memory used to be like, before you started noticing any problems. If you have had memory testing before, then the clinician would be able to compare your current scores with your previous ones. Most people, however, wouldn't have had any reason to have memory testing done before they noticed a problem. In those cases, clinicians have to make an educated guess about how your memory used to be, by looking at memory scores from people who are similar to you. We know that age, education, and intelligence can all affect memory ability: better memory is associated with younger age, more education, and higher intelligence. So, your memory scores would be compared to scores obtained by people having a similar age, education, and intelligence as you, in order to determine whether your memory problem is greater than expected. This can be a complex process, which means that the clinician working with you needs to use his or her clinical judgment to decide whether your score indicates true memory impairment. These ideas are illustrated in the case vignettes in Box 1.4.

3. No generalized cognitive impairment. In amnestic MCI, other nonmemory cognitive abilities are relatively intact. These other abilities may include attention, language, visuospatial abilities, and problem solving. Sometimes, a clinician will use a basic cognitive screening measure, such as the Mini-Mental State Examination or the Montreal Cognitive Assessment, to look at a number of different cognitive areas. Alternatively, a neuropsychological assessment would examine these areas in more detail.

Box 1.4 Case Vignettes of Amnestic MCI, Illustrating the Criterion of Objective Memory Loss

Hank is a 75-year-old retired store clerk with 8 years of formal education. He has noticed increasing memory problems over the past several years, and he tells his doctor that he is misplacing things at home and is having trouble remembering names of acquaintances. His doctor assesses his physical health and sends him for detailed cognitive testing. The neuropsychologist finds he has an average IQ. On memory testing, he is able to remember 7 out of 12 words and 3 out of 6 figures that were shown to him 30 minutes earlier. Taking into consideration his age, educational and occupational backgrounds, and IQ, his memory performance is determined to be normal for his age, and is not representative of MCI or dementia.

Barbara is a 52-year-old business executive with a master's degree. She has recently noticed problems remembering names of clients and getting turned around while on business trips in unfamiliar cities. On neuropsychological testing, she is found to have an IQ that is well above average. Similar to Hank, her memory scores are 7 out of 12 words and 3 out of 6 figures. For Barbara, however, these scores are significantly lower than normal for her age, background, and IQ, and are interpreted as representing an objective memory impairment.

Similar to the previous criterion of objective memory impairment, a lack of impairment in other cognitive areas is based on consideration of what is normal for the individual's age, education, and intelligence. Scores that are normal for one person may indicate a generalized impairment in another person. This requires clinical judgment by the diagnosing clinician, and there are no hard-and-fast rules.

4. Intact functional activities. One of the several differences between MCI and dementia has to do with a person's ability to carry out his or her daily activities. By definition, individuals with MCI are able to do these activities with little or no help from others. Also by definition, individuals with dementia do require this kind of help.

Functional activities that may be considered as part of this criterion include planning and preparing adequate meals, shopping, paying bills, driving or traveling on public transportation, dispensing medications, and arranging and keeping appointments. These are activities that are important for your ability to live independently. To evaluate your functional abilities, your doctor will most likely ask you questions about the things you are doing on a day-to-day basis and whether you are having any difficulties managing these. The doctor may also want to confirm your description by asking a family member or someone else who knows you well. There are also paper-and-pencil questionnaires that can be used to measure your functional abilities. These are discussed in more detail in chapter 6.

Regardless of how this is measured, a health professional will be looking for any *change* in your ability to do these activities. If, for example, you and your spouse have always divided household tasks, then you would be evaluated according to only the tasks that you normally would have been responsible for. If doing the finances has always been your spouse's job, your ability to do this would not be evaluated. Also, the interest is in how cognitive changes—not physical changes—have affected your daily activities. If you have stopped driving because of problems with your vision, or need help carrying groceries because of back pain, you would nevertheless meet criteria for "intact functional abilities" because these changes in your daily activities were due to physical, not cognitive, changes.

It is possible to have some subtle changes in your ability to participate in your daily activities and still meet this criterion. If you have amnestic MCI, you may find that you rely more on shopping lists, use a pill box to remember to take your medications, or make extensive use of a calendar for remembering appointments. The important distinction is whether you are still able to manage your daily activities *independently*. If your spouse has to remind you to take your pills every day or your son or daughter has taken over your finances, then you would be dependent for these activities, and you would not meet the criterion of "intact" functional activities.

5. No dementia. This final criterion is made on the basis of your doctor's clinical judgment using the previous four criteria. Because one of the main differences between MCI and dementia is functional independence, this criterion really hinges on degree of functional impairment. If you have mild cognitive changes but are functioning independently, the best classification is MCI. On the other hand, if you have cognitive changes that are sufficiently severe that you need assistance with your daily activities, you may meet criteria for dementia.

MEMORY CHANGES IN AMNESTIC MCI

Now that you have the bigger picture about how amnestic MCI is diagnosed, let's look in more detail at how memory, specifically, changes with amnestic MCI. First, we'll look at the memory problems that are reported by individuals with MCI, that is, their subjective memory complaints. Next, we'll review research findings that reveal the processes and types of memory ability that are impaired in MCI. These constitute the objective memory impairments associated with MCI.

Subjective Memory Changes

The best way to find out about subjective memory change is to look at the results of surveys and questionnaires that have been given to individuals with MCI. Interestingly, people with MCI tend to report the same types of memory slips as people with "normal" memory ability who are the same age. The most common problems reported by both groups are forgetting names of people, having difficulty remembering appointments, and not remembering where they put things. Another common problem is difficulty remembering to do something that they intended to do, like forgetting to take something with them or forgetting to tell someone something. Also, many people report problems remembering things that have happened in the recent past, like social events, stories in the news, what they watched on television, or something they were told.

If you have MCI—and even if you don't—at least some of these memory slips will probably ring true to you. Keep in mind, though, that this list of slips is an amalgamation of what is reported by a large number of individuals with MCI. You may experience some of these problems but not all of them. You may be good at remembering where you put things, but bad at remembering stories in the news. Equally likely, you may be good at remembering the news but be constantly searching for items you have misplaced. There are many variations between individuals in terms of their memory strengths and weaknesses.

Objective Memory Changes

As mentioned earlier in this chapter, objective memory impairments are detected through a process of administering and scoring formal memory tests. Standardized tests are used in clinical settings, and experimental memory tests that have not yet been standardized may be used in research settings. Fortunately, many individuals with MCI have volunteered to be in research studies or have agreed to allow their clinical test data to be used in clinical research. This allows scientists to look at the common patterns in memory performance that are associated with MCI, adds to our understanding of the experience of MCI, and also helps clinicians recognize MCI when they see it.

We can think of memory changes in two different ways. We can look at different memory *processes*, which are the things that happen when you learn and remember. We can also look at different memory *types*, which have to do with the nature of the information that you learn and remember. We'll review each of these concepts in turn.

Memory processes. In order for you to successfully learn and remember something new, three things have to happen. You have to get the new information into your memory, hold onto the information over time, and get the information back out when you need it. These three processes are called *encoding*, *storage*, and *retrieval*, respectively. Although there has not been a lot of research that has looked at how these specific memory processes change in MCI, the studies that do exist tell a similar story. MCI can be associated with some degree of change in all three of these processes, and in particular with changes in encoding and storage.

An *encoding* problem is particularly obvious in situations in which you have trouble remembering something very soon after you heard or saw the information. For example, if you have difficulty remembering the name of a person you were just introduced to, this may be an encoding problem. When this happens, people sometimes report feeling like the information "just did not register." As you would expect, if you don't encode the name in the first place, you will have a lot of difficulty trying to retrieve it later when you see the person.

Problems with *storage* are reflected in rapid forgetting of information. This means not being able to remember something that you used to know. Some degree of forgetting over time is completely normal. You have likely had many experiences of being quite familiar with new information right after you experience or learn it, but eventually forgetting details over time. For example, you may be able to discuss a movie in great detail soon after watching it, but a few months later not remember who the central characters were. Although some storage loss is normal, if you have MCI, your rate of forgetting is probably even faster than it used to be. You may find that you have more trouble remembering information that you seemed to know even an hour earlier. Another way to think about this is that your memory isn't as reliable as it used to be. You may be able to learn and remember something in the short term, for example, that you and your spouse agreed this morning to meet for dinner at your favourite café. Even if you remember the conversation half an hour later, that doesn't necessarily mean that you will still remember the information when it is time for you to head to the café later in the day.

Retrieval problems are common for everyone, including individuals with MCI. You know you are having a retrieval problem when you forget information momentarily but it eventually comes to you. The most common example of this is when you run into someone you know well and can't immediately come up with his or her name. Chances are, if you give yourself a few minutes, you will think of it. At the very least, if you hear someone else use the name, you will recognize it as the correct name.

As you might have guessed, all three of these processes—encoding, storage, and retrieval—have to be working in order for you to successfully learn and remember something over time. If any of these processes fail or partially fail, you will remember little or none of the information you wanted. Fortunately, there are a number of memory strategies that can be used to help you work around such memory problems. These are discussed in detail in chapter 15. As you'll see, most strategies focus on improving encoding, because this is the "gateway" into memory processing. If you improve your ability to encode, this will make storage more robust and retrieval easier.

On the other hand, if encoding is poor to start with, there isn't much information to store or to retrieve.

Memory types. Another way to look at memory is by memory *type*. This refers to the nature of the information that you are remembering. For example, some memory types involve recently learned information, whereas others involve very old information. Memory types may involve remembering the past or remembering to do something in the future. They may involve remembering factual information or how to do something. Research on the specific types of memory that are impaired (or not) in MCI is evolving, and we do not yet know a lot about this. In this section, we'll look at some of the types that have been studied to date. (We will return to this topic in chapter 2, as we discuss the more extensive research about changes in specific types of memory in normal aging.)

The memory type that has been studied the most in MCI is *recent memory*. As the name implies, recent memory has to do with your ability to remember events and information that you experienced recently. Examples of recent memory are remembering the name of someone you met last week, what you watched on TV yesterday, and directions that someone told you just a few minutes ago. When you have your memory tested by your doctor or a neuropsychologist, most of the emphasis will be on recent memory. Trying to recall words that were read to you 5 minutes ago or 30 minutes ago is a test of recent memory. This type of memory is, indeed, impaired in MCI.

There is some evidence that *prospective memory* is impaired in MCI. This is your ability to remember to do something in the future, such as meeting a friend for lunch at 1:00 or taking a medication before you go to bed at night. If you walk into a room and can't remember what you are there for, then you experienced a failure of prospective memory. It is fairly common to make some of these types of mistakes, whether you have MCI or not. However, if you do have MCI, you may find that you are experiencing prospective memory problems more than you used to.

Not all types of memory get worse with MCI. *Immediate memory* is the ability to remember something a few seconds after you heard it or saw it. It involves remembering information that is still the focus of your attention. This is the type of memory you use when you look up a telephone number and try to remember it just long enough to dial it. It is also what you use during a conversation or when you are reading. If you get to the end of a sentence and still remember the beginning of the sentence, you are using your immediate memory. As you might expect, this type of memory is very important for being able to make sense of the world around you. If you can't hold the gist of a full sentence in your memory, you will have a hard time understanding what you hear or read. Fortunately, this type of memory is not affected much, if at all, by MCI. It is one of the types of memory that remains strong, even through the earliest stages of dementia, for those individuals who go on to develop dementia.

To summarize, individuals with amnestic MCI show both strengths and weaknesses in memory. The difficulties that exist span a broad range of memory processes and types. Some of these problems are experienced—although to a lesser degree—by older adults with normal memory changes, and even by young adults and children. For the most part, amnestic MCI wouldn't be considered unless there was an increase in the frequency of these normal problems or slips.

OTHER MCI SUBTYPES

The criteria described earlier in this chapter are used for identifying amnestic MCI. Less research has been done with nonamnestic MCI, but a similar process is used for diagnosis. The criteria listed in Box 1.3 can be used, but it is necessary to substitute the word "memory" with "cognitive." In other words, a person may be identified as having nonamnestic MCI if he or she has a subjective cognitive complaint in a nonmemory domain such as language, attention, or visuospatial ability. The subjective complaint would be confirmed by a family member or close friend and documented on objective testing. As in amnestic MCI, there would be no generalized impairment on overall screening measures or on tests of other cognitive abilities (including memory), the individual would be independent for daily activities, and he or she would not meet criteria for dementia. See Box 1.5 for a case vignette illustrating one type of nonamnestic MCI.

Box 1.5 Case Vignette of an Individual with Nonamnestic MCI Affecting Multiple Domains

---

Carlos is a 60-year-old man who tells his doctor that he has been getting lost easily and is having difficulty building things in his woodworking shop. He is also having trouble concentrating on things he is doing, and his wife has noticed that he is sometimes confused. Results of neuropsychological testing reveal that he has an average IQ and is performing normally on tests of verbal memory, language, and problem solving. In contrast, his visuospatial abilities and attention are lower than expected for his age, education, and IQ. He continues to function independently on a day-to-day basis, although he relies more on notes and maps when he is traveling around town. He meets criteria for nonamnestic MCI multiple domain, affecting visuospatial ability and attention.

CAUSES OF MCI

As mentioned earlier in this chapter, MCI is a pathological condition resulting from a disease or condition affecting the brain. Mild cognitive impairment is not a "normal" part of aging. There are a number of different disorders that can cause MCI, although it is not always possible to tell with certainty which disorder is producing the cognitive changes in any given individual. The subtype of MCI can provide some clues about the underlying cause.

The most common form of MCI is the amnestic subtype, and many individuals with amnestic MCI eventually develop Alzheimer's disease. Barbara, whose case was presented in Box 1.4, is an example of someone with amnestic MCI who may develop Alzheimer's disease in the future. Alzheimer's disease is a slowly progressive brain disease with prominent memory impairment. Not surprisingly, the brain changes that are seen in individuals with amnestic MCI are similar to the changes seen in Alzheimer's disease, although the changes tend to be less severe. These changes include the presence of abnormal proteins, called amyloid plaques, and *atrophy* (or shrinkage) of structures in the medial temporal lobe of the brain that are important for normal memory functioning.

Another progressive disease, Lewy-body disease, does not have prominent memory impairment and is likely to start as nonamnestic MCI affecting either a single domain or multiple domains. Cognitive problems may involve attention, visuospatial abilities, and/or *executive functions* (higher-level cognitive abilities such as planning, problem solving, mental flexibility, and the ability to inhibit inappropriate impulses). Tom, whose case was presented in Box 1.5, has early cognitive changes that might mark the beginning of Lewy-body dementia. Another disease, frontal-temporal dementia, may begin with nonamnestic MCI affecting a single domain such as language or executive functioning.

Other conditions can also produce MCI syndromes that are stable or even reversible over time. Vascular changes—such as small strokes or other cerebrovascular events—can be associated with MCI affecting any cognitive domain, depending on the location in the brain where the vascular events occur. Mental-health disorders such as depression and anxiety can produce MCI affecting memory and possibly attention or executive functions. As you might expect, it is entirely possible that a person would recover from a small stroke or experience improvements in their depressed mood, and this could result in memory improvement. In chapter 3, we discuss more details about the various dementias and how they relate to MCI.

RELATED TERMINOLOGY

There are a number of terms that have been used to characterize the transition stage between normal aging and dementia. Some of these are listed in Box 1.6. The term *MCI* is currently the most widely used, and most of the research that has been done to understand the transitional stage between normal aging and dementia has used the specific criteria for MCI. This term first appeared in the medical and scientific literature within the past 15 to 20 years, with much of this work headed up by Dr. Ronald Petersen and his colleagues at the Mayo clinic. We reviewed these diagnostic criteria for MCI earlier in this chapter. Other terms have recently emerged, and it is possible that you will hear more about them in the future. For this reason, we will review them briefly here.

Box 1.6 Terms Used to Characterize the Transition Stage between Normal Cognitive Aging and Dementia

---

- Cognitive impairment, no dementia.
- Late-life forgetfulness.
- Limited cognitive disturbance.
- Mild cognitive decline.
- Mild cognitive disorder.
- Mild cognitive impairment.
- Mild cognitive impairment due to Alzheimer's disease.
- Minimal dementia.
- Minor neurocognitive disorder.
- Possible dementia prodrome.
- Questionable dementia.

The fourth edition of the *Diagnostic and Statistical Manual of Mental Disorders* published by the American Psychiatric Association is a widely used resource for clinicians containing agreed-on criteria for classifying disorders of mood, behavior, and cognition. Although the current version of the *Manual* does not have a category equivalent to MCI, there is a proposal to include the term *minor neurocognitive disorder* in an upcoming revision (fifth edition). The proposed diagnostic criteria for this disorder share some similarity with those for MCI, including the presence of a subjective cognitive decline, objective cognitive impairment, and independence for functional activities. One of the main differences is that specific guidelines have been proposed to help the clinician determine whether an individual meets the cognitive criteria. For example, cognitive impairment may be defined as test scores that fall in the lowest 16% relative to individuals with a similar background. This level of specificity will be helpful in ensuring that there is a high degree of *homogeneity* (or similarity in presentation) among individuals classified with this disorder.

The term *minor neurocognitive disorders* can be further broken down into subtypes, according to the presumed etiology (or cause) of the cognitive impairment. The Alzheimer's disease subtype of minor neurocognitive disorder has additional criteria with specific features that are common in Alzheimer's disease. These include having prominent memory impairment, a gradual rather than sudden onset of the memory symptoms, and a pattern of worsening over time. In addition, to boost the chance that the cause is related to Alzheimer's disease, the criteria require that there are no other medical disorders that could fully account for the cognitive deficits.

Another term, *mild cognitive impairment due to Alzheimer's disease,* is similar in concept. The term was recently developed in 2011 by a working group of experts convened by the National Institute on Aging and the Alzheimer's Association. In addition to the usual criteria for MCI and the clinical features of Alzheimer's disease, this conceptualization of MCI has provisions for the use of genetic information as well as experimental *biomarkers* (measures of physiological brain changes) associated with Alzheimer's disease. You will learn more about this in chapter 3. The goal of these specific criteria is to be able to diagnose Alzheimer's disease as early as possible.

A very different way of identifying the transition state between normal aging and dementia is from the administration of scales that are commonly used by medical professionals to rate the severity of dementia. For example, scores on a dementia severity scale may indicate the presence of preclinical, mild, moderate, or severe dementia. *Preclinical* means that an individual exhibits some of the early changes associated with dementia (for example, mild memory changes) but does not meet all of the criteria for a clinical diagnosis of dementia (for example, does not have significant functional difficulty). The terms used on dementia scales to characterize the preclinical stage vary from one scale to another and include *limited cognitive disturbance, mild cognitive decline, minimal dementia, questionable dementia,* and *possible dementia prodrome.* It is important to note that these terms are used primarily in conjunction with their specific rating scales, whereas other terms like MCI or minor neurocognitive disorder can be applied regardless of which tests or scales were used to determine their presence.

There are additional terms that are used to refer to cognitive changes that happen in normal, healthy older adults. These include *age-related cognitive decline, age-consistent memory impairment,* and *age-associated memory impairment,* for example. Despite the similarity in wording of these terms and some of those listed in Box 1.6, it is important to keep in mind that they represent very different concepts. We will return to this issue in chapter 2.

A FINAL WORD

In this chapter, we have given you a definition of mild cognitive impairment and outlined the criteria that health professionals use to determine whether someone has MCI. You may have noticed that, for some individuals, the cognitive changes associated with MCI can be quite subtle and difficult to distinguish from the normal cognitive changes that everyone experiences as they age. Similarly, as MCI progresses, it can be difficult to tell when a person no longer has MCI and, instead, meets criteria for dementia. In the next two chapters, you'll learn more about the cognitive changes of normal aging and of dementia, and how these differ from MCI.

Box 1.7 Questions to Ask Your Doctor if MCI Is Suspected or Confirmed in Yourself or in Your Family Member.

---

1. What is your usual plan for managing MCI? In other words, how often will I see you for follow-up, will I be referred to a specialist, will I have brain imaging, and so on?
2. Is it clear which subtype of MCI I have? (This could include amnestic or nonamnestic MCI affecting a single domain or multiple domains. See Box 1.2.).

2

How Mild Cognitive Impairment Differs from Normal Aging

Now that you have an understanding about the changes that happen in mild cognitive impairment (MCI), we will turn to a discussion of changes that are associated with normal aging. As you will see, although there are some similarities between MCI and normal aging, they differ in fundamental ways, with very different causes and outcomes.

DEFINITIONS

By definition, "normal" age-related cognitive changes are those that happen to healthy individuals who do not have any diseases or disorders that affect memory or other cognitive abilities. In other words, they are not related to the presence of plaques or tangles that can be seen in the brains of individuals with MCI or Alzheimer's disease. Neither are they related to any other abnormal or "pathological" changes in the brain. Rather, they are related to normal or typical age-related changes in the brain. These are discussed in more detail later in this chapter. So how do we know what is "normal" and what is not in terms of cognitive changes? To answer this question, it is important to note that there are many differences among individuals in the type, degree, and timing of cognitive changes that occur with age. Your experiences may be different from those of other people your age, just like other signs of aging: you may have noticed your first grey hair at age 35 but know of others who enter their 60s with nary a grey hair in sight. Similarly, your memory may have changed more or less than another person the same age, but both of your experiences could well be considered to be normal. What is considered "normal" or "average" is determined by taking into account the experience of the majority of individuals of a given age. For cognition, this is measured by how people perform on cognitive tests. Generally speaking, *average* performance on a cognitive test includes the range of scores achieved by the middle 67% of healthy individuals (which, if you're interested in statistics, represents one standard deviation from the mean score). Scores that are higher or lower than this middle range are considered "above average" and "below average," respectively. Scores that are considered to be *normal* make up a slightly larger range, achieved by up to 90% of healthy individuals, or about 1.5 standard deviations from the mean. Scores falling in the bottom 5% are generally considered to be "impaired" and those in the top 5% are "superior."

NORMAL MEMORY CHANGES

Memory changes that are associated with normal aging begin gradually and relatively early. Over your lifespan, your memory skills increase from birth through adolescence. Sometime during one's late teens or early 20s, some—but not all!—memory skills peak and then very gradually begin to decline. Because the changes occur so slowly, you are not likely to notice them right away. It isn't until a few decades have passed that the small changes start to build up to the point they are noticeable to most of us. Often, people begin noticing subtle memory changes sometime in their 40s or 50s, and these become more noticeable in the decades that follow. The case vignette in Box 2.1. describes an individual with memory changes that are related to normal aging.

In chapter 1, we talked about subjective and objective memory changes in MCI. We will take a similar approach in this chapter, and discuss how the same memory processes and types are affected by the normal aging process.

Self-Reported Memory Changes

The results of surveys and questionnaires asking healthy older individuals to describe their most common memory mistakes provide

---

Box 2.1 Case Vignette Illustrating Normal Memory Changes

Rosemary is a 73-year-old woman with no major health problems and a generally happy disposition. When she gets together with her friends, the conversation sometimes turns to the ups and downs of aging. Like many of her peers, Rosemary finds it challenging to remember the names of new people she has met and sometimes even the names of acquaintances she has known for many years. Fortunately, she notices that if she gives herself enough time, the name will often come to mind spontaneously. She also finds that she really has to pay attention to where she puts things, such as her keys and her purse, so that she doesn't waste time searching her house for them when she is in a hurry to go somewhere. Having been a recreational ballroom dancer in her youth, she and her husband recently decided to take a few dance lessons again so that they could better enjoy the occasional night out dancing. Many of the dance moves came back to her quickly. However, she found that, when learning new dance routines, it took her quite a bit longer to memorize the steps than it did when she was younger. Overall, she finds that the changes in her memory can be inconvenient and require extra planning in order to cope, but they have not interfered with her ability to do the things in life that are important to her.

---

us with valuable information about what is normal and what is not. What we find is a remarkable similarity—but with some important individual variations—in the types of memory changes that people describe. By far the most common memory challenge is remembering names, including names of new acquaintances as well as names of people known for a long time. This seems to be a particular challenge when you run into someone you know in an unexpected place, such as seeing your neighbour when you are on vacation in another city.

Some commonly reported memory mistakes relate to how well you are paying attention to the task at hand. You've likely had the experience of not remembering where you put something, such as your keys or your reading glasses, and this probably happened because you were not paying attention when you put the item down. Similarly, when your attention wanders, you may find yourself forgetting what you were just about to do, such as walking into the kitchen and not remembering why you are there. Other commonly reported memory mistakes include having difficulty remembering important numbers (such as PIN numbers, phone numbers, and passwords) and dates (such as birthdays and anniversaries). If these are the types of nuisance memory problems you experience, and they are not causing major disruptions to your lifestyle, then you are in the same boat as the majority of individuals over the age of 40 or 50.

Just as interesting as the similarities in memory mistakes we all experience is the fact that a number of memory mistakes are often experienced by some people and not others. Some individuals are great historians, with an impressive ability to remember details from events that happened long ago. Other people may have more vague recollections of events that are lacking in detail. Similarly, many people feel that they "never forget a face," whereas other people—like at least one of the authors of this book—find it difficult to recognize faces. One of us has had the embarrassing experience of being acknowledged by someone she met a few days earlier and not recognizing her, leading the new acquaintance to remark, "You have no idea who I am, do you?" Luckily, those of us who experience these types of memory slips are not alone. Although not everyone reports these experiences, they are certainly not unusual. We can chalk such variations in memory up to individual differences. For a number of human qualities, differences between individuals are the norm rather than the exception. Just as there are many variations in human physical characteristics such as height and hair color, there are a number of normal variations in mental and social characteristics such as memory, intelligence, and personality.

Objective Memory Changes Noted on Memory Tests

Another way to find out what constitutes "normal" memory change is to look at scientific research that has examined actual memory abilities in healthy older adults. Such research typically involves laboratory studies in which individuals of different ages are given some kind of information to remember, such as a list of words or a page of geometric designs, and then they are asked to recall the new information later. There is quite a large body of research on this topic that has spanned many decades and has contributed immensely to our understanding of normal age-related cognitive changes. As in chapter 1, we will look at two different types of memory changes: Changes in memory *processes*(that is, the things that happen when you learn and remember) and changes in memory *types*(that is, the nature of the information you learn and remember).

Memory processes. Memory processes include getting information into your memory (*encoding*), holding onto it over time (*storage* or *retention*), and getting it back out when you need it (*retrieval*). Normal aging has different effects on these memory processes. There is little effect of normal aging on the process of storage. At any age, as time goes by since you learned something new, you are less likely to remember it. You may have noticed this when you were in school, and you could study hard and do well on an exam the next day, but remember hardly any of that material a month or so later when studying for the final exam. A natural decrease in storage over time is also the reason why you are more likely to remember an article you read in the newspaper this morning than one you read last week. This phenomenon is similar for younger and older adults.

With normal aging comes a slight decline in encoding. In other words, it can be a bit more difficult to get new information into your memory than when you were younger. This is when it becomes particularly important to use memory strategies to boost your ability to encode new information. If you don't already use memory strategies regularly, these can be learned. You can read more about these strategies in chapter 15.

By far the largest change in memory processes with normal aging involves retrieval. Although retrieval slips happen at all ages, they are much more common as we grow older. As mentioned previously, the most frequent memory complaint is remembering names. This is often a failure of retrieval, such as in the example of running into someone you know and not remembering the name right away. Most likely, the name will eventually come to you. At the very least, if someone tells you the name, you would probably react with "Of course! I knew that." Research studies show that older adults are not as good as younger adults at coming up with information without any cues. This is called *free recall* and makes considerable demands on the retrieval process. In contrast, younger and older adults are equally good at pinpointing the correct information when it is presented along with other options, as in a multiplechoice test. This is called *recognition*, and makes much lower demands on retrieval.

It is worth pointing out that encoding, storage, and retrieval are all interrelated processes. Although we have talked about each one separately, they do not operate independently. For example, how well you retrieve information that you learned is obviously related to how well you encoded the information in the first place.

If you remember from chapter 1, this pattern of age-related differences in memory processes is different from what we see in MCI. Normal aging is associated with relatively less change in storage, more noticeably decreased encoding, and significantly decreased retrieval. On the other hand, MCI is associated with more global changes that affect encoding, storage, and retrieval. So, despite the fact that normal aging and MCI are both associated with increased reports of memory problems in general, the nature of these difficulties are rather different.

Memory types. There is quite a bit of research about how different types of memory are affected by the normal aging process. We'll start by discussing some of the types that change with age, but keep in mind that memory is not entirely a downhill course. Just as with memory processes, some memory types decline more substantially with age and others are stable or can even improve with age.

Types of memory that generally decline with normal aging include prospective memory, associative memory, and recent memory. *Prospective memory* is the ability to remember to do something in the future, such as make a telephone call at 10:00 or stop at the grocery store on your way home from visiting a friend. When prospective memory is tested in the laboratory on simulated tasks such as pressing a computer key every 10 minutes, older adults tend to do worse than younger adults. However, on more naturalistic tasks, such as mailing a letter on a particular day, older adults do just as well as younger adults. This indicates that aging is associated with changes in the basic cognitive processes involved in prospective memory, but that older adults are often able to compensate for these in everyday situations. At all ages, prospective memory is enhanced when you use external reminders, such as setting an alarm to ring at 10:00 or posting a note on your car's dashboard to stop at the store. We'll talk more about this type of strategy in chapter 15.

Item memory involves remembering individual pieces of information, such as a name or a face. This contrasts with *associative memory*, which involves remembering which items go together, like which name goes with which face. There are age-related changes in item memory, but the changes in associative memory are generally more extensive. Less-than-perfect associative memory is the cause of common experiences such as knowing that you bought stamps but not remembering where you put them, or knowing that you saw a particular movie but not remembering where you saw it or who you were with. This can also be the reason that we repeat ourselves: We may remember an amusing joke but not remember to whom we have already told the joke.

Another type of memory that declines with age is *recent memory*. This memory type has to do with your ability to remember events and information that you experienced recently. Examples of recent memory are remembering where your parked your car when you went into the store, or remembering what you had for lunch two days ago. Recent memory declines with normal aging, although it depends on how it is tested. If tested using free recall (What did you have for lunch on Tuesday?), there are substantial age differences. If tested using recognition (Did you have spaghetti, tomato soup, or a grilled cheese sandwich?), there are smaller age differences. This relates back to our discussion of encoding, storage, and retrieval. When recent memory tasks require a lot of retrieval, age differences are prominent, but when they require less retrieval, age differences are smaller.

Recent memory contrasts with *remote memory*, which is the ability to remember things that happened years ago. This may include remembering your first day of work, your wedding ceremony, or last year's family reunion. Younger and older adults tend to remember these remote events differently, but no better or worse than each other overall. Younger adults are good at recalling details, such as what they were wearing, the weather that day, or specific comments that were made. Older adults have more difficulty pulling up these details. They are, however, better at putting past events into context, such as knowing what else was going on in their lives at that time or why it was a significant event to them personally.

We'll add an interesting aside here about recent and remote memory. Many people are struck by the seeming contradiction of being able to remember remote events with clarity but of having no idea what happened a few hours or days ago. It is difficult to imagine how our memory could work this way—if we can't remember something soon after it happened, how can we remember it much later? The answer is that we are often comparing the equivalent of apples and oranges when making this observation. Remote events that are crystal clear tend to be significant events that were full of emotion, for example, a frightening childhood injury, the joyful birth a child, or a tragic death in the family. In addition, as time passes, we tend to think about and discuss these significant events often, and this repetition helps us remember the event better. Unfairly, we contrast these memories with mundane recent memories of uninteresting conversations or what we had for dinner last night—events that were not unique, emotional, or repeated. When we compare apples and apples, we see a different relationship between recent and remote memory. Can you remember what you had for dinner the Tuesday before your wedding? Most likely, this would be more difficult than remembering what you had for dinner last Tuesday. In general, it is more difficult to remember the same type of information when it occurred many years ago than when it occurred within the past few hours or days.

Procedural memory is the ability to remember *how* to do something, such as how to crochet, type on a keyboard, or swing a tennis racket. Some of these skills seem to be retained for a lifetime, even if not used. You may have heard people say, "You never forget how to ride a bike," and there is certainly evidence that this is true. Granted, your endurance on the bike may be decreased and your speed of typing or crocheting may be slower, but your memory for how to do these activities does not decline substantially with age.

We've saved the best news for last. *Semantic memory*—your memory for general facts or knowledge—is related to experience and has plenty of room for improvement with age. As you gain more experience within a particular domain, your knowledge in that area increases. If you start doing crossword puzzles or playing Scrabble for the first time, for example, you will gradually learn lots of words that are useful in those contexts that you didn't otherwise know. This knowledge is likely to keep on increasing as you continue to partici- pate in those activities. Similarly, your knowledge of financial ter- minology and financial planning likely increased from the time you started your first job (and had few finances to speak of) to the time when you started planning for your retirement and had more com- plicated investments. Although your ability to access semantic knowl- edge may slow down a bit as part of the natural process of age-related slowing or changes in retrieval, at any age there is no limit to the amount of information you can put into your semantic memory.

To sum up, there are age-related memory changes that may affect your ability to remember to do things in the future, to associate indi- vidual pieces of information, and to remember events that happened recently. There is little change in your memory for how to do some- thing or for your general knowledge. Interestingly, this particular pattern has some similarities to that which is seen in MCI, although the extent of the memory difficulty is by definition greater in MCI than normal aging.

WHY MEMORY CHANGES WITH AGE: CHANGES IN THE BRAIN

As you likely know, normal aging is associated with changes to a number of systems and organs in the body. If you look around, you will notice that aging is commonly associated with changes in hair color, skin structure, and eyesight. Although you can't see them, there are also structural changes in internal organs such as the heart, lungs, muscles, and the brain. There are very specific changes at the level of brain cells, or *neurons*, and these are more predominant in some brain areas than others.

A general finding with age is *atrophy* (decrease in size) of some brain structures. Some of the brain areas that show the most signifi- cant atrophy include the frontal lobes and the temporal lobes. Both of these areas are involved in memory, although they play different roles. The frontal lobes are important for strategic aspects of memory, such as applying memory strategies or systematically searching through memory stores. The temporal lobes, which include the hippocampus, are important for associating and retrieving learned information over time, among other things. The cause of the age-related shrinkage of these structures includes some loss of neurons as well as decreases in the size and branches of existing neurons.

Another general finding with age is a change in the structure of the *white matter*(connecting tissues) in the brain. These are vascular changes and are called *white matter hyperintensities* because they show up as small bright spots on MRI scans of the brain. It is unusual to see these hyperintensities in the brains of young, healthy individuals, but very common in older adults. White matter is important for relaying messages from one neuron to another in the brain. Thus, one of the most significant impacts of change in the white matter is a general slowing of the speed of thinking.

There are also changes in the chemical structure of the brain with age. Certain neurotransmitters, including acetylcholine and dopamine, important for communication between neurons, decline with age. Also, metabolites such as n-acetylaspartate that reflect the functioning of brain cells decline with age.

These brain changes are thought to occur in normal aging for a variety of reasons. They appear to be associated with stress-related hormonal factors, recurrent inflammation, exposure to toxins, and cardiovascular risk factors such as hypertension. The good news is that many of these factors can be modified by being proactive with your health and making good lifestyle choices. It is important to manage hypertension, counteract the effects of stress through relaxation, and maintain an active and physically fit lifestyle. You'll learn more about lifestyle factors in later chapters. Although having a healthy, active lifestyle won't stop brain changes from occurring at all, it can help counteract some of the factors that cause these changes.

CLASSIFICATION SYSTEMS FOR NORMAL COGNITIVE CHANGES

As we mentioned in chapter 1, there are specific terms for describing the normal cognitive changes that occur with age, and many of these have their own definition or set of criteria. This is similar to the idea of using diagnostic criteria to identify the presence of MCI. The purpose of having criteria for normal cognitive aging, however, is somewhat different from that of having criteria for MCI and other cognitive disorders. It is unlikely that anyone would be "diagnosed" with normal cognitive aging for the purpose of their medical care. The term is more likely to be used in order to confirm that no abnormal cognitive problems are present. In addition, having a standard set of criteria is useful in research studies to verify that a person is a normal, healthy older adult. In this way, we can be sure that findings from the research are indeed indicative of normal aging as opposed to any cognitive disorder.

Terms for normal age-related cognitive change appeared in the medical and scientific literature as early as the 1920s. These earliest terms included *normal senility* and *normal senescent decline*, and were descriptive in nature. In the mid 1980s, a group of experts was convened by the National Institute of Mental Health to create formal criteria for characterizing individuals with normal memory changes. The term that resulted from this conference was *age-associated memory impairment*. The criteria are listed in Box 2.2. Briefly, this category is defined by individuals age 50 or older who have subjective memory complaints and obtain scores on standardized memory tests that are lower than what is seen for *younger* adults. The reason the comparison is with younger adults is that this implies there has been a change in memory related to age, and it also excludes individuals who have superior memory abilities for their age. Additional criteria for age-associated memory impairment, similar to those for MCI, include an absence of a decline in intelligence, dementia, or any history of health conditions that could affect cognition. Modifications to this basic definition have been made in order to increase the reliability of the classification. Some of the modifications included changes to the term, resulting in similar but new terms, including *age-consistent memory impairment* and *age-associated memory decline*. It has been suggested, and we tend to agree, that it is inappropriate to use the word "impairment" when describing memory changes that are normal. In this sense, "decline" is more fitting.

More recently, the term *age-related cognitive decline* is used in the current *Diagnostic and Statistical Manual of Mental Disorders*.

Box 2.2 Criteria for Age-Associated Memory Impairment

---

1. Inclusion criteria (these must be present):
   a. Males and females age 50 years or older.
   b. Complaints of memory loss, such as problems remembering names, locations of objects, tasks to be performed, or telephone numbers. Onset of memory problems must be described as gradual, with no sudden worsening.
   c. Memory test performance that is at least 1 standard deviation below the mean for young adults on a standardized test of recent memory with adequate normative data.
   d. Evidence of adequate or normal intellectual function on an IQ test.
   e. Absence of dementia, as measured by a general cognitive screen.
2. Exclusion criteria (these must not be present):
   a. Delirium, confusion, or other disturbances of consciousness.
   b. Neurological disorders that affect cognition.
   c. Infective and inflammatory diseases of the brain.
   d. History of head injury, psychiatric diagnoses, or alcoholism.
   e. Use of drugs that affect cognition.
   f. Any medical disorder that could produce cognitive deterioration.

This condition is defined by the presence of an objectively identified change in cognition (such as memory or problem solving) that is within the normal range for the person's age and is not caused by a psychiatric or neurological condition. Although by definition this is not considered to be a "mental disorder," it may still be the focus of clinical attention, which is why it is included in this clinical manual.

COMPARISON OF AMNESTIC MCI AND NORMAL COGNITIVE AGING

Let's go back to the diagnostic criteria for amnestic MCI to see how they compare with the definition of normal cognitive aging. The MCI criteria were presented in Box 1.3 in chapter 1. As we make our comparisons, you'll see that there are many similarities between these concepts, but there is at least one crucial difference.

By definition, neither amnestic MCI nor normal cognitive aging is associated with generalized cognitive impairment. In other words, nonmemory cognitive abilities such as attention, problem solving, language, and visual-spatial abilities are within the normal range for the individual's age.

Another similarity is that both MCI and normal cognitive aging are characterized by intact functional activities. This means that any memory changes that are present are not severe enough to interfere with the individual's ability to carry out his or her normal daily activities such as shopping, cooking, or managing basic finances. Given that MCI and normal aging both involve normal generalized cognition and normal daily functioning, none of these individuals meet criteria for dementia. That is, they do not have multiple cognitive impairments for their age and they are not dependent on others for their daily functioning.

One of the MCI diagnostic criteria may or may not apply to individuals with normal age-related cognitive changes. This is the presence of a subjective memory complaint. Because normal aging is indeed associated with subtle cognitive changes, some individuals may report a significant decline over time, whereas others may not notice them as much or may not find them problematic. As we mentioned in chapter 1, some individuals with MCI may not be aware of the degree of their memory decline. As such, the presence or absence of a subjective memory complaint cannot be used to distinguish between individuals with MCI and those experiencing normal age-related memory changes.

The primary difference between MCI and normal memory decline is the degree of objective memory loss. As we reviewed in this chapter, normal, healthy cognitive aging is associated with changes in some memory processes and some memory types. By definition, individuals with memory scores that fall within the average range for their age are considered to be experiencing normal age-related cognitive changes. Individuals with MCI obtain memory scores that are considerably lower than average for their age, generally in the lowest 5% of individuals with a similar age and background.

Box 2.3 Comparison of Amnestic MCI and Normal Cognitive Aging

Criterion	Amnestic MCI	Normal aging
Subjective memory complaint	Usually present	Present or absent
Objective memory	Impaired for age	Normal for age
Generalized (nonmemory) cognitive abilities	Normal for age	Normal for age
Functional activities	Normal	Normal
Dementia	Absent	Absent

Box 2.3 presents a summary of the similarities and differences between amnestic MCI and normal cognitive aging.

OTHER CAUSES OF MEMORY CHANGE

Memory changes, of course, can be caused by factors other than normal aging and MCI. There are a number of medical and other causes of memory change. The good news is that some of these can be reversed or at least stabilized by appropriate medical treatment and by making important lifestyle modifications.

Your Health and Memory

Any health condition that affects your brain has the potential to impact your memory. The most obvious example of this is dementia. Dementia is usually associated with memory loss. One type of dementia, Alzheimer's dementia, almost always begins with memory loss—except in rare variations of the disease—and always progresses over time. You'll read more about the different dementias and their respective cognitive effects in chapter 3.

Head trauma can also cause memory loss. If you have ever hit your head in a fall or in a motor-vehicle accident and the injury was serious enough to cause you to lose consciousness or to feel ill, then you likely sustained some level of injury to your brain. In most cases, the cognitive problems associated with head trauma are mild and last a few months or less. More severe head trauma, for example if it was associated with an extended coma, can result in more significant and longer-lasting cognitive problems.

Another type of brain injury, cardiovascular accidents, occur when there is a blockage of blood flow (*ischemia*) or a bleed (*hemorrhage*) in your brain. The more common word for cardiovascular accident is *stroke*. If you have had a stroke, your memory may have been affected if the damage occurred in a brain region that is important for memory. As with head trauma, the degree and duration of the memory impairment will also depend on the severity of the damage to the brain. Some strokes are small and the effects are temporary. These are called transient ischemic attacks, TIAs, or ministrokes. A single transient ischemic attack will not result in long-term problems, but if there are many of them, the effects can accumulate. Large strokes can result in extensive problems with memory, language, other cognitive abilities, or motor function. Although these impairments always show some level of improvement over time, they may not completely return to normal.

Dementia, head trauma, and stroke are all fairly obvious conditions that can be associated with memory problems. If you experience any of these, you or those close to you would know that something major has happened. Other health conditions that can affect memory are not as noticeable right away. The symptoms may be more gradual and may never become severe. It is important for you to be aware of these so that you know when it is time to talk to your doctor. In many cases, treating these conditions can result in full (or nearly full) restoration of your memory ability to its former level.

The most common subtle medical problems that affect memory in older adults are thyroid disease and vitamin deficiency. The thyroid is a gland located in your neck behind your voice box that produces and releases hormones into your body. An underactive thyroid gland results in *hypothyroidism*, which can cause mild difficulty with attention and memory. There are also physical symptoms of hypothyroidism, including fatigue, feeling cold, weight gain, depression, and constipation. It is important to tell your doctor if you are experiencing these symptoms. Hypothyroidism can be easily treated with medication, and the symptoms are usually well controlled after ongoing treatment.

Vitamin B$_{12}$ deficiency can result from too little of this vitamin in your diet or, more likely, from problems absorbing the vitamin. The symptoms of vitamin B$_{12}$ deficiency are usually vague, and can include feeling tired, difficulty with attention and memory, irritability, and depression. If vitamin B$_{12}$ deficiency is suspected, it is easy to diagnose with a simple blood test and easy to treat with vitamin pills or injections. Treatment is usually associated with improvement in the cognitive symptoms including memory problems.

Other health conditions can affect your cognition because they are related to heart health. A condition you will learn more about in chapter 11, *metabolic syndrome*, is defined by the presences of multiple medical conditions including high blood sugar, high blood pressure, elevated cholesterol and fat, obesity around the waist, and insulin resistance. A related condition, *diabetes*, is also a risk factor for heart disease. Although not everyone with these conditions experiences cognitive impairments, there is evidence that these metabolic disorders can be associated with cognitive changes such as slowed speed of thinking and subtle general cognitive difficulties. If you have any of these conditions, it is important to ensure that they are treated.

Another health factor that can impact your memory is sleep. Sleep is known to be important for retaining information that you learn. In other words, when you learn something new, you will be able to recall it better the next day if you sleep well than if you sleep poorly that night. There is some evidence that this is because high-quality sleep helps to optimize the activity in the hippocampus, which is one of the brain regions that is important for memory. In chapter 8, you can learn more about changes in sleep that are seen in individuals with MCI and how this impacts their memory performance.

The final category of health issues that we'll address in this section involves the substances that you take into your body: alcohol, cigarette smoke, caffeine, and medications. Light to moderate alcohol consumption, such as drinking 1 or 2 glasses of wine per day, does not have a negative effect on cognition in healthy middle-aged and older adults. There is even some research that shows a slight positive effect of moderate alcohol consumption over abstinence. However, as you might expect, heavy drinking on a long-term basis is not good for your brain or your cognitive abilities. Heavy alcohol consumption can result in atrophy of neurons and the brain overall. Cognitive impairments associated with heavy drinking can include problems with attention, memory, and visual-spatial skills such as map reading. These impairments can remain even after prolonged abstinence, which means that part of the brain damage is permanent.

Cigarette smoking has a negative effect on memory, although the effect is indirect. Smoking does not have an immediate impact on your cognitive abilities. However, prolonged smoking puts you at increased risk of having a stroke or even *vascular dementia*—a serious cognitive problem associated with multiple strokes.

Having a bit of caffeine everyday, on the other hand, may be good for your memory. There is evidence that people who drink coffee or tea habitually tend to do better on memory tests than people who do not drink caffeinated beverages. In particular, if you tend to lose energy over the course of the day, having some caffeine in the afternoon can be helpful for your memory at that time of day. The reason this happens is that caffeine can make you feel more alert and help you pay attention, and this results in better memory. Interestingly, there is also some evidence that caffeine can stimulate the growth of neurons in areas of the brain important for memory, namely the hippocampus, and this could also contribute to the positive effects of caffeine on memory.

A number of prescription and over-the-counter medications can also affect your memory. The effect of medication on memory may be for the better or for the worse. Some medical and mental health conditions—such as hypothyroidism, vitamin deficiency, depression, and anxiety—cause memory problems. Successful treatment of these conditions with medication can result in improvements to memory, although in some cases it depends on the particular medication that you take. Medications that make you feel sleepy or sedated can have a negative impact on your memory. Some examples are first-generation antihistamines (for example, diphenhydramine) used to treat allergy symptoms, and tricyclic antidepressants (such as amitriptyline and desipramine) that are used to treat depression. Other medications that can have negative effects on memory include benzodiazepines used to treat anxiety, and antiseizure medications used to treat epilepsy.

This discussion is not meant to discourage you from taking your medications. If you are taking any of these medications, it is important that you continue to do so in order to treat the underlying medical or mental-health problem. The risk of not treating epilepsy or depression, for example, may far outweigh any negative effects on memory. This information is presented here so that you can have a better understanding about what types of factors may be impacting your own memory. If you suspect that your medications may be affecting your memory, you can talk with your doctor to find out if there are any alternative medications that treat the underlying condition with fewer effects on memory.

To sum up the effects of heath on memory, in order to maximize your memory, talk to your doctor if you think you may have thyroid disease or a vitamin deficiency, consider having a glass of wine every day, stop smoking, enjoy your coffee or tea, do your best to get a good night's sleep, and take a careful look at the medications you are taking. Other ways to maximize your memory through lifestyle factors such as diet and exercise are discussed in chapters 11 and 12.

Memory and Mental Health

A variety of mental-health disorders can be associated with cognitive symptoms, the most common of which are depression and anxiety. Most people experience some symptoms of depression now and then, such as feeling sad or losing interest in activities that they normally enjoy. Clinical depression is diagnosed when these symptoms persist over time and interfere with the ability to function at work or at home. Cognitive problems that can accompany depression include decreased attention, slowed thinking speed, and difficulty learning and retrieving new information. Fortunately, depression can be successfully treated in most individuals through psychotherapy or medication. As the mood symptoms of depression improve with treatment, so do the cognitive symptoms.

Another mental health issue is anxiety. Everyone feels nervous or worried from time to time, such as when faced with new situations or upsetting events. In a more severe form, anxiety can involve unrealistic or excessive worry along with physical symptoms such as shaking, muscle tension, and shortness of breath. It is diagnosed as a clinical disorder when the symptoms are sufficient to interfere with a person's ability to participate in their normal activities. As with depression, anxiety disorders are associated with cognitive problems involving attention, speed, and memory. Fortunately, anxiety can be treated with psychotherapy and medications. Cognitive problems tend to diminish with treatment, along with improvement in mood and physical symptoms.

A closely related concept is that of the "worried well." This term specifically applies to individuals who fear they have a medical problem, but don't actually have that medical problem. Of relevance here is the worry about having Alzheimer's disease. The worried well who fear Alzheimer's disease are often individuals who have a family history of this disease. Even without a family history, some people worry about this disease when they start to notice changes in their memory. Given that virtually everyone who reaches a certain age will experience some decline in his or her memory, this worry can affect a large number of individuals. For some people, educating themselves about the difference between normal aging and dementia, by reading the material listed in the recommended readings sections of this book, is helpful. For others, a trip to the doctor for screening and reassurance may be needed.

The Role of Stress

Stress is something that is experienced by most everyone. Stress is defined as a reaction to a perceived loss of control over situations or events that are typically new or unpredictable. Stressors can be physical, such as major surgery or an illness, or psychological, such as having too much to do and not enough time to do it. They can involve positive events, such as a new job or going on vacation, or negative events, such as a divorce or financial difficulties. Although stress happens at all stages of life, some common stressors are more likely to occur later in life, such as the death of a spouse, retirement, or health problems.

Exposure to stress causes a physiological response in your body. Your adrenal glands, which are located on top of your kidneys, produce hormones such as cortisol and epinephrine in response to stress. Cortisol is beneficial in short doses for short periods of time. For example, it can give you a boost of energy that helps you pay attention and work more efficiently when you are getting close to a deadline. When present in higher doses for longer periods of time, however, cortisol can have negative effects, suppressing your immune system, causing insomnia, and increasing your blood pressure.

Cortisol has direct effects on the brain. In high doses, it inhibits the formation and retention of new neurons in the hippocampus. Some studies have shown that individuals with chronically high stress and high levels of cortisol have measurably smaller hippocampal volumes as seen on MRI images of the brain. As you can imagine, if your hippocampus isn't healthy, you will experience more problems with your memory. You may have noticed that, during times of stress, you tend to make more memory mistakes than during times that your life is more stressfree. This is because stress and cortisol can have a negative effect on attention as well as on the encoding and retrieval of information from memory. The effect of stress on memory is illustrated in Box 2.4.

Some degree of stress is unavoidable in life. Fortunately for all of us, though, the negative effects of stress on the brain and on memory are reversible. When cortisol levels return to normal after being elevated, the brain eventually returns to normal, as does memory. The way that stress is counteracted is through relaxation. Stress and relaxation are opposites, and when one goes up, the other goes down. It is important to find activities that you find relaxing and engage in them often. Informal ways of relaxing may involve listening to music, taking a walk along a river, or having a cup of tea with a good friend. More formal methods include learning how to do deep-breathing, progressive muscle relaxation, or visual imagery. Many forms of exercise, such as Tai Chi and yoga, can also help you feel relaxed. You will learn more about stress and relaxation in chapter 9.

Attention and Distraction

Attention is an important precursor to memory. If you are not paying attention to something—such as a conversation or what you are reading—you are unlikely to remember much of the content later.

Box 2.4 Case Vignette of Normal Memory Changes, Illustrating the Effect of Stress on Memory

---

Ichiro is a 68-year-old gentleman who has been reasonably happy and healthy for most of his life. However, in the past year, a number of significant events have occurred. He retired from his job after 35 loyal years with the same company, his wife suffered a mild stroke, their house needed some major repairs, and his last medical check-up indicated a need for further testing for possible prostate cancer. On top of all this, he found that his mind was wandering from whatever task was at hand, and he was forgetting simple things such as where he parked the car and what he planned to make for dinner. Fortunately, over the next few months, he developed new hobbies that captured his interest and helped fill his time, his wife's health improved, the house repairs were finally over, and he learned that his prostate required medical monitoring but no immediate treatment. He also realized that he was not as distracted and was not making as many careless errors as in the past. A year later, everything was still stable, and he was able to chalk up the short period of increased forgetfulness to the stress he was encountering at that time. And that gave him even one less thing to worry about!

We have to pay attention in order to ensure that we encode. There is an interesting field of research that has looked at the relationship between attention and memory. Researchers can manipulate how much attention participants pay to information that they are told to remember, such as a list of words, by having them do a second task at the same time, such as working out math problems. Not surprisingly, when you have to do a second task at the same time, you don't learn new information very well.

In everyday life, this means that it is important to decrease distractions by working in a quiet place when you are trying to learn something new. If you are reading the instruction manual for your new smart phone or digital camera so that you can learn how to use it, turn off the television and the radio and go to a room where no one will interrupt you. In a similar vein, you should focus on only one thing at a time. Don't try to check your e-mail or have a conversation with someone at the same time that you are studying the manual.

MEMORY CHANGES THAT ARE NOT "NORMAL"

As we've discussed in this chapter, there is a wide range of memory changes that can be considered to be normal with age and, therefore, no cause for alarm. Generally, you are in good company if you experience occasional memory slips—such as problems remembering names, where you put something, or what you were just about to do—and particularly if you remember the information eventually or with a reminder. Sometimes these memory mistakes can be the cause of frustration when you waste time looking for lost items, or embarrassment when you pause noticeably before retrieving the name of an old acquaintance. If these are the worst consequences of your memory problems, then you likely have little to worry about.

So how do you know if your memory problems are beyond what is normal for your age? There are certain "red flags" that may indicate a problem, some of which are listed in Box 2.5., and you should talk to your doctor if you experience any of these. One of these red flags is

---

Box 2.5 When You Should Talk to Your Doctor about Your Memory

Tell your doctor if you have any of these memory problems:

- Asking questions or making comments repetitively, usually within a conversation.
- Getting lost in familiar places.
- Not remembering names of people that you know well, even after giving yourself some time to think about it.
- Not remembering something after a reminder.
- Not remembering important, meaningful events soon after they happened.

Tell your doctor if any of the following are true:

- Others mention problems with your memory that you were not aware of.
- You spend an excessive amount of time checking or organizing in order to cope with your memory changes.
- You give up activities you used to enjoy because they are more difficult or awkward.

if other people tell you that you are repeating yourself or if *they* have more concerns about your memory than *you* do. This may indicate that you are not fully aware of the extent of the memory mistakes you are making. You should also take note of memory problems related to information that you should know well, such as the names of family members or close friends, or how to find your way around familiar places.

Memory mistakes that are not attributable to retrieval problems should also be noted. Momentarily "blanking" on a friend's name is not unusual, but the name should eventually come to you. If you don't remember a recent conversation or event, even after others who were involved describe it to you, this is a significant memory problem reflecting something more than retrieval failure.

Important or emotional events are usually well remembered. Thus, if you have trouble remembering a momentous occasion shortly after it happened, this may indicate a more serious memory failure.

Another way to gauge the seriousness of a memory mistake is to look at the consequences. As we mentioned before, many memory mistakes can be frustrating or embarrassing, and this is a normal consequence of many age-related memory problems. Memory mistakes are more significant if they result in you withdrawing from activities that you used to enjoy, for example, no longer attending your bridge club because you can't remember what cards have been dealt or because you have trouble remembering the names of other club members. Another significant consequence is having to spend an excessive amount of time checking things, writing notes, or organizing yourself in order to compensate for your memory failures. Some degree of this type of activity is a good thing, but when it consumes a large portion of your day, it likely means that you are having more trouble coping with the memory change. Clearly, if there are safety or financial consequences to your memory changes, such as leaving pots on the stove or forgetting to pay bills, it is time to talk to your doctor. Finally, if you are starting to depend on others to help you with your normal daily activities such as shopping, cooking, taking your medications, or remembering your appointments, this is an indication that your memory problems are more than what would normally be expected with age.

A FINAL WORD

For many people, knowing what to expect regarding age-related memory changes is a challenge. You can't always tell whether or to what extent others your age are experiencing memory problems, making it difficult for you to have a comparison point. It can be helpful to educate yourself about normal aging. There are many books about memory and aging written for the general population, and some of these are listed in the "recommended readings" at the end of this chapter. You can also find lots of information from reputable sources online. Another way to educate yourself informally is to talk to other people your age about their own memory experiences. You will likely feel relieved if they report the same challenges that you have experienced.

An important way to deal with memory changes is to learn strategies to help you improve your memory and to engage in a lifestyle that promotes a healthy brain and memory. You will learn more about these approaches in section 3 of this book.

After you have educated yourself and have made reasonable attempts to manage your memory, you may still find that you are worried about your memory. If so, you should make an appointment to talk to your doctor. You may benefit from a formal evaluation of your memory to determine whether your memory changes are normal for your age or whether they indicate some cause for concern. Sometimes memory changes are reversible, particularly when they are related to treatable health conditions or stress. Working closely with your doctor is the best way to ensure that you are managing your cognitive health in an optimal way.

Box 2.6 Questions to Ask Your Doctor if MCI Is Suspected or Confirmed in Yourself or in Your Family Member

---

1. Do the memory mistakes that I describe to you sound normal for my age?
2. Are you able to conduct a cognitive screen in your office to determine whether my thinking abilities are normal for my age?

(continued)

Box 2.6 (Continued)

---

3. Have you noticed any unusual changes in my cognition? (Ask this if your doctor knows you well.)
4. Do you think my level of concern about my cognition is out of keeping with my level of actual cognitive ability? In other words, am I overly concerned?
5. Are there side effects to any of my current medications that could be contributing to my cognitive problems?
6. Should I be cutting back on my intake of caffeine and/or alcohol?

RECOMMENDED READINGS

Einstein, G. O., & McDaniel, M. A. (2004). *Memory fitness: A guide for successful aging.* New Haven: Yale University Press.

Strauch, B. (2010). *The secret life of the grown-up brain: The surprising talents of the middle-aged mind.* New York: Viking.

3

How Mild Cognitive Impairment Differs from Dementia

You now have a good sense of what mild cognitive impairment (MCI) is, and how it differs from normal aging. It is also important for you to understand how MCI differs from dementia. In this chapter we will introduce you to various kinds of dementia, and point out how MCI differs from them. We will start by asking, what is dementia?

Dementia is a brain disorder that causes disturbances in memory and other cognitive functions and often, also, in emotional control, social behavior, or motivation. Let's unpack that. Dementia arises from a disease of the brain; although later in the course of the disease, people with dementia may have symptoms such as poor balance or incontinence, these symptoms are ultimately the result of brain systems breaking down, sending improper signals to the body, and not due to problems with the legs or bladder. Another term you may run across describing dementia is *neurodegenerative*. This term is really a combination of the fact that dementia is a brain disorder (neuro) and progressive (degenerative). Disturbances in cognitive functions mean that abilities like memory, attention, problem solving, and language are affected.

Dementia is an umbrella term—just as there are different kinds of arthritis, there are different kinds of dementia, and each kind has a different cause. Most of these causes are still poorly understood, but we will share with you what is currently known about their causes. Years ago, all these kinds of dementia were lumped together and referred to

47

as "senility." However, our understanding of different types of dementia and the quality of our diagnostic tools has improved to the point where it is easier to determine the type of dementia a person has. This process is still not fool proof, however, as different types of dementias share many common features, and people can have mixed dementias, meaning that they have more than one type. This is particularly true for vascular dementia, as we will discuss later.

Millions of people worldwide are living with dementia, and the number of people with dementia is going to rise dramatically in the coming years due to shifting demographic trends. The Alzheimer's Association in the United States (www.alz.org) reported in 2010 that 5.1 million Americans have some form of dementia, and that, by the year 2030, this number will rise to 7.7 million. The Alzheimer's Society of Canada (www.alzheimer.ca) published a similar report, stating that, in 2010, half a million Canadians were living with some form of dementia, and that this number will rise to 1.1 million by 2038. Similar trends are found in other countries, especially in those

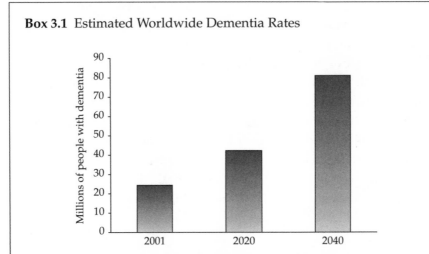

Box 3.1 Estimated Worldwide Dementia Rates

Adapted from Ferri, C. P., Prince, M., Brayne, C., Brodaty, H., Fratiglioni, L., Gangluli, M., Hall, K., Hasegawa, K., Hendrie, H., Huang, Y., Jorm, A., Mathers, C., Menezes, P. R., Rimmer, E., Scazufca, M., Alzheimer's Disease International. (2005). Global prevalence of dementia: A Delphi concensus study. *Lancet, 366,* 2112–2117, with permission from Elsevier.

countries that experienced a post-World War II baby boom similar to what occurred in North America. Worldwide estimates are shown in Box 3.1. The costs of such an increase in dementia rates are enormous, both in terms of health-care spending and on the personal lives of those living with dementia and their loved ones. This provides great impetus to develop better methods to diagnose, treat, and prevent dementia. The primary goal of this book is to provide you with information and tools to help you decrease the chance that you will develop dementia.

GENERAL DIAGNOSTIC CRITERIA FOR DEMENTIA

For years, professionals typically followed the *Diagnostic and Statistical Manual of Mental Disorders-IV-TR,* or *DSM-IV-TR* published by the American Psychiatric Association (www.psych.org) when diagnosing dementia, and this was often complemented by additional disease-specific criteria. These criteria require that at a bare minimum, the patient has a significant impairment in memory plus one other domain (for example, problem solving, language), *and* that these impairments are persistent and severe enough to interfere with the patient's work, usual social activities, or relationships. It should be noted that the requirement of memory impairment in the diagnosis of dementia has been contentious. Some forms of dementia, as you will see, affect other thinking abilities primarily, like language, and memory is relatively spared. The next version of the *DSM,* the *DSM-V,* is due to be launched in May of 2013, and, currently, a working group is proposing to do away with the term *dementia* altogether and replace it with a category title of *Major Neurocognitive Disorders,* and also to allow for the cognitive deficits to be in any relevant domain. Readers can keep updated on these changes at this Web site: http://www. dsm5.org/Pages/Default.aspx. In parallel, the U.S. National Institute of Aging is working in partnership with the Alzheimer's Association to develop new criteria for the diagnosis of dementia. They, too, are recommending that these criteria no longer require memory impairment for diagnosis. This group's criteria for all-cause dementia, that is, dementia due to any cause, are listed in Box 3.2.

Box 3.2 The National Institute of Aging-Alzheimer's Association
Diagnostic Criteria for All-Cause Dementia

Dementia is diagnosed when there are cognitive and behavioral
(neuropsychiatric) symptoms that:

- Interfere with the ability to function at work or at usual activities.
- Represent a decline from previous levels of functioning and
  performing.
- Are not explained by delirium or major psychiatric disorder.
- Cognitive impairment is detected and diagnosed through a combination of (1) history-taking from the patient and a knowledgeable
  informant and (2) an objective cognitive assessment.
- The cognitive or behavioral impairment involves a minimum of
  two of the following domains:
    - Memory
    - Reasoning
    - Visual-spatial abilities
    - Language
    - Personality, behavior, or comportment

Adapted from McKhann, G. M., Knopman, D. S., Chertkow, H., Hyman, B. T.,
Jack Jr., C. R., Kawas, C. H., Klunk, W. E., Koroshetz, W. J., Manly, J. J., Mayeux, R.,
Mohs, R. C., Morris, J. C., Rossor, M. N., Scheltens, P., Carrillo, M. C., Thies, B.,
Weintraub, S., & Phelps, C. H. (2011). The diagnosis of dementia due to Alzheimer's
disease: Recommendations from the National Institute on Aging-Alzheimer's
Association workgroups on diagnostic guidelines for Alzheimer's disease.
Alzheimer's & Dementia, 7, 263–269, with permission from Elsevier.

Regardless of how the name and diagnosis of dementia changes
in the near and more distant future, what is important is that the
memory and other cognitive deficits present in MCI are usually less
severe than they are in dementia, and people with MCI do not have
significant limitations in their ability to work or engage in normal
social activities.

In the remainder of this chapter, we review the major types of
dementia. Alzheimer's disease, either alone or in combination with
other kinds of dementia, accounts for 50–75% of cases of dementia. It is, thus, not surprising that almost everyone has heard of
Alzheimer's disease. The other types of dementia are less common

Box 3.3 Most Typical Cognitive Symptoms of Different Types of Early Stage Dementia

	Memory Deficit	Visual-spatial Deficit	Attention Deficit	Executive Deficit	Language Deficit
Alzheimer's Disease	Significant	Mild	Mild	Mild	Mild
Vascular Dementia	Mild	None	Moderate	Significant	None
Frontotemporal–Frontal variant	Mild	None	Mild	Significant	None
Frontotemporal–Temporal variant	Mild	None	None	None	Significant
Parkinson's Dementia	Mild	None	Mild	Mild	None
Lewy Body Disease	Mild	Moderate	Significant	Significant	None

than Alzheimer's disease, but many of you will have heard of at least one of the types we discuss here. To help appreciate the similarities and differences among the different forms of dementia, Box 3.3 describes the most typical cognitive symptoms of each of the types we discuss in this chapter. This chart is intended for broad descriptive purposes only, because how a particular form of dementia affects cognitive abilities can be highly variable across people, and, in general, as any form of dementia progresses, more cognitive abilities are affected. Nevertheless, we feel that it is important to describe these various forms of dementia in this book because MCI can develop into almost any one of them. In addition, we hope that you find this information to be a valuable resource that you can return to in the future if need be.

ALZHEIMER'S DISEASE

Alzheimer's disease is far and away the most common of the different kinds of dementia. It is named after German physician Alois Alzheimer who first described the disorder in 1906.

For a definition of dementia due to Alzheimer's disease, we can add to the definition we provided earlier for dementia in general: Dementia due to Alzheimer's disease is *an insidious, progressive brain disorder that causes disturbances in memory and other cognitive functions and often also in emotional control, social behavior, or motivation. Insidious* means that it creeps up on you; its onset is not abrupt, like the sudden loss of movement or speech after a stroke, but gradual, so that it is often difficult to pinpoint exactly when it started. *Progressive* means that it continues to get worse. Although there may be periods of plateau when symptoms are stable, this is followed by continuing decline.

For many years, professionals used criteria spelled out by the *DSM-IV-TR* and/or the National Institute of Neurological and Communicative Diseases and Stroke—Alzheimer's Disease and Related Disorders Association (now known as the Alzheimer's Association) when diagnosing Alzheimer's disease. However, our knowledge about this disease has grown tremendously in the past decade, and so recently the National Institute of Aging and the Alzheimer's Association charged a group of experts to revise the criteria for Alzheimer's disease. These criteria were published in 2011, and are listed in Box 3.4. Like their predecessors, these criteria distinguish between dementia due to "Probable Alzheimer's Disease" and "Possible Alzheimer's Dementia," because it is still true today that Alzheimer's disease cannot be definitively diagnosed unless characteristic brain pathology is obtained from a brain biopsy or via a postmortem examination. A "Probable" diagnosis occurs when everything points in the direction of Alzheimer's and other potential causes of the symptom have been ruled out. A "Possible" diagnosis occurs when a professional is fairly certain that Alzheimer's disease is present but cannot fully rule out other causes of the symptoms, or in cases in which the onset, course, or symptoms are not classic (for example, if *agnosia*, which is the inability to recognize objects accurately, is the primary presenting symptom). However, it is important to note that this group does not endorse a diagnosis of dementia due to Alzheimer's disease if the symptoms suggest that another form of dementia dominates.

Finally, a third set of tools is used to determine where along the spectrum from normal aging to severe dementia a patient is. The

Box 3.4 National Institute of Aging—Alzheimer's Association Criteria for Dementia due to Alzheimer's Disease

Probable Alzheimer's disease

The person has cognitive or behavioral symptoms that meets the criteria for dementia listed in Box 3.3, and have the following characteristics:

1. Insidious onset.
2. Clear-cut history of worsening of cognition by report or observation.
3. The initial and most prominent cognitive deficits are evident on history and examination on one of the following categories:
   a. Amnestic presentation.
   b. Nonamnestic presentation (language presentation, visual-spatial presentation, or executive dysfunction presentation).

Diagnosis of dementia due to probable Alzheimer's disease is more certain if there is evidence of progressive cognitive decline on subsequent evaluations or evidence of a causative genetic mutation (described later in this chapter).

Possible Alzheimer's disease

The person has cognitive and behavioral symptoms described for probable Alzheimer's disease, but either of the following is true:

A. Atypical course: either has a sudden onset of cognitive impairment or insufficient historical detail or objective cognitive documentation of progressive decline.
B. Mixed presentation: for example, concomitant cerebrovascular disease (stroke or white matter disease, defined later in this chapter), features of Lewy Body Disease, or evidence of another neurological or non-neurological condition.

Adapted from McKhann, G. M., Knopman, D. S., Chertkow, H., Hyman, B. T., Jack Jr., C. R., Kawas, C. H., Klunk, W. E., Koroshetz, W. J., Manly, J. J., Mayeux, R., Mohs, R. C., Morris, J. C., Rossor, M. N., Scheltens, P., Carrillo, M. C., Thies, B., Weintraub, S., & Phelps, C. H. (2011). The diagnosis of dementia due to Alzheimer's disease: Recommendations from the National Institute on Aging-Alzheimer's Association workgroups on diagnostic guidelines for Alzheimer's disease. *Alzheimer's & Dementia*, 7, 263–269, with permission from Elsevier..

Clinical Dementia Rating rates patients in six different functional areas (orientation to date/place, memory, language, functioning at home, social activities, and personal care) and results in an overall score where 0 is normal, 0.5 is questionable dementia, 1.0 is mild dementia, 2.0 is moderate dementia, 3.0 is severe dementia, 4.0 is profound dementia, and 5.0 represents the terminal stage.

Early-Onset versus Late-Onset Alzheimer's Disease

The vast majority of people who develop Alzheimer's disease do so in their later years, after the age of 65 but most often in one's 70s. This form of the disease is called late-onset for obvious reasons. About 5–10% of people with Alzheimer's disease develop it before the age of 65, in which case it is called early-onset. A number of risk factors for Alzheimer's disease have been identified. These risk factors will be discussed in detail in chapter 5. What is important to note here is that none of these factors can predict with certainty who will and who will not develop Alzheimer's disease. Indeed, late-onset Alzheimer's disease is sometimes called *sporadic*, meaning that it can occur with no obvious inheritance of the disease.

There is also a genetic early-onset form of Alzheimer's disease. This form of the disease is particularly devastating for two reasons. First, people with it have a 50–50 chance of passing it along to their children. Second, symptoms most typically develop when people are in their 50s, but can begin earlier, so it affects people at the peak of their occupational and child-rearing lives. This form of the disease accounts for only 1–2% of people with Alzheimer's disease. If you do not have a family history of relatives developing Alzheimer's at a young age, it is unlikely that you have this form of dementia. We will describe these genetic factors in more detail in chapter 5.

Neuropsychological and Behavioral Symptoms of Alzheimer's Disease

The primary neuropsychological characteristic of Alzheimer's disease is typically memory impairment, although, as the disease progresses, more and more cognitive, behavioral, and physiological functions become affected. In terms of memory, early in the course of the disease patients will complain that they can remember personal events from long ago quite well, but cannot seem to remember more recent events. Although people usually describe this as a problem with short-term memory, the real difficulty is in storing information from recent or short-term memory into long-term memory, a process that scientists called *consolidation*. As the disease progresses, the ability to retrieve information already stored in long-term memory gradually erodes as well. Other forms of memory are relatively spared, at least until later stages of the disease. These include *semantic memory* for general factual knowledge and *procedural memory* for how to do things. These other types of memory are described in detail in chapter 2.

Recall that, according to the older diagnostic criteria, for someone to be diagnosed with dementia he or she has to have memory impairment *and* an impairment of at least one other higher cognitive function. In Alzheimer's disease, processes such as mental flexibility (for example, switching back and forth between two tasks), being able to name objects, the ability to understand complex speech and complex visual skills are often affected, especially later in the course of the disease. Getting lost is a common problem, due to difficulties remembering familiar routes, and to more complex disruptions in spatial processing. In the early stages of the disease, there can be subtle behavioral effects such as low mood, apathy, or suspiciousness (for example, believing that people are stealing personal belongings). In later stages of the disease, it is not uncommon for patients to have behavioral or psychiatric symptoms, sometimes quite severe, such as agitation, verbal outbursts, or aggression. Box 3.5 provides an illustration of some of the early signs of Alzheimer's disease.

Brain Pathology in Alzheimer's Disease

The hallmark brain pathologies associated with Alzheimer's disease are *plaques*, which are deposits of beta-amyloid protein between nerve cells, and *tangles*, which are twisted filaments of a protein called tau. Most of us eventually develop plaques and tangles, but those with Alzheimer's disease typically have far more of them. However, there is not good agreement on what contribution these pathological features make to the symptoms of Alzheimer's disease, as the amount of pathology is poorly related the severity of patients' symptoms. Some

---

Box 3.5 Case Vignette of an Individual with Probable Alzheimer's
Disease

Susan is a 73-year old homemaker and married mother of four grown
children. Since retiring eight years ago, she has volunteered at the
church as she had since her children were little, and has been busy
helping take care of her three grandchildren. In the last few years,
her husband Bill has noticed her misplacing things about the house,
which is highly unusual because she had always been a very organized person. Susan has also forgotten some important events, like
her promise to watch her son's children during a school professional-
activity day, and is getting more and more stuck for words. For the
last few months Susan has relied on Bill accompanying her on shopping trips, as she was forgetting to purchase important items and
sometimes forgetting to visit certain stores altogether. Last week, she
phoned Bill to ask him how to get home from the drycleaners. This
really alarmed Bill, because she had been going to that drycleaners
for years. His concern for Susan's safety prompted Bill to schedule a doctor's appointment. After what seemed like weeks of tests
and visits, Susan and Bill received the news that she had probable
Alzheimer's disease. Bill and Susan were connected with the local
chapter of the Alzheimer's Society, and as a family they are making
plans for the future to ensure that Susan stays engaged and active in
a safe way.

---

scientists believe that plaques and tangles do not *cause* the impairments associated with the disease, but instead are by-products (like
waste products) of the disease or represent the brain's way of trying
to protect itself from some ongoing injury.

Other procedures can help diagnose Alzheimer's disease, but
many of these procedures are not routinely performed, especially
outside large metropolitan hospital settings that are affiliated with
a university. Computed tomography (CT) or magnetic resonance
imaging (MRI) can show shrinkage, or *atrophy*, in particular brain
regions. These include the medial (that is, toward the inner surface)
temporal lobes, especially the hippocampus, early in the course of
the disease, progressing to lateral (that is, toward the outer surface)
temporal lobes and parietal lobes later in the course of the disease,

when enlargement of the cavities holding cerebral spinal fluid (the ventricles) becomes more prominent (see Box 3.6). One problem with using such measures diagnostically is that simple, automatic ways to get these measures are still in development. There is a wide range of brain sizes among healthy people, which makes it necessary to correct for head size, which can also take some time to do. Also, our brains shrink with age, and so age-related changes in brain size also have to be corrected for. Collecting these brain images at two or more time points, spread out in time (for example, over a two-year period) can help in this regard, to identify progressive atrophy over time.

Additional methods examine functional brain activity using single photon emission computed tomography (SPECT), which measures blood flow, or fluorodeoxyglucon positron emission tomography

---

Box 3.6 Illustration of Slices of a Healthy Brain (left) and a Brain with Alzheimer's Disease (right). Reproduced courtesy of Alzheimer's Disease Research, a program of the American Health Assistance Foundation. (c) 2012.

Notice how the brain regions primarily involved in memory and language are much smaller in the brain with Alzheimer's, and how the cavities that hold cerebrospinal fluid, the ventricles, are larger in the brain with Alzheimer's disease. Reproduced with permission of the American Health Assistance Foundation.

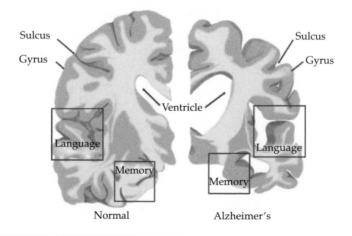

(FDG-PET), which measures glucose metabolism in the brain. In these images, one often sees less blood flow or glucose metabolism in the same regions that show atrophy as the disease progresses. SPECT is not as sensitive as FDG-PET for picking up changes, but FDG-PET is less available and relatively expensive. It also possible, now, to image beta-amyloid in the brain, using another kind of positron emission tomography measure, but given the uncertain relationship between brain amyloid and clinical symptoms, up to now this has been regarded as a research tool and not routinely used in clinics. In the future, it may become more widely used for people with MCI to help diagnose people who may be more likely to progress to Alzheimer's dementia.

Finally, scientists have begun to identify markers of Alzheimer's disease including decreased beta-amyloid and increased tau proteins in the cerebral spinal fluid of patients, obtained by way of a spinal tap. One problem with this latter approach is that these markers can be present in other forms of dementia as well, which may reduce their utility in making a specific diagnosis of Alzheimer's disease. Although these latter procedures are receiving increasing attention in research studies, they are not yet routinely used in clinical practice.

Treatment of Alzheimer's Disease

The drug treatments currently available for Alzheimer's disease treat the *symptoms* of the disease, but they do not directly prevent or cure the disease itself. In other words, the medications may be able to impact the course of progression, perhaps by alleviating symptoms to some degree for a time, but ultimately they cannot prevent disease progression. The production of a brain chemical that is important for learning and memory, called *acetylcholine*, is reduced in people with Alzheimer's disease for reasons no one really understands. Cholinesterase is a brain chemical that breaks down acetylcholine. The main drug treatment for Alzheimer's is a set of cholinesterase inhibitors that prevent the breakdown of acetylcholine, thereby making more acetylcholine available in the brain. The analogy of gasoline in your car might help here. Alzheimer's disease can be thought of as running out of fuel. We can't just refuel the brain with acetylcholine like we can put more gasoline in the car, because there is no way to get it in where it's needed and have it be distributed the way it should be. What we can do, however, is make the use of that fuel more efficient. Cholinesterase inhibitors are like those agents adding efficiency. The three cholinesterase inhibitors that are approved in most markets for use are Aricept, Exelon, and a third that is called Reminyl in Canada and the United Kingdom or Razadyne in the United States (see Box 3.7). These drugs have been found to delay worsening of symptoms for 6 to 12 months for an average of half of patients. One other drug, memantine, called Ebixa in Canada and the United Kingdom or Namenda in the United States works through a different brain chemical called *glutamate*, which is

Box 3.7 Drug Treatments for Symptoms of Alzheimer's Disease

Generic Drug Name	Brand Name	Disease Stages Approved For	Drug Type	Common Side Effects
donepezil	Aricept	all stages	cholinesterase inhibitor	nausea, vomiting, loss of appetite, increase frequency of bowel movements
galantamine	U.S.: Razadyne Canada: Reminyl	mild to moderate	cholinesterase inhibitor	nausea, vomiting, loss of appetite, increase frequency of bowel movements
rivastigmine	Exelon	mild to moderate	cholinesterase inhibitor	nausea, vomiting, loss of appetite, increase frequency of bowel movements
Memantine	U.S.:Namenda Canada: Ebixa	moderate to severe	Glutamate receptor antagonist	headache, constipation, confusion and dizziness

important for learning and memory. When cells die, they release glutamate, and if levels get too high, glutamate can become toxic to other living brain cells. Mematine blocks entry of too much glutamate into the healthy cells while preserving the lower level of glutamate entry necessary for nerve-cell functioning. It has been found to be most effective for those with moderate to severe symptoms of Alzheimer's disease.

The choice of whether to try any of these drugs—and if so, which one—will depend on a discussion with the patient's doctor about the severity of the disease, other health conditions and medications the patient is taking, and consideration of the side effects. If you were to be prescribed one of these drugs, your doctor would likely start you out on a low dose, and then, after a period of time, slightly increase the dose, and so on, until the benefits of the medication are maximized and the side effects are minimized. Often, people who report mild side effects from these medications initially find that their symptoms dissipate as their bodies become accustomed to the drugs. It is important nonetheless to keep your doctor informed of any kind of side effects (and benefits!) you are experiencing from any medication.

Saying "cholinesterase inhibitor" or "glutamate receptor antagonist" is a mouthful for sure, which is no doubt why the general population often refers to them as "memory pills." Whether they have a direct beneficial effect on memory is unclear, however. Some scientists have argued that any memory benefits derived from these drugs might be secondary to improvements in attention or to alleviation of mood and other psychiatric symptoms of the disease.

In addition to these drug treatments of the symptoms of Alzheimer's disease, we cannot stress enough the importance of education and counseling for the loved ones of patients with Alzheimer's disease. By better understanding the disease, you are more knowledgeable about how to respond to your loved one with Alzheimer's, and about the range of changes to the environment and the social and living settings that can help keep your loved one safe and comfortable.

VASCULAR DEMENTIA

Vascular dementia is the second most common form of dementia, accounting for 29–75% of all dementia cases. It is most commonly the result of strategically placed small strokes (a *stroke* is brain damage caused by blockage or bleeding from a blood vessel), or as a result of many very small strokes throughout in the brain (see Box 3.8). It can also result from inflammation of brain arteries, a condition that is called *vasculitis*. Small strokes most often occur in subcortical regions. What that means is that they most often occur in the *white matter*, the long axons that carry information from one nerve cell to another that lie beneath the *cortex*, which is the layers of nerve cells in the outer rim of our brain. We are sure that you have heard the terms *silent stroke, ministroke,* or *TIA* (which stands for transient ischemic attack). These are tiny *infarcts*, or areas where small blood vessels have burst or become blocked. The reason why the term *silent stroke* has been used is that sometimes people are not even aware that it has occurred. The main reason that there is such a wide range of estimated prevalence is that it can be difficult to identify these tiny infarcts on brain images and know for certain that they are vascular in nature. Finally, vascular dementia can also be caused by strategically located larger strokes. Larger strokes are either *ischemic*, due to an obstruction of a blood vessel by fatty deposits that deprives brain tissue beyond the blockage of blood and the oxygen and nutrients it carries, or *hemorrhagic*, due to a rupture of a weakened blood vessel. Collectively, when brain imaging shows spots in the white matter (these spots are sometimes called *hyperintensities* because they are brighter, or more intense in particular forms of imaging) this is referred as *white matter disease*. White matter disease does not refer to any particular type of disease; rather, it just indicates some kind of vascular disease process happening in the white matter.

Pure vascular dementia is rare, estimated at only about 9% of dementia cases. Many people with Alzheimer's disease and other forms of dementia also have some form of vascular pathology. Why? Because the risk factors for vascular dementia are so common: high blood pressure, high cholesterol, diabetes, excessive weight, and smoking. Many of us are living with one or more of these conditions, especially as we get older. It is also the case that the presence of vascular pathology increases the risk of developing Alzheimer's disease pathology; as we describe in more detail in chapter 5, one type of brain pathology seems to make the brain more vulnerable to another.

Box 3.8 Brain MRI images of White Matter Disease

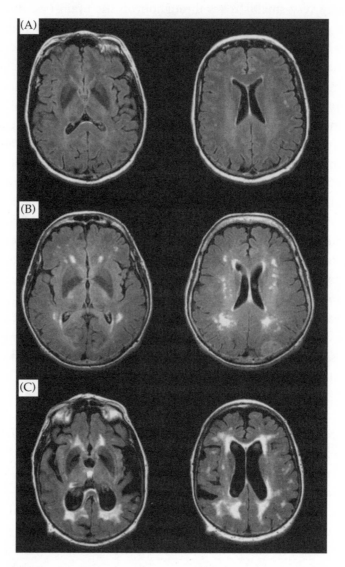

(A) A 71-year-old healthy woman with only a few small white spots called hyperintensities. (B) A 72-year-old woman with moderate white matter disease diagnosed with vascular mild cognitive impairment. (C) An 88-year-old woman with extensive white matter disease who was also thought to have Alzheimer's disease. Images courtesy of Dr. Sandra E. Black of Sunnybrook Hospital and the Rotman Research Institute of Baycrest.

Mild cognitive impairment can be due to early vascular dementia, particularly if is of the nonamnestic variety or multiple-domain amnestic MCI. As we will describe in chapter 6, it is critical for you to have a thorough physical examination to assess your vascular risk factors and treat them if necessary.

Neuropsychological and Behavioral Symptoms of Vascular Dementia

Because vascular dementia is the result of a single or multiple small strokes, the cognitive effects progress in a more stepwise fashion than they do in Alzheimer's disease, in which the progression is more gradual. So a patient may find that, one day, all of a sudden, certain abilities such as naming objects or doing mental arithmetic are more difficult. The specific type(s) of cognitive deficits depend on the location and number of infarcts in that area, but because they are often subcortical, executive function difficulties (for example, doing two things at once, problem solving, maintaining attention in the face of distraction), psychomotor slowing (that is, being slower to think and do things), and difficulties retrieving information from memory are common. Depression is very common among people with vascular dementia.

Treatment of Vascular Dementia

One of the most exciting advances in recent years has been the development of "clot-busters" to treat ischemic strokes. The most common of these drugs is *tissue plasminogen activator*, or *tPA*. If administered less than about 4.5 hours after the onset of stroke symptoms, this drug can help break down the blood clot developing at the site of a vessel obstruction and prevent further brain damage. The short time window within which this drug is effective underscores the importance of seeking emergency treatment (by dialing 911 or your local emergency number) as soon as possible after noticing symptoms of a stroke such as difficulty speaking or understanding speech, paralysis on one side of the body, or vision impairments, or sudden severe headache. Visit www.heartandstroke.ca or www.strokeassociation.org to learn more about symptoms of stroke.

In addition, the good news about vascular dementia is that, unlike other forms of dementia, it has *preventable* and *treatable* risk factors. Staying fit, eating healthy, and not smoking can go a long way toward minimizing the risk of vascular dementia, and getting these factors under control can help slow down the worsening of vascular dementia by preventing further strokes. We make specific recommendations and provide workbooks to help you in these healthy activities in chapters 11 and 12.

FRONTOTEMPORAL DEMENTIA

Frontotemporal dementia is also called frontotemporal lobar degeneration, and just to confuse matters more, it has also been called Pick's disease after the neurologist who first described one of the classical subtypes of it. It is actually not a single dementia, but, rather, it describes a family of dementias that cause progressive atrophy in the frontal and/or temporal lobes of the brain. Approximately 10–20% of dementia cases fall under the frontotemporal lobe umbrella. There are two main variants of the disease, a frontal behavioral variant, and a temporal language variant. The latter is further split into two subtypes, as described in the following section.

It is possible that someone's MCI could reflect the very earliest signs of frontotemporal dementia. This would be particularly true if the dominant symptoms were behavioral, executive, or language oriented, but very unlikely to be the case if memory impairment was a dominant symptom and one was given the diagnosis of amnestic MCI. This is because frontotemporal dementia generally spares memory, as you will see next.

Frontal Variant of Frontotemporal Dementia

The frontal variant of frontotemporal dementia shares some characteristics with Alzheimer's disease, but two main features help to distinguish it. First, the age of onset of the frontal variant is typically earlier than that of Alzheimer's dementia, often times in one's 50s or 60s. Second, because the frontal variant affects the frontal lobes of the brain, which are important in behavioral control, the most striking symptoms are personality and behavioral changes. A previously staid and proper woman with this disease can start swearing like a sailor, a formerly impeccably dressed gentleman may start to ignore his personal hygiene and grooming, and someone known for his or her kindness can fail to show social tact. As illustrated in Box 3.9, patients with the frontal variant of frontotemporal dementia sometimes have run-ins with the law for activities like stealing, sexual impropriety, or causing a public disturbance. The patients themselves often have poor insight into these changes and may dismiss them, so it is critical that family members provide this information to clinicians.

Because this variant primarily involves the frontal lobes, patients may perform normally on neuropsychological tests of general intellectual functioning and memory (especially earlier in the course of the disease). Deficits are often apparent, however, on tests of executive functioning. Tests requiring a shift from one set of problem-solving rules to another or to multitask pose a particular challenge.

Structural brain scans such as computed tomography (CT) or magnetic resonance imaging (MRI) often show atrophy of the frontal lobes (see Box 3.10), and fluorodeoxyglucose positron emission tomography (FDG-PET) and single photon emission computed tomography (SPECT) will also typically show reduced glucose

---

Box 3.9 Case Vignette of Frontotemporal Dementia, Frontal Variant

Phillip is a 58-year old chartered accountant by training. He was encouraged to quit work two years ago after numerous customer complaints of him being verbally aggressive and accusing his clients of lying to him. Since last year, he has been caught shoplifting three times, and the last time the mall security officer almost charged him with assault until his wife Ruthann stepped in and explained his diagnosis. Ruthann now feels that she has to accompany her husband on all of his outings, which she describes as being "exhausting" as Phillip is not one to sit at home everyday. Ruthann and her sons have arranged for home care to give Ruthann time to do her errands and some respite time to herself.

Box 3.10 Brain MRI Images of Frontotemporal Dementia

The images on the left in each row are of an 80-year-old woman with frontotemporal dementia; the images on the right in each row are of a healthy adult. The top row shows *saggital* (side) views of the left *hemisphere* (half) of the brain, with the face pointing to the left. The bottom row shows *coronal* (top to bottom) views through the frontal lobes. Notice the striking amount of *atrophy* (shrinkage) in the frontal lobes, indicated with white arrows, compared to the healthy individual. Images courtesy of Dr. Tiffany Chow of the Rotman Research Institute of Baycrest.

metabolism and reduced blood flow, respectively, in the frontal and temporal lobes of the brain. In contrast to patients with Alzheimer's disease, patients with frontotemporal dementia rarely have a build up of beta-amyloid in their brains.

Temporal Variant of Frontotemporal Dementia

As mentioned previously, there are two distinct types of the temporal variant of frontotemporal dementia, both of which involve atrophy and reduced blood flow and glucose metabolism in the left temporal lobes or bottom of the frontal lobes. Both of these types have been called *primary progressive aphasia*: the word *primary* means that the language impairments are the most salient feature of the disease, *progressive* means that the condition continues to worsen over time, and *aphasia* is a disorder of language. Patients with both types of primary progressive aphasia have word-finding problems and difficulty naming objects, but for very different reasons.

Nonfluent Primary Progressive Aphasia

In the early stages of nonfluent primary progressive aphasia, the symptoms are restricted to a difficulty coming up with words when speaking, leading to halting, labored speech. Now, we all get stuck for words from time to time, especially as we get older, and this can be worse in people with MCI. But the word finding difficulties in someone with nonfluent primary progressive aphasia are much more severe, and these patients do not have difficulties in other cognitive domains. So general intelligence, spatial abilities, and memory are all preserved. As the disease progresses, verbal output becomes even more restricted, leading eventually to *mutism* (loss of all speech), and comprehension of language can become affected. The brain often shows shrinkage in the lower portions of the left frontal lobe and sometimes in the left parietal lobe. Some people who show these brain changes also develop stiffness of the right arm and leg and may have difficulty carrying out learned movements such as doing up one's shirt buttons (a condition called *corticobasal syndrome*).

Fluent Primary Progressive Aphasia

Fluent primary progressive aphasia has also been called *semantic dementia*. By contrast to the nonfluent type of primary progressive aphasia where patients know what words mean but get stuck retrieving them, patients with the fluent variety of this disease lose the meaning of words (the *semantics* of words). At first, the fine details or particular characteristics of meaning are lost; as the disease progresses, more general properties of memory are lost. For example, when a patient with early semantic dementia is asked to identify a picture of a German Shepherd, he or she may not be able to retrieve the name German Shepherd but may instead call it a dog, whereas a patient with more advanced disease might only manage to call it an animal. Box 3.11 illustrates some of the early symptoms of semantic dementia. The loss of word meaning is also evident in drawing as

---

Box 3.11 Case Vignette of Semantic Dementia

Helen is a 75-year old sculptor and widowed mother of two children. For about three years now, her daughter Carol has been noticing her mother have more and more word-finding problems. It started with the common "what's his name?" slip of acquaintances or actors, but since then her daughter has noticed a progression, with her mother using descriptions in place of the names of common objects, long pauses in her speech, and most recently, the sense that her mother doesn't understand what she is talking about when they are discussing topics that they used to have lively debates about. Last week Carol was visiting at her mother's house and realized that she needed to call a friend to say she would be a bit late. When Carol asked Helen, "Can I use your telephone?" Helen did not understand until Carol tried again, "Your phone. Can I make a call using your phone?" On Carol's prompting, they visited her family doctor, who referred Helen on to a behavioral neurologist, who diagnosed her with semantic dementia. Carol is now attending her local Alzheimer's Association chapter to learn more about semantic dementia and how to help her mother best manage her condition.

---

shown in Box 3.12. These patients have marked shrinkage of the anterior part of the left temporal lobe. Occasionally, temporal shrinkage predominates in the right hemisphere, in which case the symptoms are more typically psychiatric, such as depression or delusions, and the patient may also have trouble recognizing faces.

DEMENTIA OF PARKINSON'S DISEASE AND LEWY BODY DISEASE

Dementia of Parkinson's disease and Lewy body disease are put under one umbrella because they share common symptomatic and pathological features. Some physicians argue that they are really the same disease that, early in its course, can present with more motor than cognitive symptoms, or more cognitive than motor symptoms, but other physicians argue that they are two related but separate conditions. Regardless, patients are likely to be diagnosed with one or the

Box 3.12 Examples of the Drawings of Patients with Fluent Primary Progressive Aphasia (Semantic Dementia)

Model   Delayed copy

The pictures in the left column were shown to the patients then removed, and then after a 10-second patients were given the name of the animal and asked to draw it again. Reproduced from Patterson, K., Nestor, P. J., & Rogers, T. T. (2007). Where do you know what you know? The representation of semantic knowledge in the human brain. Nature Reviews Neuroscience, 8, 976–987, with permission from Nature Publishing Group.

other label, and so we describe them here separately. The causes of Parkinson's disease and Lewy body disease are not fully understood, but science is uncovering clues about possible genetic and environmental triggers. More information about these can be found at www. pdf.org.

Almost everyone has heard of Parkinson's disease, but few are aware that it can lead to dementia in about a third of patients with this disease. Parkinson's disease occurs when the brain stops producing enough *dopamine*, a neurochemical that is important for motor movements and that is also involved in some higher cognitive functions. The decline in dopamine causes motor control problems like tremors and repetitive movements of the hands. When patients with Parkinson's develop dementia, they are often found to have Alzheimer's pathology, Lewy body disease (see later) and other pathologies. The cognitive functions that are most affected are memory, attention and other executive skills, verbal fluency, and cognitive and motor speed. They can also develop *micrographia*, which describes letter sizes getting progressively smaller as one writes, especially when writing on unlined paper (see Box 3.13). Depression is also very common in patients with Parkinson's disease and even more so in those who develop dementia. Parkinson's dementia can respond well to the cholinesterase inhibitors outlined in Box 3.6.

Lewy body disease is a spectrum of disorders with an average age of onset in the 60s and 70s that is characterized by the presence of protein deposits in the cortex of the brain that are called Lewy bodies

---

Box 3.13 Example of Micrographia

The sentence reads "In winter the mountains are covered with snow."

Reprinted from McLennan, J. E., Nakano, K., Tyler, H. R., & Schwab, R. S. (1972). Micrographia in Parkinson's disease. *Journal of the Neurological Sciences, 15*, 141–152. Used with the permission from Elsevier.

after the scientist who first discovered them. It accounts for 5–15% of all cases of dementia. Patients with dementia due to Lewy body disease develop impairments in attention, alertness, and in visual-spatial functions before or within a year after they develop the motor symptoms of Parkinson's disease. Indeed, one basis on which some scientists separate dementia of Parkinson's disease and Lewy body disease is the relative time course of cognitive versus motor symptoms, with cognitive symptoms lagging behind motor symptoms usually by years in dementia of Parkinson's disease, and cognitive symptoms preceding or occurring soon after motor symptoms in Lewy body disease. The motor symptoms of dementia of Parkinson's disease and Lewy body disease typically also differ, with the former characterized by tremor, and the latter by problems with balance and rigidity. Regardless, the most remarkable features of dementia due to Lewy body disease are well-formed visual or auditory hallucinations, and vastly fluctuating attention and alertness, which is illustrated in the case vignette in Box 3.14. Patients are prone to falls and temporary loss of consciousness. It typically progresses faster than Alzheimer's dementia, and, in fact, it often coexists with Alzheimer's especially in older individuals. Importantly, the antipsychotic medications that

---

Box 3.14 Case Vignette of Lewy Body Dementia

Saul is a 72-year old retired architect and married father of three children. About four years ago, he started forgetting how to get to places he had visited frequently, and difficulty doing things he used to do well such as when his son asked him to draw blueprints for a home renovation. Not long after, Saul started having vivid hallucinations most often when he is falling asleep at night, such as insisting that a soldier in full army gear has walked into his room. Saul's wife also describes his "energy" as unpredictable; she says that much of the time he is "his old self," but without warning he is suddenly "completely out of it." More recently, Saul has been having motor problems mainly affecting his walking. Three months ago, his neurologist prescribed donepezil, and he has been having less severe problems with his memory and fewer hallucinations.

help minimize or eliminate hallucinations for people with psychosis are *not* recommended for people with Lewy body disease, because they can exacerbate the motor symptoms of Parkinson's disease and have other very serious side effects including death. Although not officially labeled for this disease, the cholinesterase inhibitors are often used for cognitive and behavioral symptoms in Lewy body disease and especially because they can help reduce the hallucinations. Also, patients with dementia due to Parkinson's or Lewy body disease can have disturbed sleep, and they may physically act out their dreams. This can be present for years before the disease fully develops.

It is possible that one's MCI could be due to Parkinson's or Lewy body disease, representing the earliest stages of these kinds of dementia, as described in Box 1.5 in chapter 1, but this does not describe the vast majority of patients with MCI. Relative to these types of dementia, in the typical patient with MCI the cognitive symptoms are far less severe, and the motor impairments are lacking.

A FINAL WORD

We hope that this chapter served you well as an introduction to the most common forms of dementia. We should note that there are many more types of dementia, including dementia related to Huntington's disease, corticobasal degeneration, progressive supranuclear palsy, a slew of inherited or acquired metabolic disorders, toxins and drugs, and infections. Most of these are extremely rare, however, and MCI is not considered a risk factor for any of them. The next chapter discusses what types of dementia MCI *can be* a risk factor for.

Box 3.15 Questions to Ask Your Doctor if MCI Is Suspected or Confirmed in Yourself or in Your Family Member

---

1. If any of your blood relatives have had dementia, but you don't know what type, describe the symptoms to your doctor and ask, "Can you make an educated guess about what type of dementia it might have been?"

(continued)

Box 3.15 (Continued)

2. "Are there any medical tests that would be recommended for me, such as brain imaging or genetic testing?"
3. If you have a blood relative who developed dementia at a young age (in their 50s or younger), consider whether you should have genetic counseling and ask, "What is your advice on this matter?"

RECOMMENDED READING

Genova, Lisa (2009). *Still Alice*. New York: Pocket Books. This is an award-winning debut novel about a 50-year-old professor as she deals with the onset and progression of early-onset Alzheimer's disease. We recommend it because it is not only factually correct (Lisa Genova earned a PhD in neuroscience from Harvard University), but also portrays the lived experience of this disease for the professor and her family with grace and humanity.

Sutton, Amy (2011). *Alzheimer disease sourcebook: Basic consumer health information about Alzheimer disease, other dementias, and related disorders* (5th Edition). Detroit, MI: Omnigraphics.

Levine, Robert (2006). *Defying dementia: Understanding and preventing Alzheimer's and related disorders*. Westport, CT: Praeger Publishers.

The following Web sites are great resources for many different types of dementia: www.alz.org and www.alzheimer.ca.

4

Possible Outcomes of Mild Cognitive Impairment

If you have been diagnosed with mild cognitive impairment (MCI), a question you undoubtedly have asked yourself is, "What does my future hold?" Only time can answer that question with certainty but researchers have started to map out the most likely outcomes of MCI. There are three possible outcomes of MCI. It can progress to dementia, remain stable as MCI, or revert back to normal aging. In this chapter, we discuss these three possible outcomes in turn. We use the word *progress* to describe the change from MCI to dementia, although, in other papers or books, you might see the word *convert* used in this context. In our view, conversion implies that something has changed qualitatively; that is, that the person has some new pathology or disease features that she or he didn't have previously. Progression, on the other hand, implies that things changed quantitatively; the person has the same disease as she or he had before, but just more of it. It is our opinion that the evidence is stronger that MCI progresses rather than converts to dementia, and, indeed, the proposed new diagnostic criteria for MCI described in chapter 1 reinforce this. Regardless of which term is used, it is important to remember that not all people with MCI develop dementia—some people's cognitive symptoms remain stable, and some people's cognitive abilities go back to normal.

DEMENTIA AS A POSSIBLE OUTCOME OF MCI

MCI has gained so much attention in the medical research fields because people with MCI have an elevated risk of developing dementia of one type or another. We reviewed some of these types of dementia in chapter 3. In this chapter, our focus is in the outcomes of MCI. To start this discussion, we focus on these various forms of dementia that different subtypes of MCI most typically progress to. Box 4.1 displays the same classifications that we showed you in chapter 1, but we've added another layer.

As you can see in this chart, the most typical outcome of MCI depends on the subtype. Another way to view these outcomes is that they represent clinicians' best guess about the most likely *cause* of the different MCI subtypes. You know from chapter 3 that there are many different kinds of dementia, and one way to view MCI is as a very early, preclinical phase of these different forms of dementia. Thus, there are different subtypes of MCI simply because they reflect the earliest signs of these different forms of dementia. ·

Box 4.1 Most Likely Outcomes of Different Subtypes of MCI

		Type of impairment:	
		Memory impairment	Non-memory impairment
Number of impairments:	1 impairment	**Amnestic MCI single domain** Alzheimer's disease Depression	**Nonamnestic MCI single domain** Frontotemporal dementia
	2 or more impairments	**Amnestic MCI multiple domains** Alzheimer's disease Vascular dementia Depression	**Nonamnestic MCI multiple domains** Lewy body disease Vascular dementia

Most Typical Dementia Outcomes of Amnestic MCI

Most people who are diagnosed with amnestic MCI, whether single-domain or multiple-domain, are later diagnosed with Alzheimer's disease. It is now recognized that the brain changes of Alzheimer's disease, including the atrophy or shrinkage in the temporal lobes and particularly in the hippocampus that are so crucial for memory, begin decades before someone is diagnosed with this disease. For these people, amnestic MCI represents the period of time when these brain changes are significant enough to cause memory problems, but not advanced enough to limit their ability to carry out activities of daily living. Amnestic multiple-domain MCI also can lead to vascular dementia. This possibility is more likely if you have the cardiovascular risk factors for stroke, including high blood pressure, high cholesterol, or diabetes; if there is evidence of small strokes in brain images; and if the other, nonmemory domain affected is processing speed or executive functioning (for example, planning, problem solving, mental flexibility, or inhibition). Remember from chapter 3 that it is common for people to have both Alzheimer's disease and vascular dementia, a mix that is more common after multiple-domain than single-domain amnestic MCI.

Most Typical Dementia Outcomes of Nonamnestic MCI

Nonamnestic MCI is usually not due to the early changes of Alzheimer's disease, although that is a possibility. More typically, someone with nonamnestic single-domain MCI will develop frontotemporal dementia, specifically the frontal variant, if the domain affected is executive, or the temporal variant, if it is language. Individuals with nonamnestic multiple-domain MCI are most likely to develop Lewy body disease, especially if attention and visual-spatial problems, sometimes along with motor symptoms such as poor balance and *rigidity* (muscle stiffness), are prominent symptoms, or vascular dementia, if cardiovascular disease and executive impairments are present.

Rates Progression from MCI to Dementia

Research studies that follow people with amnestic MCI over time who are attending a memory-disorders clinic or dementia clinic find that 10–15% of them develop Alzheimer's disease per year. This rate is considerably higher than the approximate 2% risk of Alzheimer's disease per year among older adults who do not have MCI. What do these numbers mean? They mean that, if you followed a really large group of adults aged 65 and older who do not have MCI for a year, 2% of them would develop dementia sometime within that year. However, if you followed a similarly large group of adults aged 65 and older who do have amnestic MCI for a year, 10–15% of them would develop Alzheimer's disease within that year. Annual rates of progression from amnestic MCI to Alzheimer's disease are considerably lower, in the 5–10% range, in epidemiological studies that recruit people from the community instead of from memory clinics. This makes sense, because people who have sought medical attention at a memory disorders or dementia clinic for cognitive problems likely have more advanced MCI than people in the community who have not sought such medical attention. Less is known about progression rates of nonamnestic MCI to dementia, because those forms are less common and people with problems affecting cognitive domains other than memory seek medical attention less often.

Very little research is available describing progression from MCI to other dementias, but it does appear that individuals presenting with MCI after having had a stroke are more likely to develop vascular dementia than their peers who were cognitively normal after recovering from a stroke. Box 4.2 describes someone who developed vascular dementia after a few years of having multiple-domain amnestic MCI.

Predictors of Progression from MCI to Dementia

There are a host of factors that research has found help predict who with MCI will develop dementia (see Box 4.3). At this point in your reading of this book, you'll likely find some of these factors pretty obvious. For example, individuals with more severe cognitive impairments are more likely to develop dementia, most likely because they are further along the continuum from MCI to dementia. The faster cognitive functioning declines over time, the more likely one is to develop dementia, too. Along those same lines, individuals with multiple-domain MCI are more likely to develop dementia than are people with single-domain MCI, which might reflect involvement of

---

Box 4.2 Case Vignette of MCI to Dementia Progression

Cheryl is a 73-year old woman who has high blood pressure and diabetes but is otherwise in good health. She raised four children and has been enjoying time with her husband Tony since he retired seven years ago. About five years ago, Cheryl's daughter Anne started noticing that her mother was having memory problems. Cheryl would tell Anne the same things over and over, and would forget the details of upcoming events, like the time Cheryl forgot that she needed to pick up one of Anne's children from school while Anne was at the dentist. Cheryl also had difficulty staying on task, and seemed overwhelmed planning events such as holiday meals. Four years ago, Cheryl saw her neurologist, who ordered a neuropsychological assessment and an MRI. Those test results showed that Cheryl's language abilities were within the normal range, but her memory and executive skills were impaired for her age, and the brain images showed evidence of her having had a number of small strokes. Cheryl was diagnosed with multiple-domain amnestic MCI. Since then, things have been getting worse. Cheryl is more easily confused and asks multiple times a day what her and Tony's plans are for the day. Cheryl used to handle all the household bill payments, but after Tony recognized that she had been missing payment due dates and once sent a check to the wrong utility company, Tony took over that duty. Last month, Cheryl's neurologist diagnosed her with vascular dementia, adjusted her heart and diabetes medications, and set up appointments for her with a dietician and physical therapist to start improving her diet and exercise habits.

---

more brain regions. The presence of greater atrophy or faster atrophy over time of the hippocampus and nearby structures in the temporal lobes that are important for memory is associated with higher rates of developing dementia. Individuals who are older and have MCI are more likely to develop dementia than their younger counterparts with MCI. In addition to these more obvious factors, people who carry the ε4 allele of the apolipoprotein E gene are more likely to progress from MCI to dementia, particularly to Alzheimer's disease. We discuss this genetic risk factor in greater detail in chapter 5. Discovery of high amounts of the pathological changes associated with Alzheimer's

---

Box 4.3 Factors Predicting a Greater Chance of Progressing from MCI to Dementia

---

- Greater cognitive impairment, and faster rate of cognitive decline.
- Multiple-domain MCI (versus single-domain MCI).
- More and faster atrophy of medial temporal lobe regions including hippocampus.
- Apolipoprotein E e-4 allele presence.
- Positive evidence of amyloid on positron emission tomography imaging and/or a high ratio of tau protein relative to a particular amyloid protein (Aβ-42) in cerebrospinal fluid.
- Other cerebrovascular risk factors such as high blood pressure and diabetes.

---

disease, namely amyloid protein on brain positron emission tomography (PET) imaging and/or a higher ratio of the tau protein relative to a particular amyloid protein, Aβ-42, in cerebrospinal fluid, have also been linked to higher rates of progressing from MCI to dementia (for more on these pathologies, see chapter 3). Finally, people with cardiovascular risk factors and MCI develop dementia at a higher rate than people with MCI but who do not have these risk factors. As mentioned in chapter 3, high blood pressure, high cholesterol, diabetes, smoking, and obesity, are all risk factors for vascular dementia, but those factors can also increase the risk of developing Alzheimer's disease from MCI.

NONDEMENTIA OUTCOMES OF MCI

As we mentioned in chapter 1, the good news is that not all people diagnosed with MCI develop dementia. As shown in Box 4.4, some people remain diagnosed with MCI for years and years without developing dementia (stable MCI in Box 4.4), and still others are found to be within the normal range on reassessment (MCI to Normal in Box 4.4). In the remainder of this chapter, we discuss stable MCI and reversion from MCI back to normal aging.

Previously we said that the annual rate of progression from MCI (particularly of the amnestic forms) to dementia is somewhere on the

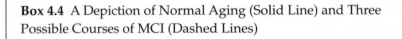

Box 4.4 A Depiction of Normal Aging (Solid Line) and Three
Possible Courses of MCI (Dashed Lines)

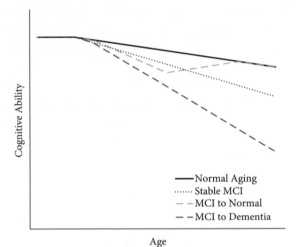

——Normal Aging
······ Stable MCI
— – MCI to Normal
— – MCI to Dementia

Age

Note the three possible courses of MCI: (a) Progression from MCI to dementia (dark
wide dashed line), (b) Stable MCI (dotted dashed line), and (c) Reversion from MCI to
normal (light wide dashed line).

order of 10–15%—higher in clinical samples, and lower in community samples, but averaging out to 10–15%. So after one year, 10–15%
of a large group of people with MCI will have developed dementia;
after two years, 20–30% of the original group will have dementia;
after three years, 30–45% will, and so on. Does that mean that after
10 years, everyone from the original group will have dementia? No,
it doesn't. What happens to the rest of the people? Some continue to
meet criteria for MCI, and others later test within the normal range.
We discuss these outcomes next.

Stable MCI

Some people continue to meet criteria for MCI for years and years
after initial diagnosis. No one knows with certainty why this is,
but two possibilities are most likely. First, MCI may progress faster
for some people than for others, just like any other disease or
condition. For example, rheumatoid arthritis progresses quickly in

some people, leaving them debilitated and unable to perform their regular activities within a few short years, while other people can have the condition for decades without it getting much worse. Mild cognitive impairment may be like that too, when, for reasons not currently understood, it progresses faster for some people than for others.

The second good explanation for why some people remain diagnosed with MCI for years without developing dementia reflects our limitations in diagnosing MCI. Remember from chapter 1 that, in order to be diagnosed with MCI, you have to be performing worse than expected for your age and educational background in one or more cognitive domains. How is that determined? This is spelled out in more detail when we describe how MCI is diagnosed in chapter 6, but usually, your scores are compared to a set of *norms*, or distributions of scores on a given test from people of your same age. Simply put, the diagnostic cognitive tests have been given to many people of different ages in order to establish the norm for your age and background, and we compare your scores to those norms. Three typical causes for stable lower performance that have nothing to do with MCI or impending dementia are learning disabilities, lifelong cognitive weaknesses, and medical events.

Learning disabilities have only been routinely recognized and diagnosed in the last few decades, and so people with learning disabilities who are currently 60 or older are very unlikely to have ever had it diagnosed. A neuropsychologist will ask you questions about your school experiences to try to identify a never-diagnosed learning disability. Even in the absence of a frank learning disability, people differ in their cognitive strengths and weaknesses. Almost no one is good in all cognitive areas. So it is possible that you scored low on memory tests, for example, because you never were very good at memory, for whatever reason.

In a small proportion of cases, certain medical events can cause cognitive impairments. For example, there can be *anoxia*, or periods of low oxygen supply to the brain, during certain surgeries like open-heart surgery that can cause memory difficulties (see Box 4.5). A head injury from a car accident or fall from a bike 30 years ago may be the culprit, particularly if at the time you lost consciousness or have no

---

Box 4.5 Case Vignette of Someone with Stable MCI

Guy is a 62-year-old married father of one, and he is a university-educated owner of a successful printing company. Guy developed clogged heart arteries in his early 50s just like his Dad had at a similar age. Seven years ago, some problems with a heart valve were also detected, and Guy underwent open-heart surgery. Unfortunately, there were complications during surgery, and there was a couple of minutes when Guy's heart was not pumping and delivering oxygen to his body and brain. Guy recovered well from the surgery, but noticed that his memory wasn't the same since. Two years after the surgery, he received a neuropsychological assessment, and it was found that his performance in all cognitive domains ranged from average to high average for his age, except memory, which fell below expectations for his age. He was told that the cause of his memory problems was unclear, but they could be due to anoxia during his heart surgery because brain regions like the hippocampus, which are important for memory, are particularly sensitive to oxygen deprivation, or they could be due to the earliest signs of Alzheimer's disease. The neuropsychologist recommended that he be reassessed in 18 months. At two regular 18-month intervals since then, Guy has had the neuropsychological assessment repeated, and each time his performance has been the same as last time. Guy was very relieved when, at the last visit, the neuropsychologist said that, most likely, his memory problems are due to the heart surgery, and they are unlikely to get markedly worse.

---

memory of the period around the accident; both are symptoms of head injury that may be responsible for your cognitive difficulties.

Doctors and neuropsychologists do their very best to rule out these other causes of poor performance by reviewing medical charts and conducting an extensive interview with you and your loved ones. If one of these conditions applies to you, the best way to figure out if your current low scores reflect a real decline from your previous level of functioning is to repeat the assessment at a later date, usually in one to two years. In that repeat assessment, if your performance is the same, it is more likely due to a cause other than a dementia (for example, in the case vignette in Box 4.5, brief oxygen deprivation during a complicated heart surgery). If, on the other hand, in that repeat assessment your performance is even worse than the first time, then it is more likely to be a type of MCI that is due to the earliest signs of some form of dementia.

Reversion from MCI Back to Normal Aging

A surprisingly high percentage of people initially meeting criteria for MCI later perform within the normal range when the assessment is repeated. This percentage varies depending on the study, but is usually about 25%. That is, about a quarter of people initially diagnosed with MCI may in fact be normal. The proposed *Diagnostic and Statistical Manual of Mental Disorders-V* (see chapter 1) suggests that MCI should be renamed minor neurocognitive disorder, and classified under the general category called neurocognitive disorders. This category includes major neurocognitive disorders such as Alzheimer's disease and the other dementias. Similarly, the proposed revised criteria prepared by the U.S. National Institute of Aging along with the Alzheimer's Association suggest the name MCI due to Alzheimer's disease dementia. The danger with these proposals is that many people may jump to the conclusion or be told by their physicians that what they have is a very mild form of dementia, when, in fact, they have a fairly good chance of testing normal later. It is extremely important for health-care professionals and agencies such as the Alzheimer's societies to emphasize that not everyone with MCI or minor neurocognitive disorder develops dementia.

There are many reasons that someone might be initially diagnosed with MCI but then later improve and test normal. For some people diagnosed with MCI, particularly those diagnosed with amnestic MCI, it turns out that their cognitive symptoms were due to depression (see Box 4.1). People with depression have difficulty attending to information, which limits their ability to get that information into memory. Research studies also find that the average size of the hippocampus is smaller in groups of people with depression than in groups of healthy individuals, a difference that has been linked to changes in certain hormones such as cortisol. The fact that depression can mimic amnestic MCI underscores the need for your doctor to carefully assess your mood for symptoms of depression. As we describe in greater detail in chapter 5, if your memory problems are due to depression, your memory is likely to improve once you are treated for depression with medications, counseling, and/or lifestyle changes.

In research studies, higher rates of reverting to normal are reported in community samples than in clinical samples, likely because, in large community-based studies MCI "diagnosis" relies often on applying strict cognitive test cut-offs, in contrast to a more clinical approach in which an individual's history and other performance on other tests indicating your overall level of cognitive functioning are given more weight. As described in chapter 6, studies that include a smaller set of diagnostic tests are more likely to falsely diagnose people with MCI. This is because it is not uncommon for people to do poorly on a single cognitive test without having a true impairment in that domain. If you didn't sleep well the night before your assessment, you may perform worse on the more difficult tests. If you're worried about your performance, or thinking about what you're going for have for dinner, you won't do too well either! For this reason, it is important that your diagnoses be based on reliable problems across multiple (two or more) tests within a domain. In addition, repeated medical and neuropsychological assessments after a year or two are crucial for more certainty about the diagnosis. Finding normal performance on a repeated assessment would rule out a diagnosis of MCI, but finding that your cognitive problems are stable or even worse means that you likely had MCI in the first place.

Going through cognitive testing can be very anxiety provoking. In the best of situations, most people do not like being evaluated or having their intellectual skills put to the test. This is all the more scary when you are going through the testing because you are concerned that you might have dementia. If you have other stressful events going on in your life, having your thinking skills tested only adds to the anxiety, as described in Box 4.6. When we are anxious, it is difficult to give our full attention to the task at hand and to perform our best. Finally, because of this anxiety, or because of a more chronic sleep problem, people often have disrupted sleep the night before testing, which again can interfere with your best performance. To perform your best, you need a good night's sleep. Avoid caffeine and high energy activities

Box 4.6 Case Vignette of Someone for Whom MCI Reverted to Normal

When first seen at a memory disorders clinic, Stephanie was a 65-year-old married mother of two who was retiring from her career as a librarian. Although mandatory retirement at age 65 was abolished a few years prior, Stephanie had felt that she couldn't keep up at work. She reported that she had been making mistakes and found the workload overwhelming. On assessment, the doctor found that Stephanie was in good general health. Her weight was in the normal range, and her blood pressure was good, but her thyroid was underactive. Stephanie also reported that she had just stopped smoking, and that she was very worried about her son who was going through a divorce. Neuropsychological testing showed that Stephanie's intelligence was in the high average range, her language skills were superior, and visual-spatial skills were average for her age. However, Stephanie's performance on attention and memory tests fell in the borderline-impaired range. During feedback, Stephanie was told that her results suggested that she might have multiple-domain amnestic MCI. Her doctor prescribed thyroid replacement therapy, told her about the various options to help her quit smoking, and asked her to come back in a year. Stephanie's family physician monitored her thyroid levels over this time and was pleased that she had successfully quit smoking. Her son's divorce, although by no means easy, was resolved and he seemed to be moving on. On reassessment a year later, Stephanie's attention and memory skills were in the average range for her age.

in the late afternoon and evening, but avoid sleeping pills if you can, because you might still feel groggy the next morning.

Knowing more about the nature of the assessment can also go a long way to easing your fears. Comprehensive descriptions of typical medical and neuropsychological assessments are provided in chapter 6. There you will read that many tests used in neuropsychological assessments are difficult for most people, or start easy and get more challenging as they go on. The tests are not designed this way to torture you, but rather to be able to detect people who are having cognitive problems; if tasks were too easy, everyone would do well on them and the tests would be unable to identify people who are having difficulties. Going into the assessment knowing that some of the tests are challenging for everyone who takes them can motivate you to simply do your best.

There are also a host of *treatable* medical conditions that can interfere with cognition, particularly memory. These are listed in Box 4.7. Some of these conditions can cause severe cognitive problems that mimic dementia. For example, if someone is severely dehydrated, they can become confused and delirious. More often, however, these conditions cause milder forms of cognitive problems that might be just enough to push someone over the line between normal and MCI. Let's take sleep apnea as an example. *Sleep apnea* refers to multiple, short periods during sleep when people stop breathing. Risk factors for sleep apnea include obesity, smoking, and age. Recent studies have revealed cognitive impairments in people suffering from sleep apnea that look a lot like MCI. The good news, however, is that sleep apnea is treatable, commonly with a continuous positive airway pressure, or CPAP device that forces air through the airway while people are sleeping. Cognitive symptoms usually lessen once people are properly treated for apnea. This is a great example of the fact that some reversion from MCI to normal may be accounted for by those people who, in receiving the medical attention necessary to be diagnosed with MCI, have another medical condition that was causing cognitive problems recognized and treated. The important message for you is

---

Box 4.7 Common Treatable Medical Conditions That Can Disrupt Cognition (Particularly Memory)

- Alcohol or drug intoxication, including barbiturates or benzodiazepines (common in sleeping pills).
- Untreated hypo- or hyperthyroidism.
- Sleep apnea.
- Vitamin B12 deficiency.
- Depression and anxiety.
- Dehydration.

that you should request a full physical examination, with blood work, and be sure to discuss with your doctor any recent life stressors or changes in mood, in order for your doctor to best identify any other conditions that might be contributing to your cognitive problems.

A FINAL WORD

Despite the rather formal and conclusive look of Box 4.1, we emphasize that predicting outcomes of MCI *is not an exact science*. Although most people with a particular subtype of MCI develop the kind of dementia noted in Box 4.1, some people develop other types of dementia. For example, someone with a single-domain nonamnestic MCI due to deficits in areas such as language or visual-spatial perception could develop Alzheimer's disease, as the disease does not start and progress exactly the same way in all people. Also, as described in this chapter, progression to dementia is not the only outcome of MCI. Some people remain stable with MCI for years and years and never progress beyond it, and a sizable minority of people with MCI reverts back to normal aging.

We need to emphasize that all the evidence about progression from MCI to dementia comes from group studies, and *no one can predict whether you will develop dementia*. Even if we knew your age, your cognitive scores, your apolipoprotein E allele status, the size of your hippocampus, and so on, and could use that information to come up with your odds of developing dementia, it would be just that—an odds ratio. Anyone who has placed bets at a casino or a horse track knows how dangerous it can be to place bets based on odds. In this context in particular, the danger is even more real because it can have an unnecessary impact on your life. For example, if we were able to calculate that you have a 75% chance of developing dementia, how would that affect you? Would you give up, become depressed, stop exercising and socializing? If so, you're almost certain to decline further. This could all be for naught because you could be one of the 25% with your cluster of risk factors that does not develop dementia. What if you calculated that you had a 2% risk of developing dementia? Would you feel in the free and clear and so start leading an unhealthy lifestyle? These extreme examples illustrate that, although these predictions are useful to scientists to better understand the factors that affect progression from MCI to dementia and point the most important factors for interventions, they are less useful and possibly even dangerous for individual use.

The discussion in this chapter highlights the need for you to share with your medical team anything that you think might be relevant. This should include your full medication list, any over-the-counter medications or supplements that you take, anything of significance from your schooling history, any previous major surgeries or accidents, and whether you have noticed changes or problems with your mood or sleep. No one can predict which course your MCI will take, but we hope that the information in this book helps you to navigate your course in the best way possible.

Box 4.8 Questions to Ask Your Doctor if MCI Is Suspected or Confirmed in Yourself or in Your Family Member

---

1. Refer to the decision tree in Box 4.1, and ask "What do you think is causing the MCI?"
2. Ask, "How would you know if the MCI is progressing? How would my care plan change if it does progress?"
3. Refer to the examples in Box 4.7 and ask, "What other medical conditions could be contributing, and how could those be treated?"

5

Risk Factors for Mild Cognitive Impairment and Dementia

If you or a loved one has been diagnosed with mild cognitive impairment (MCI), at some point you probably have wondered, "Why me?" or "Why him/her?" In this chapter we will describe an array of genetic, health, and lifestyle factors that influence the risk of developing MCI. Compared to the considerable body of knowledge about the risk factors for dementia, a lot less is known about the risk factors for MCI, mainly because MCI is a relatively new diagnosis and there has not been the time for scientists to do the research necessary to understand what factors might contribute to MCI risk. However, given that MCI is often the very early, preclinical stage of dementia, the risk factors for MCI and dementia are likely quite similar. In this chapter, we will be careful to point out when there is specific evidence about the role of these factors for MCI in particular, or when the evidence is only available for their role in dementia.

Before we get started, we would like to emphasize three important points. First, there is no way to determine for sure whether any one particular person will develop MCI. In medicine, a *risk factor* is something that influences the probability of a medical event occurring. Risk factors are discovered by studying large numbers of people, and then identifying which factors are associated with higher rates of a particular condition such as MCI. As you will see later, brain injury is one of these risk factors, but that does not mean that everyone who has had a brain injury develops MCI. So as you read this chapter keep in mind that even if you or a loved one has a few or even many risk factors for MCI, these risk factors simply increase the probability of developing MCI but do not guarantee it will happen.

Box 5.1 Case Vignette of RR: A Case of Dementia with Few Known Risk Factors

---

RR is an 83-year-old twice-married father of five children. He studied economics and sociology in college, and enjoyed playing on the college football team and acting in school plays. He continued acting on television and in movies for nearly 30 years, and he served as the president of the Screen Actors Guild. He ran for and served as governor of California for two terms prior to winning the leadership of the Republican Party. RR served two terms as president of the United States. Five years after leaving office, he announced to the world that he had been diagnosed with Alzheimer's disease.

The identity of the person described in Box 5.1 should be pretty obvious: It is President Ronald Reagan. We share his story as a prime example that no one can predict who will develop MCI or dementia. Regardless of your political leanings, you have to agree that President Reagan was an educated, successful man who rose to the top of his two careers. Although information about his health status (for example, his genetic make-up or cardiovascular risk factors) is not in the public domain, he appeared relatively healthy and fit. Despite his relative lack of risk factors (as far as we know), President Reagan succumbed to Alzheimer's disease. His example drives home the point that, although the study of risk factors has identified what is associated with higher or lower rates of MCI and dementia in large groups of people, it is impossible to predict whether any one person will develop these conditions.

The second important point is that all but one subclass of factors that we will describe in this chapter are *risk* factors for MCI or dementia, not *causal* factors, meaning that most of the factors described here do not directly *cause* MCI or dementia. Age and education are risk factors for both MCI and dementia, as you will see, but being older or having a lower education does not *cause* either condition. We aim to explain how these factors might influence the risk of developing MCI when scientific evidence or theories are available, but in many cases the intermediary causes have yet to be identified.

Finally, the third point we want to emphasize is that some risk factors are under your control, whereas others are not. The risk factors that are under your control are called *modifiable* risk factors. Modifiable risk factors are particularly important because the opposite of every risk factor is a protective factor. A *protective factor* has the same definition as a risk factor: it is something that influences the probability of a medical event occurring, but whereas a risk factor is associated with an increase in the probability that a medical event will occur, a protective factor is associated with a reduced probability that it will occur. Advanced age is a risk factor for MCI, but younger age is a protective factor against MCI. Hypertension is a risk factor for MCI, but normal blood pressure is a protective factor against MCI. Age is not a modifiable risk factor (you can't do anything about getting older), but hypertension is often modifiable: In many cases you can control or at least improve your blood pressure. We hope that learning about these modifiable risk factors will empower you to make lifestyle choices that reduced your own risk, and to encourage your loved ones to do the same. In the sections that follow, we first discuss the nonmodifiable risk factors for MCI and dementia, followed by the modifiable risk factors. These are listed in Box 5.2.

Box 5.2 Risk factors for MCI and dementia.

Nonmodifiable Risk Factors
- Age
- Sex
- Genetics
- Previous brain injury

Modifiable Risk Factors
- Education and intellectual engagement
- Vascular and metabolic factors
- Apathy and depression

AGE

Rates of MCI and dementia increase with age. Let's break that down. First of all, what do we mean by MCI or dementia rates? As mentioned in Chapter 1, scientists distinguish between prevalence rates and incidence rates. *Prevalence* refers to the number of people within a large sample who have a particular condition such as MCI or dementia when assessed at a given time point. *Incidence* refers to the number of people who develop a condition like MCI or dementia in a given period of time (e.g., over one year).

Prevalence rates of MCI vary widely across studies, mainly due to use of different methods to diagnose MCI (e.g., different tests, different test cut-offs) and the site of participant recruitment (community versus memory clinics). Nevertheless, the average prevalence rate is about 10–15%, meaning that 10–15 people in a group of 100 older adults who have not been diagnosed with dementia meet criteria for MCI. Incidence rates also vary across studies for the same reasons, but average to about 5%, meaning that about 5 people out of 100 older adults who have not been diagnosed with dementia develop MCI in a given year.

Does age *cause* MCI or progression from MCI to dementia? Of course not! If it did, *everyone* would develop MCI and dementia eventually, but we know that isn't the case. Instead, with increasing age comes a host of other physical changes that are likely more directly related to MCI and dementia risk. There is no good scientific evidence to say for certain what these are, but some likely culprits are loss of neurons and connections between neurons, the build-up of plaques and tangles in the brain (we described these in chapter 3), reduced physical and cognitive activity, and common obesity-related disorders such as a high waist circumference, high blood pressure, high cholesterol, and high blood sugars. Although age itself is not modifiable, we hope you've noticed that many of these possible "links" between aging and MCI and dementia are modifiable, and we discuss them separately later. Addressing these modifiable culprits can help reduce your risk of developing MCI, or progressing from MCI to dementia.

SEX

Some good news is that most studies find no effect of sex on rates of MCI. Now that we've piqued your curiosity, what we really mean is that the results of most studies are that men and women have a comparable risk of developing MCI. One recent exception was a study out of the Mayo clinic that found higher rates of MCI among men than women. This result is surprising given the higher prevalence of Alzheimer's disease among women than men (see later), but the authors suggested that the finding might be due to differences in the age at which men and women first develop MCI or alternatively to other risk factors that differ between the sexes. Indeed, an interesting study conducted in France found that women and men had different risk factors for MCI. Women who were in poorer physical health, had insomnia, and had weaker social networks were more likely to develop MCI than their female counterparts who were healthier, slept better, and had richer social networks. Men who were overweight, had diabetes, or had suffered a stroke were more likely to develop MCI than their male counterparts that were slimmer and did not have diabetes or a history of stroke. This study is important because it suggests that sex itself may not be an important risk factor for MCI, but *sex-specific* health and lifestyle factors influence one's risk of developing MCI. We caution against drawing conclusions from a single study, because particularities about their participants or study methods may have influenced the findings, but we hope that more studies take this approach of identifying common and distinct MCI risk factors for men and women.

Sex does make a difference for Alzheimer's disease. Considerably more woman than men have Alzheimer's disease. However, women live longer than do men. In most studies that control for the ages of the participants in the study, the prevalence of Alzheimer's disease does not differ between men and women under the age of 80 to 90, depending on the study, but among people older than that, the prevalence is higher among women than men. There is also evidence that men and women have different risk factors for Alzheimer's disease. One of these factors concerns *estrogen*, a sex hormone that is in much greater abundance in women than men. Estrogen helps support the growth of new *dendrites*, the neurons' branches that receive signals from other neurons, particularly in the area most important for memory, the hippocampus, and estrogen is related to better cognitive functioning. With menopause, women undergo a drastic decline in estrogen production and, consequently, can experience side effects such as hot flashes and mood changes. These symptoms led to the wide-spread use of hormone-replacement therapy until 2002, when the Women's Health Initiative Study reported that the combination of estrogen and another female sex hormone, *progesterone*, was related to an increased risk of stroke and breast cancer (for details about this study and its findings, see http://www.nhlbi.nih.gov/whi/estro_pro. htm). Since those reports, however, other studies have found lower dementia rates in women who took hormone replacement therapy for a limited number of years after the onset of menopause, although use of hormone-replacement therapy in older women who are well-past menopause is associated with an increased risk of dementia. Undoubtedly the coming years will bring much discovery about the likely multiple interacting causes of dementia and MCI, and the importance of sex differences in these causes.

GENETICS

Genetics of Alzheimer's Disease

Genetics certainly plays a role in risk for Alzheimer's disease (for a little refresher on human genetics, see Box 5.3). There are two distinct subtypes of genetic risk for Alzheimer's disease: causal mutations and susceptibility genes. Causal mutations are autosomal dominant mutations; this means that if someone inherits one of these mutations from one of their parents, it doesn't matter whether the gene they inherited from their other parent is normal—the mutation will dominate and cause disease. Three causal mutations have been identified so far. These are amyloid precursor protein on chromosome 21, presenilin 1 on chromosome 14, and presenilin 2 on chromosome 1. If someone inherits one of these mutations from one of their parents, that individual is certain to develop early-onset Alzheimer's disease, with symptoms typically starting in their 50s, although sometimes earlier. However, as we mentioned in chapter 3, only 1–2% of patients with Alzheimer's have this autosomal dominant version of the disease.

A number of additional susceptibility genes for Alzheimer's disease have been identified, in which certain mutations increase one's risk of developing the disease but do not guarantee it. Far and away the most important of these is the apolipoprotein E gene on chromosome 19,

---

Box 5.3 Basic Human Genetics

- Our bodies contain about 100 trillion cells, and each of them contains a long, winding molecule called *deoxyribonucleic acid* (DNA).
- About 99% of DNA is the same between any two people; nevertheless, the 1% that is different is important because it determines things from your hair and eye color to your risk for developing certain health conditions such as MCI and dementia.
- We have 23 pairs of tightly packed DNA, called *chromosomes*.
- We inherit one copy of each chromosome from our mother, and one from our father.
- Our 23rd pair of chromosomes determines our sex. Women have two X sex chromosomes, and men have one X and one Y sex chromosome.
- Chromosomes contain *genes,* which are sections of DNA that code for features of a living organism; in total, we have some 20,000 genes.
- A particular gene can have different variants across people (different groupings of nucleotides). These variants are called *alleles*. It is usually a particular allele type that is associated with a higher risk for a particular condition.
- Some allele types are *autosomal dominant* whereas others are *recessive*. Autosomal dominant alleles will determine the presence of a particular feature, condition, or disease regardless of what variant you inherited from your other parent, but for recessive features, conditions, or diseases to occur, you need to have inherited two copies of the alleles.
- The allele for brown eyes is autosomal dominant, for example. If one member of a couple has two copies of the allele for brown eyes, their children are certain to also have brown eyes. However, if for example, mom and dad both have one dominant brown-eye allele, and one recessive blue-eye allele, then the kids have a 3 out of 4 chance of having brown eyes—only if the two recessive blue-eye alleles are passed on will a child have blue eyes.

---

a gene that is abbreviated to APOE. One function of this gene is to make a protein that combines with cholesterol and other fats to carry them through the bloodstream. There are three variants, or *alleles*, of the APOE gene: ε2, ε3, and ε4, and we each have two alleles of any combination (e.g., ε2/ε3, ε4/ε4). The ε3 allele is most common, with most people carrying two copies of this allele, and it does not appear to modify the risk of developing Alzheimer's disease. The ε2 allele is least common, but many studies find that it is associated with a *lower* risk of Alzheimer's disease and, hence, it is considered to be protective. The main reason that the APOE gene receives so much attention, however, is because of the ε4 allele, of which about 40% of us carry one or two copies. The ε4 allele has been associated with an *increased* risk of developing Alzheimer's disease. People who have one ε4 allele are 3 times more likely to have Alzheimer's disease than those who do not, whereas those who have two ε4 alleles are 9 times more likely to have Alzheimer's disease. That degree of elevated risk is frightening, but it is important to remember that the ε4 allele is still just a susceptibility gene: Many people who have two ε4 alleles never develop Alzheimer's disease, whereas many people with no ε4 allele do succumb to this disease. Because APOE status does not tell us with certainty whether someone will develop Alzheimer's disease, the vast majority of centers will not test APOE status for clinical purposes. A person with no ε4 allele may wrongly feel "in the clear" and ignore other modifiable risk factors or early signs of problems, whereas a person with one or two ε4 alleles may feel doomed and give up hope.

There are a number of other genes that have been identified to have weaker associations with Alzheimer's disease than the ones we have mentioned here. However, reviewing them all is outside the scope of this book. You can browse the very technical website www.alzgene.org if you are interested in learning more about these additional genes.

Genetics of Other Forms of Dementia

Most common forms of vascular dementia have no known causal genetic mutations, excepting some very rare forms such as cerebral autosomal dominant arteriopathy with subcortical infarcts and leukoencephalopathy (CADASIL). Most cases of frontotemporal dementia are also *sporadic* (seemingly random occurrences of diseases), but about 10–15% of people with this disease have one of two inherited autosomal dominant genetic mutations. These are microtubule-associated protein tau and progranulin mutations, both on chromosome 17. As with Alzheimer's, patients with these mutations have a 50–50 chance of passing it on to their children. The tau mutation is linked to deposits of the tau protein in brain cells, which you know from chapter 3 are recognized as contributing to the tangles that are also characteristic in Alzheimer's disease. The pro-granulin mutation leads to underproduction of *progranulin*, a chem-ical that promotes cell growth and wound repair. For more about the genetics of frontotemporal degeneration, we recommend reading the Web site of the Association for Frontotemporal Dementia, at http://www.theaftd.org/. The risk of developing dementia of Parkinson's disease and Lewy body disease has been associated with mutations on the glucocerebrosidase gene on chromosome 1.

Genetics of Mild Cognitive Impairment

The few studies that have aimed to specifically identify genetic muta-tions associated with MCI have found that more people with MCI than older adults without cognitive impairment have the APOE ε4 allele. This is not too surprising given that MCI, particularly in the amnestic form, most often results in Alzheimer's disease. Indeed, because MCI often, but not always (see chapter 4), represents very early stages of other forms of dementia, there is likely not a special genetic risk factors for MCI. We are certain that the coming years will bring many new discoveries about how genetics can be helpful in diagnosing and determining the possible outcomes of MCI.

BRAIN INJURY

There is considerable ongoing research examining the link between brain injury and dementia, but far less involved with looking into how prior brain injury affects risk for MCI. Brain injuries can occur for a variety of reasons, but the two causes that receive the most attention are trauma and stroke. Traumatic brain injuries most often occur during accidents like motor-vehicle collisions or falls, but they also occur in milder forms when someone has a concussion. Brains do not deal well with such accidents: Our brains are essentially float-ing in a bag of fluid (cerebral spinal fluid), and if our heads are pro-pelled forward, for example, our brains lag a bit behind and then collide with the front of our skull, then bounce backward and collide with the back of our skull, and then forward again with less force, and so on. What can result is *contusion* (bruising) of the brain where it hits the skull, and *shearing* (stretching and tearing) of the long neuronal connections inside the brain.

Traumatic brain injury has been associated with an increased risk of dementia in many studies, and there is a small but growing body of evidence that it also puts people at greater risk of developing MCI. One area that is getting a lot of attention lately is the link between repeated concussions acquired during sports play such as professional football and later risk of MCI and dementia. Traumatic brain injuries do not *cause* MCI or dementia; that is, there is no evidence that they cause a build-up of amyloid plaque or tangles. Nevertheless, they cause brain damage that makes the brain more vulnerable to the effects of dementia pathology. If traumatic brain injury is a risk factor for MCI and dementia, then we want to reduce the risk of traumatic brain injury in the first place. Using safety mechanisms such as seat belts and helmets will reduce not only your risk of damaging your brain, but also your risk of dementia.

The second main form of brain injury is stroke. As mentioned in chapter 3, strokes are the result of bleeding in the brain. Strokes put people most at risk for vascular dementia, but can also accelerate the rate of Alzheimer's disease and other dementias. Similar to the way traumatic brain injuries might be linked to dementia, strokes make the brain more vulnerable and less able to withstand the accumulation of brain pathology associated with dementia. The risk factors for stroke are primarily cardiovascular, and they are modifiable. These are discussed later in this chapter.

EDUCATION AND INTELLECTUAL ENGAGEMENT

One risk factor for dementia and MCI surprises a number of people: The more years of formal education you have had, the less likely you are to develop either disorder. There are undoubtedly many intermediary factors affecting the association between education and risk of dementia or MCI. More highly educated people earn higher incomes on average, which often affords them better health care, nutrition, and access to certain recreational activities that can help mitigate stress and provide exercise. Nevertheless, many studies take care to control for socioeconomic status, and still find a link between education or occupation and dementia risk, which suggests that there really is something protective about living an intellectually engaged life. There are intriguing explanations for how education may mitigate against cognitive decline and dementia. As we discuss in more detail in chapter 13, cognitive engagement (i.e., thinking) is known to increase connections between neurons, and, hence, spending more years actively learning may create more connected, denser networks between brain cells.

You might think that education is a nonmodifiable risk factor for MCI and dementia, because most people finish school some time between their late teens to mid-20s, but of course learning does not stop once you graduate. Many occupations require continued learning on the job, and, indeed, as discussed in greater detail in chapter 13, occupations that are more complex and, therefore, more likely to require more continuous learning are associated with lower rates of dementia. In addition, older adults who spend more time pursuing leisure activities that are cognitively engaging are also less likely to be diagnosed with dementia. We want to make it clear that we are not saying that giving yourself a mental workout can prevent MCI or dementia, but what it can do is raise your level of functioning to a level at which the impact of these conditions is minimized, potentially delaying diagnosis and increasing the number of years you have to lead an active, productive life.

Some studies have reported a downside to higher education, however, because they find that people with higher education experience more rapid cognitive decline once they have been diagnosed with dementia. You are probably thinking, "Wait a minute! It doesn't make sense that education can protect you against dementia but also put you at risk for faster decline if you do get it!" This paradox has two competing, but captivating explanations. The first explanation suggests that people with greater intellectual attainment effectively burn their brains out by all that thinking. A second explanation is more nuanced, but has stronger evidence backing it up. That second explanation is that people with greater intellectual attainment have more robust brains, in essence, and, therefore, can withstand greater brain pathology before symptoms such as memory problems appear. What this suggests is that education (i.e., learning) provides a buffer, or *reserve*, against dementia. People can have the underlying disease, but be asymptomatic for longer because of the enhanced brain networks established by years and years of hard thinking.

One compelling piece of evidence in line with this idea was gathered by Ellen Bialystok, Fergus Craik, and Morris Freedman at Baycrest in Toronto, Canada. They recorded the age at which people were diagnosed with probable Alzheimer's disease, and found that people who were lifelong bilinguals—that is people who spent most of their lives speaking two or more languages daily—were about 4 years older when diagnosed compared to monolingual patients who spoke only one language their whole lives. Dr. Bialystok has plenty of other evidence that bilinguals have better *executive functioning* (multitasking, avoiding interference) than monolinguals. Together, these results suggest that spending your entire life mastering two languages and switching back and forth between them makes your brain more robust and better able to withstand brain pathology associated with Alzheimer's disease.

Some evidence regarding MCI is also in line with this idea of brain or cognitive reserve. In one study, people with MCI who had more reserve (higher education, better intelligence, more complex prior occupations, and greater cognitive and social engagement) had *smaller* brains than their counterparts with less reserve. That is, compared to those with less reserve, those with greater intellectual attainment likely had MCI for longer, causing their brains to *atrophy* (shrink), but it took them longer to come down to the same level of cognitive impairment because they had more reserve! Two of your authors, Kelly Murphy and Angela Troyer, along with Lynn Ossher of the University of Michigan, as well as Fergus Craik and Ellen Bialystok mentioned in the previous paragraph, have found a similar association between bilingualism and age of MCI diagnosis: Bilingual people are an average of 4.5 years older at time diagnosis with single-domain amnestic MCI than are monolingual people. Interestingly, this pattern did not hold for multiple-domain amnestic MCI, which suggests that bilingualism may have a special buffering effect against Alzheimer's disease and not other forms of dementia.

Together, the evidence about education and intellectually engaging occupations and leisure activities provides a strong case for staying intellectually engaged. In chapter 13 you will find a host of suggested activities to keep you mentally engaged.

VASCULAR AND METABOLIC FACTORS

A variety of vascular and metabolic conditions have been identified as risk factors for both MCI and dementia, including hypertension (high blood pressure), high cholesterol, smoking (even past history of smoking in current nonsmokers), high body-mass index (a ratio of weight to height), and diabetes. When three or more of these are present in a person, this has been termed the *metabolic syndrome.* We have classified these risk factors as modifiable, because for the majority of people, they can be controlled by lifestyle choices. We recognize that some people have genetic predispositions to hypertension, high cholesterol, and diabetes, and for them these conditions may not be modifiable. Regardless, it is important to understand how they can contribute to MCI and dementia risk.

High cholesterol clogs the arteries with fats, smoking increases the thickness of artery walls, and diabetes reduces the reactivity of blood vessels to on-demand changes in blood flow, all of which increase blood pressure. This causes a chain reaction of sorts: First, these syndromes are associated with more *hyperintensities,* or unusually bright spots on certain MRI scans that are often caused by tiny bleeds (ministrokes). Second, these ministrokes disrupt communication between neurons in the *white matter,* the long axons transferring information from one brain region to another. Third, disrupted communication between neurons contributes to cognitive difficulties. Some good news is that many studies find that pharmacological control of these conditions, that is, medication-control of high blood pressure, high cholesterol, and diabetes, reduces their effect on MCI and dementia risk. The bad news is that some other studies find that pharmacologic control of these disorders does not modify risk of MCI or dementia. How could this be? Most likely it is because these disorders are diagnosed and treated only once they pass a certain cut-off, but that does not mean that the disorders start the day of diagnosis. Rather, they have been brewing for quite some time, doing harm. Either way, it is well worth it to aim to control these conditions if you can, through medication, diet (see chapter 11), and exercise (see chapter 12) to try to protect your brain health. To control your modifiable risk factors, you have to know that you have them in the first place! This is why it is important not to avoid your annual medical check-ups, like Theresa has as described in Box 5.4.

Box 5.4 Case Vignette of Sylvie and Theresa: The Sometimes Subtle Impact of Risk Factors

---

Sylvie and Theresa are 77-year-old identical twin sisters. Both are married and have grown children. Because they are identical twins, they share an identical genetic make-up. Sylvie is a retired emergency-room nurse, a career she was inspired to pursue because she has always been so grateful for the excellent care she received after being in a serious car accident while in her teens that left her with a broken collarbone and a serious concussion. Since retiring, Sylvie has been volunteering at an art museum and in her grandchildren's kindergarten classroom. She takes medication to control her blood pressure and cholesterol.

Theresa and her husband owned a successful restaurant. She handled all the food ordering, looked after the accounting, and hired and managed the staff. Theresa helps look after her grandchildren when needed, and she likes to read. She intends to drop the extra weight she has put on over the years, but hasn't been to see her doctor in about four years, although she thinks her blood pressure and everything else is okay. What does bother her is her memory. Theresa says that she can't seem to remember where she has put things, and her husband notes that she repeats the same questions many times each day. After her husband finally convinced her to see her doctor, she was ultimately diagnosed with high blood pressure and amnestic MCI.

Sylvie and Theresa both have a mix of protective and risk factors for MCI, but only Theresa has been diagnosed with it. It is possible that Sylvie's better management of her health and greater social and intellectual engagement in retirement have provided added reserve, protecting her against the effects of cognitive decline.

DEPRESSION

Depression is a risk factor for both MCI and dementia. Between 1% and 5% of adults aged 65 and older have a major depressive disorder, and up to 15% of community-dwelling older adults have significant symptoms of depression. Half or more of all cases of depression among older adults occur for the first time over the age of 65 (in which case it is called *late-onset depression*), whereas the other half or less are cases of recurrent depression that existed in the individuals' young or middle-aged years (called *early-onset depression*). It is still unclear whether early-onset and late-onset depression are distinct disorders, with different risk factors, symptoms, and outcomes, but, regardless, both forms are risk factors for MCI.

There are four common explanations for the link between depression and cognitive decline. The first is that depression makes people more vulnerable to cognitive decline. The idea is that a healthy mood and positive outlook may provide some reserve to combat cognitive decline. A second explanation for the link between depression and cognitive decline is that depression may be a response to very early cognitive changes. If you start finding yourself losing your keys or getting stuck for acquaintances' names, you might start getting down on yourself. A third explanation states that depression is a symptom of the underlying neurodegeneration that ultimately leads to MCI or dementia. A likely culprit here is damage to the hippocampus, which by now you know is important for memory, but it is also important for the *glucocorticoid* system that modulates stress hormones like *cortisol*. Stressors such as depression elevate cortisol, which in turn can cause further damage to the hippocampus. Another contender is vascular pathology, because people with cardiovascular risk factors such as hypertension, obesity, and high cholesterol as a group have a higher prevalence of depression than do people without these risk factors. A fourth explanation for the link between depression and cognitive decline is genetic. Certain genetic variations associated with dementia (for example, presenilin 1) have also been linked to depression, and there may be more genetic commonalities that have yet to be discovered.

Regardless of how or why depression is a risk factor for MCI and dementia, the important take-home message here is that if you are suffering from depression—mild, moderate, or severe—you should seek treatment. The first step in this path is to recognize that you have depression, and this, in turn, requires getting past the stigma. In most societies, psychiatric disorders are still taboo topics and not discussed openly. It is hard to believe that the same was true of cancer only a few decades ago. Then, people didn't mention "the C word," and were much less likely to let others know that they had cancer than they are now. Depression and other psychiatric disorders are diseases just like any other disease; they are not a sign of mental weakness.

The second requirement for recognizing if you have depression is to know the symptoms. The *Diagnostic and Statistical Manual of Mental Disorders-IV-TR* has two classifications you should know about: major depressive disorder, and dysthymic disorder. You no doubt have an inkling what depression is, but you may not have heard the word *dysthymia*, which means low mood. Of course, we all experience low mood and even symptoms of depression from time to time. That is why it is important to consider the diagnostic criteria carefully, because they aim to rule out normal fluctuations in mood and normal reactions to bad or disturbing events. The symptoms for major depressive disorder and dysthymic disorder are listed in Box 5.5.

The symptoms listed in Box 5.5 are general and are used to diagnose anyone with depression or dysthymia, but research shows that, on average, older adults present with different symptoms than do younger adults. Compared to younger adults, older adults are less likely to express feelings of depression, worthlessness, and guilt, but are more likely to display the cognitive and somatic (bodily) symptoms of depression and a loss of interest in daily activities. So whereas a younger adult with depression may complain to his doctor about not feeling worthy or feeling sad, an older adult with depression is more likely to express concerns about his or her memory and concentration and problems with sleep or energy. Memory, concentration, and sleep all do change as a part of healthy aging, so the challenge for clinicians is to disentangle whether these problems are due to normal aging, depression, or MCI. Figuring this out can be quite tricky, but a complete neurological, neuropsychological, and psychiatric/

Box 5.5 Criteria for Major Depressive Disorder and Dysthymic Disorder

Major Depressive Disorder
Depressed mood and/or loss of interest or pleasure in life activities for at least two weeks and at least five of the following symptoms that cause clinically significant impairment in social, work, or other important areas of functioning almost every day:

- Depressed mood most of the day.
- Diminished interest or pleasure in all or most activities.
- Significant unintentional weight loss or gain.
- Insomnia or sleeping too much.
- Agitation or psychomotor retardation (slowing of behavior) noticed by others.
- Fatigue or loss of energy.
- Feelings of worthlessness or excessive guilt.
- Diminished ability to think or concentrate, or indecisiveness.
- Recurrent thoughts of death.

Dysthymic Disorder
Depressed mood most of the day for more days than not, for at least two years, and the presence of two or more of the following symptoms that cause clinically significant impairment in social, work, or other important areas of functioning:

- Poor appetite or overeating.
- Insomnia or sleeping too much.
- Low energy or fatigue.
- Low self-esteem.
- Poor concentration or difficulty making decisions.
- Feelings of hopelessness.

psychological evaluation usually provides enough information to make a correct diagnosis.

If you recognize that you have depression or dysthymia, get professional help. You are no better equipped to treat your own depression than you are to treat any other medical conditions you may have. There is an array of professionals and treatment types for depression, and what works best for you will depend on the severity of your depression and on what you are comfortable with. A recent study of people who had late-life depression but did not have MCI found that a group *psycho-educational* program (a program that educates people about a particular condition and ways to manage it) and cognitive training was associated with significant improvements in memory. The results of the handful of studies that have examined the effects of antidepressants on cognitive functioning in people with MCI and on rates of progression from MCI to dementia have been more disappointing, showing little or no benefit of the medications. However, there is some promising evidence that, among people who have both MCI and depression, medication used to treat the symptoms of dementia (donepezil, see chapter 7) can delay progression to dementia. Regardless of whether treatment of depression is ultimately found to help alleviate cognitive problems in MCI or delay progression to dementia, it is still a worthwhile goal to seek treatment in order to enjoy the positive benefits on your mood and well-being.

A FINAL WORD

In this chapter, we have described a number of risk and protective factors for MCI and dementia. Now that you understand these factors, we hope that you better understand your own risk or that of a loved one, and that you are inspired to address the modifiable risk factors that you may have. In an ideal world, we would be able to plug your age, sex, education, blood pressure, and all of these other factors into a calculator and an algorithm would then tell us your risk of developing MCI or dementia. Risk assessments like this already exist for other conditions such as stroke, heart disease, and certain forms of cancer (see ww2.heartandstroke.ca, www.framinghamheartstudy.org/risk, and www.cancer.gov). These sites provide valuable information that can help you make positive lifestyle changes, and, indeed, the public availability of this information may account for some of the fact that deaths from these diseases have been on the decline over recent years. Nevertheless, we caution you to use calculators only from reputable sites hosted by governments or nation-wide health societies like the Canadian Heart and Stroke Foundation, or the American Heart Society, and to use such tools in conjunction with a discussion with your doctor who can help interpret your personal risk.

In contrast to these stroke- and cancer-risk calculators, to date there is no validated tool to calculate your individual risk of developing MCI or dementia. Nevertheless, we hope that the knowledge you have gained in this chapter will help you to make positive health and lifestyle changes. Even if you have already been diagnosed with MCI, there is considerable overlap between the risk factors for MCI and those for progressing from MCI to dementia, so making these changes now is a worthwhile goal.

Many people ask us, "Isn't it too late for these factors to protect me?" What they are asking is whether the modifiable protective factors are only effective if people practice them from a young age and throughout their life. Undoubtedly, it is better to have led a healthy lifestyle throughout your life, but there is good reason to believe that it is never too late to start. We know that people can improve their blood pressure and glucose control through exercise, and studies have shown that sedentary older adults who are started on a walking program show improved cognitive and brain functioning. In section 3 of this book, we talk about a number of positive health and lifestyle options (diet, exercise, cognitive engagement, social engagement, and memory strategies) that research shows help to improve cognitive functioning. Although the effect of these lifestyle options on dementia rates has been the focus of many studies, current scientific evidence for the power of these behaviors to minimize the risk of MCI or of progressing from MCI to dementia is scant at best. The studies needed to properly assess the impact of lifestyle changes on risk take an enormous amount of time and money, but some are currently underway. Nevertheless, in order to be diagnosed with MCI or dementia, one has to have cognitive impairments. Therefore, anything that helps to improve brain functioning should help reduce risk of a cognitive disorder such as MCI or dementia. We advise our clients *and you* to make these positive health and lifestyle changes now.

Box 5.6 Questions to Ask Your Doctor if MCI Is Suspected
or Confirmed in Yourself or in Your Family Member

---

1. "What aspects of my medical history could contribute to my risk
   of MCI or dementia?"
2. "How are my weight, blood pressure, blood cholesterol, and blood
   sugars, and should I be doing anything to improve them?"
3. If you are a woman of menopausal age, ask, "Is hormone-
   replacement therapy right for me?"
4. If you think a blood relative has one of the autosomal-dominant
   forms of dementia described in this chapter, consider whether
   you should have genetic counseling and ask, "What is your
   advice on this matter?"
5. If you have had a head injury or stroke in the past, ask, "Do you
   think this could be contributing to the cognitive changes I am
   experiencing?"
6. "What more can I do to reduce my vascular and metabolic risk
   factors?"
7. If you are suffering from low mood that has limited your activities, ask, "Are there any treatment options (medications or
   counseling) you would recommend?"

RECOMMENDED READING

Stern, Y. (2006). Cognitive reserve and Alzheimer diesease. *Alzheimer Disease and
   Associated Disorders, 20,* 112–117.
Watch an interesting HBO video on cognitive reserve at http://www.hbo.com/
alzheimers/supplementary-cognitive-reserve.html.

HOW IS MILD COGNITIVE IMPAIRMENT IDENTIFIED AND MANAGED?

6

The Process of Diagnosing Mild Cognitive Impairment

It is not unusual for adults over the age of 50 to notice that their memory is not the same as it used to be when they were younger. People often joke about memory failures with friends and are reassured by the fact that no one has a perfect memory. As depicted in Box 6.1, pretty much everyone can relate to feeling a little frustrated when they forget something.

Box 6.1 A Typical Memory Slip

"Now what was it I came upstairs for?"

In chapter 2 you learned about the differences between normal aging and mild cognitive impairment (MCI). If you have memory concerns, it's rather difficult to figure out on your own what side of the equation you fall on. Are you the "worried well" or do your concerns represent something more significant? The question is: When do everyday memory slips become cause for concern? In exploring this issue, you should consider whether there has been a notable increase in the frequency of your memory failures and whether these failures have "real consequences." For example, if you forget to stop at the mall to drop-off the dry cleaning, you might have to make a return trip to the store. If you forget to stop at the mall to pick up your friend from the dentist, then your friend will be inconvenienced and maybe even offended. An increase in memory failures that have consequences, ranging from annoying (repeat trip to the store) to more significant (standing up your friend) may be cause for concern; however, they may not indicate anything more than age-normal memory decline. The first step to getting some answers is a visit to the family doctor.

Some people worry their independence could be questioned if they bring up their memory concerns with their doctor and a problem is discovered. They don't want anyone questioning their capability to make decisions or to drive the car. These outcomes are highly unlikely in the case of MCI, because, as reviewed in chapter 1, by definition MCI does not significantly compromise your ability to manage your day-to-day responsibilities, including driving (see chapters 8 and 10 for further information on the topic of driving).

Finding out as early as possible whether your concerns are indeed representative of MCI puts you in the best position to take advantage of available treatments. The best prevention is early intervention, so we encourage you to take that first step, see your doctor, and start getting some answers. For example, see the situation faced by Evelyn and Gerry described in Box 6.2.

VISIT TO YOUR FAMILY DOCTOR

Once you decide to talk to your family doctor about your memory, there are several things you can do in preparation for the visit that can

---

Box 6.2 Case Vignette of a Couple with Memory Concerns (Part 1)

Gerry and Evelyn are a married couple, both in their late 60s and enjoying retirement. Over the past year or so, Gerry has noticed that Evelyn occasionally asks him the same question, and, once in a while, she is mixing up their schedule of commitments. She has always been the one with the great memory in the family, and these little slip-ups are not typical of her. He recently read an article in *Reader's Digest* about MCI, and he is wondering how to bring up his concerns with Evelyn. Meanwhile, Evelyn has also recognized that she is making memory mistakes more frequently and brings this up with her family doctor during her annual physical check-up.

---

assist your doctor in evaluating your concerns. In fact, the preparation steps you'll read about in the following section would also apply if your doctor decided to refer you to one of the specialist doctors described later in this chapter.

How to Prepare for Your Appointment with Your Doctor

Prior to your appointment with your doctor, stop and think about the following: How long have I been having this problem? What kinds of memory slips am I experiencing? In chapter 2 we discussed examples of common memory slips. Referring back to that chapter may help you identify some of your personal experiences. Also, consider whether events in your life could be impacting your memory. Stress, depression, excessive worry, poor sleep, and being preoccupied or distracted by something going on in your life are all factors that can hinder your memory, and some of these your doctor may be able to treat. If you can, talk to a close family member, such as your spouse/partner or friend who knows you really well and may or may not have noticed some changes in your everyday memory. Regardless of whether this person shares your concerns, it is helpful if you can have them accompany you on your visit to the doctor. Your doctor may also wish to ask them some questions. This person can also support you by being an extra set of ears to help you remember the doctor's recommendations. They can also help you remember to tell the doctor all the information and to ask all the questions you have planned. It's helpful to prepare by writing down the information that you wish to discuss and to bring what you've written along when you see your doctor. See Box 6.3 for a survey that you can download from www.baycrest.org/livingwithMCI to help you prepare for your visit with your doctor to evaluate your memory concerns.

What Will Happen at the Doctor's Office

Taking a history

Your doctor should want to take a history of your memory *complaint* (a term used by health professionals to signify that it is *your* report of *your* symptoms, it does not mean you are complaining). Any type of doctor you see about your memory will want to take this history, so if you see more than one, you may find yourself repeating the same story. It's a very important story because it helps doctors in their efforts to diagnose what might be causing your problems. The doctor will want you to describe what you feel has changed about your memory and how the change is affecting you. You will be ready for this if you've completed the survey in Box 6.3 about how to prepare. Examples of some questions you might be asked are: When did it start? How did it start? Was it gradual or sudden in onset? What kinds of changes exactly? So be prepared to provide examples of your memory slips.

Next, the doctor might want to figure out if these cognitive changes have had any impact on your ability to manage your day-to-day responsibilities by determining your level of independence in *instrumental activities of daily living.* These are everyday activities that require you to think and problem solve, such as independently getting around town, managing your own schedule, doing your own banking, your own shopping, cooking...well you get the idea. As we noted in chapter 2 both healthy older adults and people with MCI can still manage on their own, although people with MCI might find carrying out some of these activities to be more challenging or may not do them as well as they did in the past. The doctor is just look-ing for any change in the activities you normally do, so if he or she asks you about an activity you've never done, like the banking, for

Box 6.3 A Survey to Help You Prepare for Your Visit with Your Doctor

1. Specific examples of my memory or other cognitive (thinking) problems are: _____
   _____
   _____
   _____

2. These problems first started about _____
   _____ago.

3. These problems started (circle one response): GRADUALLY, SUDDENLY, or NOT SURE.

4. Since they started, these problems are (circle one response): IMPROVING, WORSENING, or STAYING THE SAME.

5. I have asked those close to me if they have noticed any changes in my memory or cognition and they said (circle one response): YES or NO. [If yes, ask your close friend or family member for specific examples of the changes and list them here): _____
   _____
   _____
   _____

6. There (circle one response) ARE or ARE NOT any significant changes in my health that started happening around the same time the cognitive changes started. If there were health changes describe them here: _____
   _____
   _____
   _____

7. I have experienced notable changes in my (circle response) LEVEL OF STRESS, MOOD, or NOT APPLICABLE. If you circled "level of stress," "mood," or both please note when these changes started _____
   _____
   _____
   _____.

8. I have blood relatives (for example, parents, siblings) who have experienced cognitive changes (circle one response): YES or NO. If yes, please specify their relationship to you. _____
   _____
   _____.

(continued)

Box 6.3 (Continued)

9. My medical history includes (list all past, including childhood, and current medical conditions): _____

_____

_____

_____

10. This is a list of my current medications (including over-the-counter medications, vitamins, and other supplements), with dosages. _____

_____

_____

_____

---

example, that activity would not be considered in evaluating your level of independence. However, if you were the one that always did the banking, but your spouse is now helping you, then the doctor will want to know why, especially if it seems linked to these cognitive changes you are reporting.

Performing a physical examination

Your doctor will want to examine you for any obvious physical or neurological symptoms that might explain your report of cognitive decline. For example, are your heart sounds and blood pressure normal? Are your reflexes normal and the same on both sides of the body? Is there any evidence of swelling or discoloration in your hands and feet? How do your eyes look? Are they clear, are your pupils the same size and are they reacting normally to light? Is your abdomen, soft, nontender and nondistended (not swollen)? What's your temperature? Doctors can learn a lot about the health of their patient from the physical examination and are equipped with the breadth of knowledge to identify and treat many kinds of ailments; however, in the case of MCI, there is usually nothing obviously wrong and your doctor will quickly move on to evaluating the less obvious causes of your impression of cognitive change.

Review of medical history and treatable causes

Your doctor will review your medical history for the presence of risk factors associated with development of *dementia* (persistent cognitive impairment causing loss of functional independence, reviewed in chapter 3). As we discussed in chapter 5, medical conditions such as high cholesterol, high blood pressure, and diabetes, as well as history of previous head injury, and family history of dementia are all associated with risk of dementia. Your doctor will want to consider these factors in your medical history when evaluating the significance of your memory complaint. Indeed, the presence of one or more of these risk factors, coupled with your subjective memory complaint, may influence your doctor to more readily consider the possibility that you may have MCI. Before pursuing this possibility, she or he will also want to review whether there are any obvious treatable causes.

As you know from reading chapter 4, there are treatable causes of cognitive decline, such as side effects of medications, vitamin deficiencies, problems with hormone regulation, or a change in mood that could be impacting memory. The doctor will want to assess whether you could be experiencing any negative side effects from any medicine you might be taking. He or she will also want to confirm that you are taking your prescribed medications properly. With respect to side effects, some medications can have side effects that can be almost nonexistent or very small in some people and larger in others. It is important to take your medicine to control conditions such as high blood pressure, high cholesterol, and diabetes, because these are associated with increased risk of dementia and decreased heart and brain health. (The link between these medical conditions and dementia is reviewed in chapters 5 and 11).

Feeling very depressed, anxious, or stressed can also influence your attention and memory abilities, so the doctor will want to ask you about whether or not you are experiencing any of these negative symptoms and why. This is critically important, because if mood or stress problems are causing your symptoms, then you may find considerable improvement in your thinking skills when some of the symptoms improve. You may be experiencing these negative symptoms for no obvious reason, or these feelings could be linked to some significant life event. For example, a recent move of your residence, divorce, a death in the family, a wedding you were responsible for, financial burdens that are troubling you, and so on. The important point is your doctor can be key in helping you, either by providing you with (or referring you to) counseling support, medication, or some combination of both to treat your experience of these negative feelings and their impact on your cognition.

Order lab tests

Lab tests might be ordered to rule out or identify some physical causes of your cognitive symptoms. For example, blood tests can determine if you have a thiamine (Vitamin B12) deficiency or thyroid dysfunction, both of which can cause memory problems, which can be minimized or reversed with treatment. These "reversible" causes of memory decline are mentioned in chapter 2 in the section on "your health and memory" and again in chapter 4 in the section on "reversion to normal aging." Brain scans, also referred to as neuroimaging tests, may be ordered. These scans are essentially a picture of the brain and its interior that are taken to help rule out whether or not the memory changes you are experiencing are due to an abnormality in your brain, such as an undetected mild *stroke* event (area of brain damage due to a disturbance in blood supply) or a *tumor* (an area of abnormal tissue growth). The scans may also be used to determine whether there is greater than expected *atrophy* (brain shrinkage in a specific area or all over) for your age or any areas of inefficient blood circulation in your brain. Your family doctor may order one of the *brain scans* or your doctor may defer to one of the specialists you will read about later on in this chapter who will likely order one of these kinds of scans. The types of scans most commonly ordered by doctors and specialists are described in Box 6.4.

Cognitive screening

Your doctor may want to give you a brief test that involves answering questions, following commands, drawing a simple design, and writing something. These brief screening tests check that you know

Box 6.4 Examples of Common Types of Brain Scans (Neuroimaging Tests) and Their Purpose.

Test	Purpose
Computed [axial] tomography (CT or CAT)	Takes a picture of the structure of the brain to check for a previously undetected stroke event, tumor, and/ or greater than expected atrophy (shrinkage of the brain) for age.
Magnetic resonance imaging (MRI)	Same as a CT scan, but the resolution is much better, thereby improving accuracy for detecting any structural brain abnormalities.
Single photon emission computed tomography (SPECT)	To examine blood flow in the brain, looking for areas that might be getting too little blood.

the date and where you are, and they will examine different kinds of cognitive abilities such as attention, memory, language, and simple spatial drawing skills. On screening tests it is the total score that is examined, rather than performance in any one thinking area. Most people with an average level of education, who are being tested in their first language, should have no trouble scoring within the normal range on a screening test. Indeed as noted in chapter 2, people with MCI perform similar to their same-aged peers classified as "normal aging" on cognitive screening tests.

What the Doctor Will Do Next

Your doctor will consider all the information she or he has gathered from you and will likely want to arrange to meet with you again to monitor the symptoms you have reported, to see if there have been any further developments, or to review the results of your lab tests (if ordered). Although medical tests can help to rule in, or out, the possible physical causes of your cognitive problems, there no lab test that can conclusively detect MCI.

THE STATE OF MEDICAL LAB TESTS FOR DETECTING MCI

There are currently no medical tests that can definitively diagnose MCI. Scientists are actively investigating for such a test and efforts in this regard do look promising. Structural scans such as those described in Box 6.4 of people with MCI often look totally normal. Thus, other types of lab tests and scans are under investigation for use in detecting and even subtyping MCI. Some examples of these tests are described in Box 6.5. Importantly, although these additional tests may show evidence of brain disease in people with MCI, scientists do not yet know how much disease is normal. In other words, we do not yet know the exact ranges of "normal" and "abnormal"

Box 6.5 Examples of Some of the Types of Medical Tests Scientists Are Investigating as Tools for Detecting MCI

Medical Test	Purpose
Amyloid positron emission tomography (PET)	To look for evidence of areas of brain pathology by injecting a tracer substance into the blood stream that is attracted to areas where there is an accumulation of *amyloid plaques* (areas of protein build-up outside the brain cells that represent areas of disease).
Fluorodeoxyglucon positron emission tomography (FDG-PET)	Measures *glucose metabolism* (efficiency of brain cells to use a simple sugar for energy from the circulating blood supply) where brain areas of reduced metabolism indicate presence of pathology.
Lumbar puncture	A spinal tap to check for the presence of proteins described in chapter 5, in which low levels of the beta-amyloid protein along with high levels of the tau protein signal the brain pathology of Alzheimer's disease and other dementias

brain pathology in the aging brain, because there is so much normal variation from one person to another. This is further complicated by research showing evidence of significant brain pathology in the brains of older adults at autopsy who did not show symptoms of cognitive or functional decline prior to their death.

POSSIBLE NEXT STEPS IF MCI IS SUSPECTED

Do not be discouraged by the fact that there is no medical test with a definitive answer. There are several options you and your doctor may decide on if MCI is suspected. Use of the options may be dependent on a variety of factors such as ease of access through your health-care provider and geography. For example, whether you live in an urban or rural area, and whether you have health insurance or financial means are just some factors that affect ease of access to specialized tests or care. Box 6.6 provides a listing of possible courses of action depending on the nature of the information obtained on your initial visit and the lab tests (if ordered). If your doctor suspects MCI, then he or she may elect to wait and monitor the situation by making a follow-up

---

Box 6.6 Courses of Action Your Family Doctor Could Take when MCI Is Suspected

Monitor

- Track cognitive symptoms (Are symptoms stable, improving, or worsening?).
- Promote management of modifiable risk factors (such as diabetes).

Order Lab Tests

- Blood tests (to check for problems in hormone or vitamin levels).
- Brain scans (to check for evidence of stroke, tumor, or shrinkage).

Refer To A Specialist

- Geriatrician (focuses on health of older adults).
- Psychiatrist (focuses on mental health).
- Neurologist (focuses on disorders of the nervous system).
- Neuropsychologist (focuses on cognition and brain health).

appointment with you to assess whether the problems may be getting worse over time. Your doctor might help you focus on your modifiable risk factors, such as stricter management of medical conditions like high blood pressure and high cholesterol, and he or she may counsel you on how to prevent these conditions if you don't have them. Your doctor may also decide to refer you on to a specialist, if one is available in your community, such as a *geriatrician*, who specializes in the health of older adults, a *psychiatrist*, who specializes in mental health disorders, a *neurologist*, who specializes in disorders of the nervous system, or a *neuropsychologist*, who specializes in evaluating the relationship between cognitive functioning and brain health. In turn, these specialists may also consult with one another. The specialists will also want to review your history of memory concerns, your health history, and conduct their own investigations. If you did the preparation outlined in Box 6.3 then you will also be ready for a visit with any of the other specialists.

The Geriatrician

A geriatrician is a medical doctor who specializes in geriatric medicine, meaning in the physical health and well being of older adults. Your family doctor may want to refer you to a geriatrician because this type of specialist has expertise in how medical conditions that are common among older adults interact, such as high blood pressure, urinary incontinence, and high cholesterol, and how the medications used to treat these conditions interact. The geriatrician can also appreciate how medications, reductions in hearing and vision (sensory loss), and early signs of possible neurological disease can influence cognitive decline in older adults. Geriatricians do not treat individual conditions, like high blood pressure or an illness like a sore throat; for these you see your family doctor. Rather, the geriatrician is interested in looking at any medical problems you may have as part of the larger picture of your overall health.

Geriatric medicine takes a holistic approach to your health. A visit to the geriatrician will involve comprehensive assessment of your medical conditions (if any), your medications and vitamin intake (if any), your lifestyle (including *social history*, which refers to the people in your life, what your pastimes are, whether you exercise, what your eating habits are like, and your substance use now and in the past, such as alcohol intake or tobacco use), your physical appearance (signs of fatigue, skin problems, evidence of poor circulation, especially in your hands and feet), your balance, and how you walk.

If you are taking medications, then the geriatrician will assess whether the medications you are taking are best suited to work well together, if the time of day you're taking the medicine is the best to get the most benefit, and assess for the presence of any negative side effects. For example, some medications, if taken in the evening, can interfere with sleep. It is also possible that your medications, when taken together or even individually, can produce side effects that may be impacting your memory by affecting your ability to get a restful night's sleep.

The geriatrician will also want to evaluate your mental and mood status by conducting some screening tests involving asking you questions or having you fill out brief questionnaires. He or she will also perform a physical examination to evaluate sensory loss (in particular vision and hearing), check that your muscle tone and reflexes are normal, determine whether your heart and abdominal sounds are normal, examine neurological functions (described subsequently), and assess your level of functional independence in managing your activities of daily living. The latter includes both basic physical activities, such as bathing, getting dressed, and eating on your own, and instrumental activities, such as using the telephone, getting around town, taking your medications, shopping and managing your schedule on your own.

The geriatrician is concerned with assessing and treating any syndromes that are more common among older adults but that are not representative of normal aging, such as greater-than-expected vision and hearing loss, problems with balance and walking, depression, not getting proper nutrition, and observation of cognitive decline. Geriatricians are often part of a larger health-care team (or at least they know how to get access to the services provided by other health-care professionals), including nurses, audiologists, ophthalmologists, dieticians, physiotherapists, occupational therapists, phramacists, psychologists, and social workers. These other health-care professionals may be called on to participate as necessary in the overall goal of geriatric medicine, which is to help older adult clients maintain their quality of life, their mobility, and their functional independence. In pursuit of this goal, the geriatrician may also elect to consult with other specialists such as a psychiatrist (when a mental health disorder is suspected), or a neurologist (when neurological disease is suspected), or a neuropsychologist (when no medical, neurological, or psychiatric conditions account for the reported cognitive decline and cognitive screening is not sensitive or specific enough to conclusively diagnose MCI and the type of MCI).

The Psychiatrist

A psychiatrist is a medical doctor who specializes in identifying and treating mental-health disorders. Mental-health problems could be related to disorders of personality, development, mood, sleep, dementia, substance addictions, and many other types of conditions. It is unlikely that someone with MCI would show psychiatric symptoms severe enough to be classified as a clinical mental disorder. However, if you are experiencing changes in your mood, personality, or sleep behavior, for example, then it is important to have access to a specialist who knows how to evaluate and treat these symptoms.

Unfortunately for some people, there is a stigma associated with mental-health problems, and for this reason you may or may not feel apprehensive about being referred to a psychiatrist. Don't let this hold you back, the specialized training of psychiatrists makes them excellent resources for you and your family doctor. The practice of psychiatry draws on many disciplines including medicine, psychology, neuroscience, biology, and pharmacology. As a result, the psychiatrist utilizes a variety of tools in evaluating the mental health of their patients. You can expect to be interviewed extensively with respect to your medical, social, and developmental history. Cognitive screening (described earlier in this chapter) will be conducted. Screening for psychiatric symptoms (such as hallucinations, sleep problems, eating problems, paranoia, and depression for example), often using questionnaires, will also be conducted. Individual psychiatric symptoms could be associated with a variety of different mental-health disorders, but when present in certain combinations, they can be diagnostically meaningful. A physical exam may be performed. The psychiatrist may also want to order lab tests such as those previously described.

A number of people with MCI do experience a decline in their mental health, such as an increase in anxiety for example, and this can also impact cognition (you will read more about these mental-health changes in chapter 8). The psychiatrist will be able to determine the degree of severity of such symptoms. The most common psychiatric treatment approaches would be medication, or some form of talk therapy, or possibly a combinatin of both. If any noted mental-health changes cannot fully account for your experience of cognitive decline, then the psychiatrist will likely advise that your cognition continue to be monitored over time. He or she may also pursue consultation with another specialist. The neurologist might be consulted if it is suspected that the changes you are experiencing are the early manifestations of a neurodegenerative disease. The neuropsychologist might be consulted if the psychiatrist wants an in-depth cognitive evaluation to help differentiate whether your cognitive changes are due to a psychiatric disturbance, a neurodegenerative disease, or some complex combination of both.

The Neurologist

A neurologist is a medical doctor who specializes in identifying and treating diseases or conditions that affect the nervous system. The nervous system is comprised of a *central* part, which involves the brain and spinal cord, and a *peripheral* part, which involves all the nerves outside of the brain and spinal cord, such as those involved with the workings of your muscles and organs. There are many different types of neurological disorders related to central or peripheral nervous system damage or dysfunction, and the neurologist is an expert at identifying the pattern of symptoms characteristic of a particular disorder. The first thing the neurologist will want to do is talk with you about your symptoms and gain a thorough understanding of how and what symptoms started first and whether and how they have changed over time. You may recall from chapter 4 that the different MCI subtypes are associated with different disease processes, and the neurologist will be looking for early signs that might be consistent with one of these. The neurologist will also question you about your medical history, the medical history of your blood relatives, and previous or current drug or alcohol use. He or she will be interested in knowing if you are right or left handed because, for most right-handers, language abilities are localized more on the left side of the brain and visual spatial abilities (such as being able find your way around places) are localized more on the right side of the brain. Another interesting thing about how our brains are organized is that the left side of the brain controls movement of the right side of our body and vice versa. So if word-finding difficulty was apparent during general conversation while taking the history, and reduced sensitivity to touch on the right-side was discovered as the neurological examination proceeded, then the neurologist might suspect the person being assessed could have had an undetected mild stroke event in the left side of the brain.

As shown in Box 6.7 there are several steps to the neurological examination, which involves the following: taking a history and assessing your current mental status, the nerves in your head and neck, your muscle strength and movement, reflexes, sensory abilities (ability to smell, see, hear, and feel), as well as your balance and walking. The neurologist will want to assess whether there is a problem in any of the components of the neurological exam and if these problems appear to affect only one or both sides of the body.

The neurologist may order some more lab tests, including some of the previously described neuroimaging tests (see Box 6.4), to rule in or out certain neurological diseases. He or she will put information from the neurological examination together with any lab test results to come to a diagnosis. When changes are very mild, the neurologist may not be certain whether you are experiencing the earliest stages of a neurodegenerative disease, such as Alzheimer's disease, or a cerebrovascular disease that could lead to a vascular dementia, or some combination of both.

The neurologist may suspect MCI, but not be certain about the subtype of MCI. If this is the case the neurologist may refer you on to a neuropsychologist who will do more in-depth testing of your cognitive abilities. This can be extremely helpful because there are patterns of strengths and weaknesses in cognitive functioning that are characteristic

Box 6.7 Components of a Neurological Examination

Area Evaluated	Behaviours Examined
Neurological history	Report of onset and course of symptoms, personal and family medical history, and hand preference.
Current mental state	Level of alertness; knowing where you are, who you are, and the date; screening of cognitive abilities, such as attention, memory, language, and visual spatial skills; screening for the presence of any psychiatric symptoms such as hallucinations or delusions (false beliefs).
Cranial nerves (nerves in the head and neck)	Eye, face, tongue, neck, and shoulder movements, sensory abilities (vision, hearing, taste, smell, touch), and pupil function. For example, you might be asked to move your eyes up and down and side to side or to shrug your shoulders.
Muscle and reflex functions	Strength and tone of muscles, posture, presence of tremor or other abnormal movements. Reflexes in response to touch or tap to your knees, arms, feet, and face.
Sensory abilities	Sensitivity to sensation in the arms, legs, hands, and feet to fine touch, temperature, vibration, and position.
Cerebellar function (brain region involved in movement coordination among other things)	Finger-to-nose test (moving your finger back and forth between touching your nose and the examiner's outstretched finger), heel-to-toe walking, walking normally, moving from standing-to-sitting and back again, eye movements (following the movement of the examiner's finger with your eyes), coordination of speech, and making sure there is no tremor when intentionally moving part of your body.

of different neurological diseases, and investigating these patterns can greatly assist in *differential diagnosis* (distinguishing between different possible diseases as the cause of the cognitive decline).

The Neuropsychologist

A neuropsychologist has a PhD[1] (doctor of philosophy degree) in Psychology (the scientific study of behavior and mental processes) and has further specialized in the field of neuropsychology. Neuropsychology is the study of the relationship between brain functioning and behavior. Different kinds of cognitive abilities are governed by different parts of our brain working together (brain systems). The neuropsychologist can examine for patterns of cognitive strengths and weaknesses that can inform about the functioning of brain regions known to be involved in different cognitive processes, which, in turn, helps identify neurological disorders and assists in diagnosis. The measures used by the neuropsychologist are typically pencil and paper tests (some may be computerized) that are similar to the cognitive screening exam described earlier in this chapter and also in chapter 1, but they are much more in-depth. Instead of an overall score, each cognitive domain or area, such as attention, thinking speed, memory, and language, to name a few, is individually evaluated. How well you do (your performance level) within each cognitive domain is compared with the other domains examined and with what is expected based on your age and education. Assessment of each cognitive domain should involve the use of more than one test of the ability being examined. This is because research shows there is a possibility any one of us could perform below expectations on a neuropsychological test just due to chance factors. Therefore, finding poor performance on two or more tests of a particular type of thinking skill gives the neuropsychologist more assurance that he or she has detected a true impairment.

A comprehensive neuropsychological evaluation (described subsequently) when MCI is suspected is important because, as discussed earlier in this chapter, there are currently no medical tests that are

---

1 In some provinces the neuropsychologist may hold a MA (Master's of Arts Degree) and not the higher degree of PhD.

conclusive of MCI. Mild cognitive impairment is a cognitive disorder and, as such, can only be fully appreciated using a comprehensive assessment of cognition. This is what the neuropsychologist will do and we explain the neuropsychological evaluation in detail next.

NEUROPSYCHOLOGICAL EVALUATION

The neuropsychologist will begin your visit by first ensuring that you understand the nature and purpose of the assessment and agree to participate. Following that, there will be an interview to obtain information about your age, education, and hand preference (reviewed in the section about the neurologist), as well as your health, developmental, and social history, and history of your memory problem. This information is necessary to accurately evaluate your performance against peers of similar age and education and to determine if there are other factors that could affect the results of the tests, such as mood or sleep problems. A series of thinking tasks will be administered, either by the neuropsychologist or someone trained to administer the tests working under the supervision of the neuropsychologist. These tests will examine a broad range of cognitive abilities that are described in detail later in this section. The tests are scored and the neuropsychologist evaluates the results and writes a report interpreting the results to the referring doctor. The neuropsychologist will want to determine if the kinds of difficulties you are reporting in memory or other thinking skills are consistent in any way with the objective test findings. You will be informed of the results either through a follow-up visit with the doctor who referred you or through a return visit to the neuropsychologist.

Preparing for your Neuropsychological Evaluation

Prior to seeing the neuropsychologist, review the survey you took in preparation for your initial visit with your doctor (refer back to Box 6.3). In particular, spend some time thinking about your developmental history and whether you had any medical problems as a child, delays in the timing of when you learned to walk or talk, whether you had any difficulties in any particular subjects at school, or had troubles paying attention at school. It is important for the neuropsychologist to know about any developmental difficulties you may have experienced because this could negatively affect how you perform on some of the cognitive measures and should not be mistaken for evidence of cognitive decline due to MCI.

As mentioned previously, your performance on the tests will be compared to people of a similar age and education level. The neuropsychologist is looking to see whether you are performing within, above, or below expectations based on your age and education and in what cognitive areas. Everyone has strengths and weaknesses when it comes to thinking skills. The neuropsychologist is looking beyond the strengths and weaknesses that characterize your set of cognitive abilities for evidence of meaningful patterns within and across the different thinking domains in order to determine if MCI is present and, if so, what subtype. You will be challenged by a lot of complex thinking tasks and finding the tasks challenging is normal. It is important that the tasks be complex enough so that they are sensitive to possible changes in your abilities. If the tests were too easy, then everyone would do well on them and they would be useless in identifying people who are having difficulties. Going into the assessment knowing that no one performs perfectly on all the tests can give you the needed perspective to just try your best and see what happens.

You want to be at your best on the day of the neuropsychological assessment, so try to get a good night's sleep the night before. However, don't worry if you didn't get the best sleep the night before. Often, people do feel a little worried about this sort of thing and, as long as it's not too extreme, then feeling a bit anxious can actually optimize your test performance. The neuropsychologist is going to do his or her best to put you at ease because the goal is to see you at your best. This specialist is experienced at identifying whether someone appears unduly anxious or fatigued during testing and will be able to consider the potential influence of these factors when interpreting the test results.

The Neuropsychological Interview

The entire interview could take anywhere from 30 to 60 minutes, and you can expect the neuropsychologist will want to learn about all the kinds of personal and medical history information reviewed earlier.

He or she will also want to know how you are feeling on the day of testing. Are you depressed? Are you worried? Is there anything in your life currently causing you any stress? Are you feeling tired? You can expect the neuropsychologist to be particularly interested in how you are doing at managing your daily activities. If you have brought along a close family member or friend, this person may also be asked to corroborate your self-report concerning your level of independence in running your daily affairs. It is very helpful to have the observations and opinions of someone who knows you well. However, it is unlikely that this person will be permitted to stay in the room with you during administration of the cognitive tests. There are two main reasons why: First, the specific items comprising the tests are to be made known only to the people who are experiencing the testing in order to prevent these items from becoming public knowledge and thereby reduce the ability of the tests to detect cognitive deficits; and second, your companion may interfere with testing, for example, by making you feel self-conscious if you perceive you are not doing well on some task or by interrupting to ask questions or to provide answers for you during the testing.

Neuropsychological Testing and Interpretation
Administering and scoring the tests.

The types of *cognitive domains* (areas of thinking ability) examined and representative behaviors within each of these domains are listed in Box 6.8. Administration of the tests can take anywhere from two to four hours depending on how extensive the evaluation plan is. The number of tests used may be fewer in a brief neuropsychological evaluation, but there should always be more than one test used in evaluating abilities within a given cognitive domain. Multiple tests are necessary because research shows that assessing a cognitive domain with a single diagnostic test increases the likelihood of falsely diagnosing people with MCI.

Each of the tests used to assess these cognitive domains are standardized. This means that there are specific instructions about how to administer and score the tests. If these instructions are properly followed, then performance scores can be compared against a *normative* (representative) group of individuals who are of the same age

Box 6.8 Types of Behaviors Examined in a Neuropsychological Evaluation

Cognitive Domain	Examples of the Types of Behaviours Tested
Attention	A series of numbers may be read to you that you must repeat back in the same order, reverse order, or in sequence from lowest to highest (referred to as auditory attention span); The examiner may time how fast you can read, copy shapes, or scan patterns to find a target shape or number (referred to as thinking or processing speed).
Memory	You may be read a story or a list of words, or asked to study pictures or line drawings. Then, your memory will be tested for the information you just heard or saw, right away and then again later after 20 or 30 minutes.
Language Skills	You may be asked to describe the meanings of words or the relationships between word concepts, to name pictures of objects, or to generate as many words as you can in one-minute that start with a particular letter or are examples belonging to a particular category (such as tingle, toe, tank, for the letter *t* or seaweed, daffodil, ivy, for the category *plants*).
Visual Perception of Objects and their Spatial Relationships	You might be asked to identify or sort objects by their shape, size, or category (such as tools, vegetables, flowers), to match lines that have the same angle or orientation, to discrimination the positions of lines or circles, and to draw or construct patterns that may be well-known or novel (such as the face of a clock, a simple shape, or an abstract line drawing).

(continued)

Box 6.8 (Continued)

Cognitive Domain	Examples of the Types of Behaviours Tested
Sensory–Motor Skills	Your ability to detect the presence of visual, auditory, or touch types of information equally well on the left and right sides of your body. Manual motor skills related to fine motor control (tapping a key as fast as you can with your index finger), coordination (dexterity at quickly fitting a series of little pegs into their holes) and also strength. The ability to coordinate purposeful movements of the arms and face (showing the examiner how you would use a key, wave goodbye, or smell a flower).
Executive Functioning	You may be asked to engage in complex thinking skills that draw on all of the other cognitive domains. For example: your ability to focus attention under conditions of distraction; flexibly alternate attention back and forth between tasks; re-organize information in your mind, such as when repeating a random series of numbers in reverse sequence or in ascending sequence; make decisions about how to solve novel and practical problems; and keep track of task instructions and past actions during testing may all be assessed.

and education level as you. The normative group is a large sample of medically healthy individuals who have taken the test. For most tests, this large sample has been further subdivided according to age and educational level, which allows the neuropsychologist to determine if your performance is comparable to your peers or if it is lower or higher than expected based on age and education. Further evaluation of your mood, beyond the questions you may have answered in your interview will likely also be undertaken using self-report questionnaires. These questionnaires permit the neuropsychologist to determine if you are currently experiencing any symptoms associated with feeling depressed or anxious and whether these symptoms are within normal limits or if they are mildly, moderately, or severely elevated. Evaluation of mood is important, because as mentioned earlier your mood must also be considered when evaluating the test findings.

Evaluating the pattern of results

The graph in Box 6.9 shows the test results for Evelyn, the lady you met at the start of this chapter in the case vignette described in Box 6.2. The bars in the graph represent her overall performance level within each of the cognitive domains the neuropsychologist examined. In chapter 1 (Box 1.3) the criteria for amnestic MCI were described and what you are seeing in the graph below would be consistent with these criteria, where only the objective memory scores are low. Along the bottom of the graph are numbers representing *scaled scores* (a way of converting scores from the different cognitive tests to a common scale). Using scaled scores allows you to compare performance levels across cognitive domains to see if the levels are similar or if some are considerably better or considerably poorer than others. The range of average for scaled scores spans from 8 to 12. You will notice that Evelyn is not *impaired* (defined as a scaled score less than 5) in any cognitive domain, but her memory scores are below average (scaled score of 7), and differ from her above-average abilities in the other cognitive domains examined.

At the start of the assessment, Evelyn had expressed feeling very worried about her memory and about doing poorly on the memory tasks in particular. So, was Evelyn's poorer performance on the memory testing a self-fulfilling prophesy? Is Evelyn just a highly intelligent woman with a crummy memory? To be fair, being particularly worried about memory could have influenced her performance level to some degree; however, there are some pretty challenging problem-solving tests for which Evelyn managed to rise to the occasion, despite feeling worried about her memory. Further, there is her history to consider, which includes the fact that both she and her

Box 6.9 Graph Depicting Results of a Client Classified with Amnestic-MCI

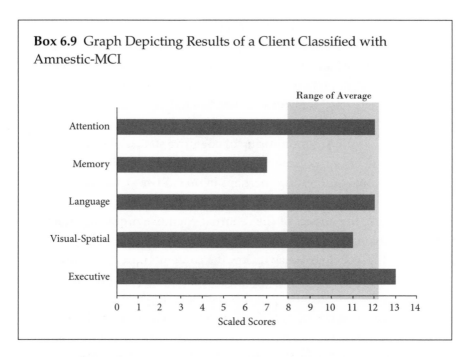

husband feel there has been a memory change, a decline from her previous level of ability.

Evelyn's case is complex because she is not clearly impaired in any one thinking area. Indeed, when she was seen by her family doctor and by a neurologist, she performed normally on cognitive screening and nothing of significance showed up on any of her lab tests. No physical cause could be identified to explain her report of memory decline. In-depth neuropsychological testing has objectively confirmed Evelyn's (and her husband's) report of her memory problems because, as seen in the graph depicted in Box 6.9, her memory is significantly weaker than her demonstrated abilities in other cognitive domains. So what happens next? First, we will tell you about how neuropsychological findings are communicated generally, and then we will return to the specific case of Evelyn.

Communicate findings

The neuropsychologist will write a report that will include information on the reason for the neuropsychological assessment, your relevant social and medical history, the onset and course of your cognitive problems, the results of your performance on the cognitive tests, the interpretation of the results, and classification of the type of MCI (if present) and suspected causes (if MCI or another cognitive disorder is identified), as well as recommendations. Possible recommendations, if MCI is identified, could include: additional lab tests (if not already undertaken); referral to community support services (if available); continued monitoring of cognitive status, given that diagnosis of MCI is a risk factor for further cognitive decline; follow-up neuropsychological testing (perhaps in one to two years); and information on specific cognitive strategies that could be implemented to minimize the impact of the reported cognitive problems on daily life and that could, perhaps, even improve functional thinking skills. The neuropsychologist may review the content of the report directly with you or this information may be communicated to you through the doctor who referred you to this specialist. You may request a copy of the neuropsychology report for your personal records. If you do, keep in mind that it was written for another health-care professional (your family doctor or the specialist doctor) and, therefore, it may contain terminology that is unfamiliar to you. The report contains your personal health information, so it is a good idea that you keep the information private. Returning to the story of Evelyn, continued in Box 6.10, may give you a better feel for how neuropsychological findings are communicated and received by the people involved.

A FINAL WORD

Once MCI has been identified, there are some immediate factors to consider, namely what treatments are available (see chapter 7), how living with MCI might affect you and your loved ones (chapter 8), and what steps you can take to take charge of your MCI and your future (chapters 9 and 10). These are the factors we shall concern ourselves with in the remainder of this second section of the book. Being aware of these factors is where the many benefits of early identification can be realized. You do not necessarily need to have access to a specialist to be able to work collaboratively with your family doctor to proactively manage your health and your future, even in situations in which MCI is suspected but not confirmed.

Box 6.10 Case Vignette of a Couple with Memory Concerns (Part II)

The neuropsychologist tells Evelyn and Gerry the results of the testing. They are not surprised to learn that memory is indeed a weakness for Evelyn. They are gladdened, however, by the fact that her memory is not frankly impaired. Rather, it's reduced relative to her other stronger thinking abilities, which likely accounts for the fact that her memory changes are not really impacting her ability to manage her daily responsibilities. They are told that Evelyn's history and cognitive test results are consistent with MCI and the subtype is single-domain amnestic-MCI. This is sobering news for the couple because, as you learned in the first part of this book, a possible etiology for this subtype of MCI is Alzheimer's disease. They wish there was a medication Evelyn could take, but the neurologist already told them there is currently no evidence of benefit to prescribing medications for cognitive decline to people with MCI. The best course of action at present is to monitor cognition to see if the decline progresses over time (perhaps by repeating the neuropsychological testing after a year-and-a-half or so); to engage in lifestyle choices that promote brain health (regular physical activity, healthy diet, and doing activities that are mentally challenging); and to develop good memory habits to minimize the occurrence of everyday memory slips. The neuropsychologist provides some practical how-to information, but, at first, the couple feel deflated by the news. It would be a lot easier to just take a medication. Upon further discussion, however, they learn about evidence (reviewed in the third section of this book) showing that the lifestyle choices Evelyn makes could significantly impact her health by delaying or even preventing the onset of symptoms of dementia. At the moment, amnestic-MCI represents a risk factor for Evelyn, one that she and Gerry feel empowered to take action on, now that they understand what they are up against.

For all of us, the best reduction of risk of dementia as we age is through good management (either through treatment or prevention) of medical conditions that we know confer risk, and through adopting healthy lifestyle choices. This is because the best prevention of dementia is early intervention. In the final section of the book, we detail what actions you can take to optimize your cognitive health.

These actions are good for all of us if we want to age well, but they may be particularly critical for someone with MCI. This is because research shows our lifestyle choices can have a real impact on our physical and cognitive health that could prevent or delay the onset of dementia for those at risk.

Box 6.11 Questions to Ask Your Doctors if MCI Is Suspected or Confirmed in Yourself or in Your Family Member

---

Questions to ask your medical doctor

1. How do you manage MCI? For example, how often will I see you for follow-up? Will I be referred to a specialist? Will I have brain imaging?
2. Can you conduct a cognitive screen in your office to determine whether my thinking abilities appear to be normal for my age?
3. Would you recommend that I be referred to a neuropsychologist for further cognitive testing? What is the process for this?

Questions to ask your neuropsychologist

1. How are you going to evaluate my thinking skills relative to what would be considered normal for someone with a background similar to mine?
2. When and how will you tell me about the results of the neuropsychological testing?
3. Will you be sending my own doctor a copy of your report, and if so, when?
4. What specific cognitive strategies should I be using, given the thinking areas that were my strengths and those that were my weaknesses according to your test results?
5. If I have MCI, what subtype do you think it is?
6. What do you think could be causing my cognitive problems?
7. What might my prognosis be over time? Do you think my MCI will develop into dementia and, if so, what type?

RECOMMENDED READING

See the Mayo Clinic website www.MayoClinic.com and the Alzheimer's Association www.alz.org for reader-friendly descriptions of MCI diagnosis and treatment approaches.

7

Treatment of Mild Cognitive Impairment

Now that you know quite a lot about what mild cognitive impairment (MCI) is, we are sure you are wondering what can be done about it. In this chapter, we cover the pros and cons of formal drug- and psycho-educational treatment approaches for MCI. The third section of this book (chapters 11–15) describes many lifestyle changes and strategies that can also help minimize the effects of MCI and improve functioning. We encourage you to consider both approaches— formal ones organized by your doctor or other health-care professionals, and informal ones that you can do on your own—to maximize the benefits for you.

First we will discuss drug-treatment approaches to MCI and Alzheimer's disease, including both drugs targeted at these conditions, as well as drugs and supplements that were developed for other purposes but that have been tried in patients with Alzheimer's disease. We include a description of the long process by which drugs get approved for clinical use, describe some of the drugs that have failed in clinical trials, and some of the drugs that are now in their final stages of clinical testing and that hopefully will be available in the next few years. These drug trials are focused almost exclusively on people with Alzheimer's disease, but we describe them here because, no doubt, as soon as successful treatments are found for Alzheimer's disease, future trials will test the efficacy of those treatments in MCI.

The second section of this chapter describes nondrug interventions, in particular psycho-educational groups that have been shown to help people with MCI. Finally, a third section of this chapter describes how to find research studies that you can participate in to help scientists in their pursuit of ways to prevent, treat, and cure MCI and dementia.

DRUG TREATMENT APPROACHES TO MCI AND ALZHEIMER'S DISEASE

The first thing you need to know is that, currently, there are no approved drug treatments for MCI. In chapter 3, we discussed medical treatment of various types of dementia. One topic we discussed was the handful of drugs that have been approved to treat the symptoms of Alzheimer's disease (see Box 3.7). These include donepezil (brand name Aricept), galantamine (brand names Razadyne or Reminyl), rivistigmine (brand name Exelon), and memantine (brand names Namenda or Ebixa). The first three of these are cholinesterase inhibitors. That is, they help prevent the breakdown of *acetylcholine*, a brain chemical that is involved in attention and memory. The fourth drug, memantine, is a glutamate receptor antagonist, that is, it prevents uptake of glutamate by one neuron from another. Glutamate is released when cells die, and in concentration that are too high, it can be toxic; thus, memantine helps protect cells by preventing the uptake of extra glutamate.

These "memory drugs," as the general population refers to them, are not approved by drug regulatory bodies as treatments for MCI. The fourth drug, memantine, is approved for use with people with moderate to severe Alzheimer's disease, that is, at the other end of the spectrum from MCI, and so this drug is unlikely to be prescribed in people with MCI. The decision not to approve the use of the three cholinesterase inhibitors for people with MCI is based primarily on clinical trials that have shown no effect of these medications on preventing progression from MCI to dementia. Another issue preventing widespread recommendation of these drugs for MCI relates to two ethical issues. First, as we described in chapter 4, people can have MCI for many years, and the effects of taking these drugs over many, many years is unknown. Second, as we also mentioned in chapter 4, a good proportion of people who initially meet criteria for MCI later test normal on cognitive tests, and the possible ill effects of prescribing these drugs to people who may not have a reduction in acetylcholine due to a preclinical dementia are also unknown. Thus, many doctors choose not to prescribe these drugs to people with MCI.

Nevertheless, physicians have some discretion in which medications they prescribe to patients, and some choose to prescribe these medications for people with MCI. One reason for this is that the line between MCI and dementia is not crystal clear. If a physician finds that someone previously diagnosed with MCI is performing worse on cognitive tests than at a previous visit, he or she may chose to prescribe a cholinesterase inhibitor. Two common reasons not to take cholinesterase inhibitors are gastrointestinal conditions and certain heart rhythm abnormalities, so if your physician knows that you have one of these conditions that could be made worse by cholinesterase inhibitors, she or he would likely not recommend that you take them.

We asked an internationally recognized geriatrician and ethicist, Dr. Michael Gordon of Baycrest in Toronto, for his perspectives on the factors that influence him to either prescribe or not prescribe "memory drugs" to the people he cares for with MCI. In addition to his prolific career taking care of aging patients, Dr. Gordon has written his own books on aging and on ethical issues of caring for older adults.

In Box 7.1, Dr. Gordon describes a scenario that is likely very familiar to many doctors, in which someone has been diagnosed with MCI and his or her condition has remained stable for some time, but the person, or the person and his or her loved ones, wants to try anything they can to help the situation. In cases like this, your doctor may (or may not) try a cholinesterase inhibitor.

So what might be some of the drugs prescribed for people with MCI? Box 7.2 should look familiar to you. It shows the classification of the four subtypes of MCI you might have, and then it lists some of the possible outcomes of each MCI subtype. We remind you that two other possible outcomes for each subtype

Box 7.1 Interview with a Geriatrician, Dr. Michael Gordon

Question: What factors affect your decision to either prescribe or not prescribe a cholinesterase inhibitor to someone who has MCI?

Answer: Prescribing cholinesterase inhibitors for patients apparently suffering from MCI can be a challenging decision. The person being assessed may be more or less "anxious" about their condition. The person may have a stronger or weaker family history or knowledge of people close to them who have suffered from dementia. And the person may be more or less intent on seeking a drug intervention after having read or perhaps a family member having read articles on the subject, of which there are many readily accessible through the Internet.

My approach is first of all to do a full and careful assessment with the patient to get a sense of where they are on the spectrum of formal cognitive testing, in addition to supplementary cognitive testing using their ability to manipulate, absorb, and recall information from current events if they claim to be interested in such sources. Of course, an assessment of how they are functioning in general is key to and one of the standard criteria for the diagnosis to be made.

If they seem to fulfill the criteria for MCI rather than "early dementia," which is usually the key to the decision-tree in terms of considering cholinesterase inhibitors, I explain that situation to the patient. If they understand the process, I usually do a follow-up in a period of 3–4 months to see if there is any objective or subjective changes in their clinical and cognitive picture. Depending on that second assessment, and that usually is coupled with some investigations to assess possible metabolic influences as well as any changes in medications that they might be exposed to that could potentially affect their cognition, I may recommend further periodic assessment to determine the trajectory of change if there is one.

After I get to know the patient in a more in-depth manner and I feel, along with them and/or their family member, that, although they are stable and have not deteriorated, that they are feeling that they want "everything done that can be done," I may consider the use of medications. I explain that, although cholinesterase inhibitors have not been shown to be effective in people with the condition that their loved one is experiencing (MCI), I might consider using

(continued)

Box 7.1 (Continued)

the medications if there is a strong desire to do so on the part of the patient who usually can participate in such a decision. If I do so, I use the same protocol that I use with patients that I feel have mild to moderate dementia. I start with a very low dose (usually half of the lowest dose recommended) and try that for two weeks, and, if tolerated, I then raise the dose and arrange to see the patient in 3 months' time for a reassessment. Depending on the result of that assessment, I usually recommend continuing the medication and undertake 3–4 months follow-up on an ongoing basis. In some situations, even though the initial assessment was one of MCI, the person or family feels that there is some beneficial effect of the medication on subtle components of their clinical picture, especially those of "sharpness" and engagement rather than pure cognitive features.

that are not shown in this chart are remaining stable at your current level of cognitive problems (stable MCI), or reverting back to normal aging. We described all these possibilities in great detail in chapter 4. Here, we have added one final layer to the chart, which lists the types of medications your doctor might prescribe. We already mentioned that if your doctor suspects that you might be heading toward Alzheimer's disease, based on worsening of memory over time and escalating difficulties doing complex activities of daily living, he or she might prescribe a cholinesterase inhibitor. If you have symptoms of depression, you very likely will be offered an antidepressant or referred for counseling or for *cognitive behavioral therapy* (a problem-solving form of therapy in which a therapist helps you to identify and deal with your problems). If you have *hypertension* (high blood pressure), *hyperlipidemia* (high cholesterol), or diabetes, you will very likely be prescribed an *antihypertensive* (a blood-pressure-lowering drug), a *statin* (a cholesterol-lowering drug), or a *hypoglycaemic agent* (a drug that helps lower your blood sugar), respectively, and your doctor may also recommend changes to your diet and exercise habits. Note that these treatments would also be recommended if you had single-domain amnestic MCI or single-domain nonamnestic MCI *and*

Box 7.2 Possible Drug Treatments of Different Subtypes of MCI

| | | Type of impairment: | |
		Memory impairment	Nonmemory impairment
Number of impair-ments:	1 impairment	**Amnestic MCI single domain** Alzheimer's disease (cholinesterase inhibitor) Depression (antidepressant)	**Nonamnestic MCI single domain** Frontotemporal dementia (antidepressant)
	2 or more impairments	**Amnestic MCI multiple domains** Alzheimer's disease (cholinesterase inhibitor) Vascular dementia (antihypertensives; statins, hypoglycemic agents) Depression (antidepressant)	**Nonamnestic MCI multiple domains** Lewy body disease (cholinesterase inhibitor; antidepressant) Vascular dementia (antihypertensives; statins, hypoglycemic agents)

hypertension, hyperlipidemia, or high blood sugars. That is, if you have one of these conditions, they will be treated even if your doctor does not think vascular dementia is the underlying cause of your cognitive problems. No specific drugs have been identified to treat frontotemporal dementia or Lewy body disease, although antidepressants seem to help many people with these forms of dementia, and so if your doctor suspects that either of these conditions are the source of your cognitive impairments, he or she may decide to see if an antidepressant helps you.

We want to remind you that, with the exception of antidepressants for the treatment of identifiable depression, none of these drugs directly targets the underlying brain pathology of their respective disorders. The effect of the cholinesterase inhibitors on the underlying brain pathology of Alzheimer's disease—that is, on the plaques and tangles—is still unclear. Some studies find that they decrease production of the plaque pathology, the build-up of the beta-amy-loid protein, or reduce its toxic effects on the brain, but other studies fail to confirm these effects. Antihypertensives, statins, and hypogly-caemic agents definitely attack the underlying high blood pressure, high cholesterol, and diabetes, respectively, but they likely have lit-tle effect on any damage these disorders already caused to the brain. Furthermore, the effect of antidepressants in frontotemporal demen-tia and Lewy body disease is certainly indirect.

In contrast to these indirect approaches to treating MCI and demen-tia, researchers are in hot pursuit of safe and effective drug treatments to fight the underlying brain pathology of these disorders more directly. Unfortunately, no attempt has yet succeeded, but to give you a sense of how hard scientists are trying, take a look at Box 7.3. This figure is from a review paper published in 2010 that described the vast array of drugs that were then currently in development to fight Alzheimer's disease. Don't worry about the names of the drugs in this figure, they really don't matter for what we are trying to portray here. What we want to impress on you is that a very large number and wide variety of drugs are being evaluated, and the hope is that this large-scale effort will one day result in the development of safe, effective drugs for treat-ing Alzheimer's disease. Before we describe some of these, we thought it would be useful to first discuss how drugs get developed in the first place, because this should give you some appreciation of the long road scientists take when trying to develop new drugs.

How Drugs Get Developed

The development of any new drug follows a rigorous sequence of studies or *trials*, most of which is overseen by government regulatory bodies such as the U.S. Food and Drug Administration and Health Canada. As shown in Box 7.4, this sequence starts with scientists pur-suing a hunch; based on what is known about the pathology of a particular disease, scientists try different ways to affect that pathol-ogy. These sorts of studies are called *preclinical studies*, and they are conducted on cells in test tubes or in Petri dishes, or in nonhuman animals such as mice. For example, a scientist who has a drug that she thinks should prevent the aggregation, or clumping, of beta-amyloid in the brain into plaques might add the drug to a Petri dish containing

Box 7.3 The Vast Array of Drugs in Development to Fight Alzheimer's Disease as of 2010

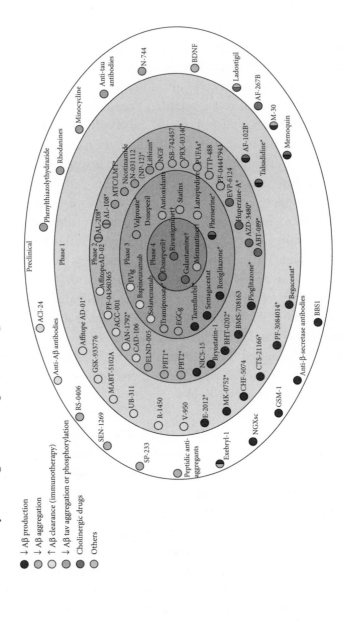

Note that they target a variety of pathological mechanisms (identified by shade of the circle). Drugs closer to the center of the circle are closer to being approved for use. Reproduced from Mangialasche, F., Solomon, A., Winblad, B., Mecocci, P., & Kevipelto, M. (2010). Alzheimer's disease: Clinical trials and drug development. *Lancet Neurology, 9,* 702–716 with permission from Elsevier.

Box 7.4 Phases of Clinical Trials

- *Preclinical:* conducted in test tubes or Petri dishes or nonhuman animals.
- *Phase I:* conducted in a small group of healthy individuals.
- *Phase II:* conducted in larger groups of healthy individuals and patients.
- *Phase III:* conducted in large groups of patients across many geographically distinct sites.
- *Phase IV:* conducted after drugs go to market to track rare or long-term side effects.

---

beta-amyloid protein to determine if it prevents aggregation. For the vast majority of these attempts, the drug development sequence stops at this preclinical phase, either because the drug doesn't work (it doesn't affect the pathology), or because it has unintended effects (for example, healthy cells are also affected).

The very few attempts that make it past this preclinical stage enter into the regulated investigational drug stages. *Phase I* trials involve trying out the new drug on a small group of healthy human volunteers. Scientists look at the safety; *tolerability* (how well patients can tolerate the drug and its side effects); *pharmacokinetics* (examining what the body does with the drug, for example how it is metabolized); and *pharmacodynamics* (examining what the drug does to the body, and what the relationship is between the drug dose and its effects). *Phase II* trials involve trying the drug out on a larger group of healthy individuals as well as on patients with the targeted disease to further test the safety and effectiveness of the drug. Of drugs that fail the regulated investigational stages, they most often fail at this stage, for the same reasons that they fail in preclinical stages. *Phase III* trials are conducted in large groups of patients across many geographically distinct sites, to determine how effective the drug is, often relative to the current "gold standard" treatment, if there is one. Because of their size, Phase III trials take the longest to conduct—sometimes years if the condition is rare! Drugs that pass Phase III trials and a thorough review of the trial data by the regulatory agencies are finally permitted to be sold. Finally, *Phase IV* trials are for postmarket surveillance, to detect any rare or long-term effects or to determine safety and effectiveness in populations that do not participate in early study phases (for example, pregnant women). All told, it can take up to 12 years and millions of dollars to get a new drug to market! Although this delay is frustrating to a lot of people, it is important to realize that it takes this long because safety and effectiveness have to be proven over and over again before drugs are made available to you. The long wait reassures all of us that the drugs our doctors prescribe and that we agree to take are likely to help us and not cause serious harm.

Anti-Alzheimer's Drugs That Have Failed

It is worth considering anti-Alzheimer drugs that have failed, because, although they were unsuccessful in treating Alzheimer's disease, it is possible that the application of these drugs in patients that already had Alzheimer's disease was simply too late. The drugs that failed in Alzheimer disease trials might be effective in treating MCI, in which the brain pathology and clinical symptoms are less severe. So what sorts of drugs have started down the clinical trials road but failed?

Most attempts at developing drugs to treat Alzheimer's disease have focused on blocking development of beta amyloid, the protein that builds up in patients with Alzheimer's disease (see chapter 3). A number of drugs developed to block beta-amyloid development have failed. Most recently, the pharmaceutical company Eli Lilly & Co. stopped clinical trials of a drug called semagacestat. Unfortunately, cognitive symptoms worsened, and there was an increased risk of skin cancer in patients who were randomly assigned semagacestat compared to patients who were assigned to *placebo* (an inactive intervention, such as a sugar pill). This example also makes it clear that unexpected events can happen in drug trials, because this drug was considered very promising in the 2010 review article from which the figure in Box 7.2 was reproduced.

Cholesterol lowering drugs, or *statins*, have also been investigated as potential anti-Alzheimer's drugs. This is based in part on the fact that the primary gene linked to a higher susceptibility to late-onset Alzheimer's disease risk, apolipoprotein E, helps our bodies to process cholesterol (see chapter 5). Early studies raised hopes when they found that groups of people who took statins to lower their cholesterol had lower rates of dementia compared to people who did not take statins. However, a recent *meta-analysis,* or an analysis of the results combined across other published studies, failed to find sufficient evidence to recommend statins for the treatment of dementia. This doesn't mean that you shouldn't aim to keep your cholesterol levels in the healthy range; you most certainly should, because we know that brain health is intimately linked to heart health. However, the verdict is still out about whether statins are beneficial in preventing MCI from progressing to dementia.

Ginko biloba, an herb derived from the ginko tree, has been found not to cure Alzheimer's disease or even have a significant benefit for cognitive functioning in healthy individuals. This was disappointing for many people, because preclinical studies showed effects of ginko biloba on blood flow in the brain, in reducing beta amyloid, and in acting as an anti-oxidant, not to mention the advantage that ginko biloba is available over the counter and considered "natural" and "safe." Ginko biloba has blood-thinning effects, however, so even though it is easy to obtain, it should be used with caution among people at risk of bleeding or with reduced clotting ability.

Medications, Nutrients, and Supplements in Late-Phase Clinical Trials

Two amyloid busting drugs are currently in Phase III trials: solanezumab and bapineuzumab. These drugs have so far avoided the pitfalls of their predecessors such as semagacestat and hopefully will make it to the market in the years to come.

Immunoglobulins are antibodies found in our bodily fluids that are made in response to bacteria, viruses, fungi, and even cancer cells to help keep us healthy. Researchers are pursuing the idea that immunoglobulins may also help fight the brain pathology (plaques and tangles) of Alzheimer's disease. A current Phase III clinical trail in the United States is following up prior positive findings that intravenous injection of immunoglobulin-g obtained from blood plasma of healthy people halted cognitive decline and brain atrophy in groups of individuals with Alzheimer's disease.

Three supplements are current hot targets for fighting MCI and Alzheimer's disease. First of all, it has been shown that patients with Alzheimer's disease have depressed levels of docosahexonoic acid (DHA), an omega 3 fatty acid. Phase III clinical trials of DHA supplementation in patients with Alzheimer's disease have been mixed, with two showing improvements in cognitive functioning but a third showing no change. The second supplement being tested in Phase III clinical trials is resveratrol. Resveratrol is a compound in grapes and wine, especially of the red variety. It has been suggested that this compound protects the brain against a range of diseases such as cardiovascular disease, cancer, and Alzheimer's disease. The specific way in which resveratrol might help fight Alzheimer's disease is unclear, but it has been shown to lower levels of beta amyloid and to promote antioxidation and DNA repair.

Finally, Vitamin E is showing some qualified hope in fighting Alzheimer's. Vitamins E and C are antioxidants that fight the neuron damaging effects of free radicals. Earlier clinical trials with Vitamin E supplements have been mixed, with some showing positive benefits on cognitive performance among patients with Alzheimer's disease but others failing to find any effect, and even worse, finding an increased risk of death! By contrast, recent studies examining the diets of older adults have shown a more promising link between amount of Vitamin E consumed through the food people eat and the risk of Alzheimer's disease. Why the conflict? It turns out that what we call Vitamin E is actually a family of eight different natural compounds, and we consume all or most of these when we eat foods such as leafy greens, nuts, and certain oils. By contrast, the clinical trials with supplements have been restricted to the one Vitamin E compound contained in supplements. In chapter 11, we provide much more information about how a healthy diet can help protect your brain health and reduce your risk of developing MCI and dementia.

It is also worth remarking that some common supplements, vitamins, and minerals can have potentially dangerous interactions with certain medications. Vitamin D and various heart medicines, magnesium or calcium and certain antibiotics, flaxseed and some diabetes medicines are just three examples of things that do not go well together. We strongly encourage you to discuss your medications with your doctor or pharmacist before adding supplements, vitamins, or minerals to your daily routine.

MEMORY INTERVENTION PROGRAMS

Another way to fight MCI is through *psycho-educational* programs, or programs that combine education, counseling, as well as practice of the strategies that are taught in the program. In this section, we highlight the MCI program that we developed at Baycrest, but we also include a table of other programs we are aware of in Box 7.5. The information in this box was acquired by contacting every author who had published a study examining the effects of a group intervention for people with MCI, and every federal and many local chapters of Alzheimer associations, and it reflects every response received at the time of publication. Any updates will be posted on the Web site for this book: www.baycrest.org/livingwithMCI.

The Baycrest MCI Program is a free program for people with MCI and their loved ones. It includes six weekly and two long-term follow-up group sessions (one and three months after the end of the initial six weeks), each lasting two hours. The first hour of each session is facilitated by a multidisciplinary team of professionals, including psychologists, nutritionists, and social workers, who provide education about what MCI is and a host of lifestyle factors affecting memory, including diet, anxiety and depression, physical exercise, and activity in the community. We discuss these in greater detail in chapters 11–14 of this book. In the second hour of each session, people with MCI are taught and practice practical, everyday memory strategies, while their family members meet in a separate group for education, support, and strategies to facilitate living effectively with a relative who has MCI. Each week, all participants are given take-home memory exercises that provide the opportunity to engage in daily practice of the memory strategy reviewed in the session. An alumni program provides graduates an opportunity to stay connected to the program and brush up on their skills.

Are such psycho-educational programs effective? In 2008, we published initial results of the MCI Program. We found that the program was successful in changing the everyday memory behavior of people

Box 7.5 A List of Memory Programs for People with MCI

#	Location	Description	Contact
1	Toronto, Ontario, Canada	**8-session group format** **Topics:** cognition, factors affecting memory **Practice:** memory strategies **For:** people with MCI+partner	Dr. Kelly Murphy kmurphy@baycrest.org 1-416-785-2500 ext. 2445

Health-care professionals can learn how to administer this program by contacting Dr. Kelly Murphy, kmurphy@baycrest.org, 1-416-785-2500 ext. 2445 This same program is also offered in

	London, Ontario, Canada and in		Dr. Jennifer Fogarty Jennifer.Fogarty@sjhc. london.on.ca 1-519-685-4000, ext. 42557
	Hong Kong		Ms. Flora Leung leunglt@ha.org.hk
2	Munich, Germany	**20-week group format** **Topics:** cognition, topics of interest (for example, music, food) **Practice:** memory strategies **For:** people with MCI	Dr. Katherina Buerger katharina.buerger@ med.uni-muenchen.de
3	Rochester, Minnesota, USA	**10-day group format** **Topics:** memory supports, emotion, wellness, exercise **Consultations:** physicians **For:** people with MCI+partner	Dr. Glenn Smith 1-507-266-5100

(continued)

Box 7.5 (Continued)

#	Location	Description	Contact
4	Montreal, Quebec, Canada	**8-week group format** **Topics:** cognition **Practice:** memory strategies **Training:** speed, visual imagery, executive control **For:** people with MCI	Dr. Bridget Gilbert brigitte.gilbert.iugm@ ssss.gouv.qc.ca 1-514-340-2800 ext. 4108

Health-care professionals can learn how to administer this program by contacting Dr. Sylvie Belleville, sylvie.belleville@umontreal.ca, 1-514-340-3540 ext. 4767 or This same program is also offered in

	Quebec City, Quebec Canada		Dr. Marie-Claude Bédard or Dr. Carol Hudon mclaudebedard@ hotmail.com Carol.Hudon@psy. ulaval.ca
5	Montreal, Quebec, Canada	**4-week group format followed by individual sessions as needed** **Topics:** Cognition, factors affecting memory **Practice:** Memory strategies, relaxation **For:** People with MCI	Dr. Nora Kelner or Dr. Lennie Babins nora.kelner@gmail.com psych104@hotmail.com

with MCI, with evidence of increased knowledge about memory strategies and how to apply them in everyday life. For example, people were given a list of scenarios, such as learning the name of a new acquaintance, and they wrote down what kind of memory strategies they would use to help them in this situation. Before the program, participants were more likely to list ineffective, or nonspecific strategies, such as "I would pay attention," without specifying exactly what was being attended to and how they would pay attention, whereas, after the program, participants listed effective, specific strategies, such as "I would think about what the name means, and try to link that meaning to a specific feature of her face." Participants also used better strategies on actual tests of their memory after the program than before. Indeed, there are now a handful of published studies that show that, at least compared to a wait-list control group (that is, a group of people with MCI who received no special intervention), these types of programs lead to significant improvements in immediate and delayed recall of information. Note that the goal of these types of programs is not to "cure" MCI, but rather to raise your level of functioning and arm you with effective strategies to promote more effective, productive, and fulfilling living. Box 7.6 is an amalgamated portrayal of the experience of people who participated in our studies and who helped to develop the Baycrest MCI program.

The number of psycho-educational programs for people with MCI worldwide is still few; this is, in part, because even health-care providers and advocacy groups are just starting to learn about MCI, and not all yet fully appreciate the need to help people with MCI. Fortunately, not everyone holds the views of one associate director of an Alzheimer's Association chapter in one large U.S. city, who replied to our e-mail request for information about ongoing programs: "At the MCI stage, people don't have a diagnosis and probably would not join a support group." The ever-present wait list for the Baycrest MCI program, along with the published results showing the positive effects of such programs, dispel that view and encourage us to keep advocating for additional programs in cities around the world. Indeed, the 2010 Rising Tide report published by the Alzheimer's Society of Canada, which you can download from http://www.alzheimer.ca/en/ Get-involved/Raise-your-voice/Rising-Tide, strongly advocates for psycho-educational programs such as this as one important way to help delay the onset of dementia, and thereby reduce dementia rates and their economic and psychological burden.

RESEARCH STUDIES

Another great way to keep mentally active and to potentially be on the receiving end of the next great treatment is to participate in research

---

Box 7.6 Case Vignette of Someone Attending an MCI Program

Charlene wasn't so sure about attending this program at Baycrest. It had only been a few weeks since she received the official diagnosis of MCI, and she and her husband Peter were still adjusting to this news. Both she and Peter had noticed a gradual decline in her ability to remember details of things he had told her, and she found herself being less organized than she had been all of her adult life. Charlene was not so comfortable about the idea of opening up about these types of problems with strangers. In any event, Charlene and Peter decided that the program was worth a shot, and they agreed that, if the first two sessions didn't go well, they would discontinue.

Charlene and Peter were both surprised at the sense of relief they felt when they realized they were in a room of people who were experiencing similar things. Sure, the particulars of the types of memory slips varied from person to person, but it was a surprising relief for them to know they were not alone. They both felt that they learned a lot of useful information about how memory works and ways they could boost and support Charlene's memory in their everyday life. Peter especially appreciated the honest and detailed session with the social workers about planning for the future. In the end, Charlene and Peter had made a number of adjustments in their everyday life. They now make sure to get out for a walk together every evening, they take time after dinner to coordinate their calendars, and work together at applying the memory strategies they learned to cement new information they need to remember into memory. They met some new friends along the way too. Although both Charlene and Peter are still apprehensive about what the future holds, they both feel better prepared to make the most of today and make adjustments along the way.

---

studies. The only way that new medical and cognitive interventions can be developed is if people like you enroll in studies so that scientists can determine the effects of the treatments that they are developing. Indeed, the first 48 participants in the Baycrest MCI program were all individuals who volunteered to be in our clinical research, and all three of us authors maintain active research programs to advance knowledge in brain health issues related to aging in order to help people like you.

Research studies take place at most universities, at many hospitals (especially those affiliated with a university), and via some independent pharmaceutical companies. Check out your local university and hospitals—the psychology, gerontology or geriatrics, neurology, and psychiatry departments are good places to start—for current research study options. The Web sites www.clinicaltrials.gov and www.controlled-trials.com/isrctn also catalogue all current and completed clinical trials, including drug trials as well as nondrug trials such as memory training or physical exercise trials. This Web site tells you whether they are still recruiting participants for the study, where the study is taking place, what the criteria are for being in the study, and who to contact. Your federal or local Alzheimer society or association likely also keeps lists of ongoing studies in your area. A list of federal societies can be found at http://www.alz.co.uk/associations.

It is important to ensure that any study you participate in has been approved by a local research ethics board or institutional review board. In most parts of the developed world, research studies have to undergo review by a research ethics board or panel that reviews the study design to ensure the safety and rights of participants. Special attention is paid toward balancing potential harms and benefits, and toward avoiding coercion and conflicts of interest. For example, although a drug study might have unanticipated side effects, the investigators have to demonstrate that the drug dosages they plan to use and the means by which that drug is delivered (for example, pills, injections) are the least harmful options relative to the anticipated benefits of the drug. Research participants cannot be made to feel that they have to participate in a study—it is always your choice whether you take part or not, and you always have the option to discontinue participation even after the study has started. Research ethics boards also ensure that the amount that participants are compensated (if any) is not so high that some people may agree to a study they don't really want to be part of just because they need the money. Finally, your decision to participate or not should not have any impact on the care you receive from your doctor or another health-care provider. Usually, research ethics boards make sure that a "third party," someone outside your circle of health care, tells you about the study and records whether you are interested in participating or not.

Almost all research studies approved by a research ethics or institutional review board must engage participants in an informed consent process as well. This means that you should be told the nature of the study, the steps required (number of sessions, the nature of any interventions), your right to withdraw your consent, and contact information of the principal investigator of the study. This is usually done in the form of a written document, but you should also be given the opportunity to ask questions and the time needed to make a decision before providing written or verbal consent to participate. We hope that this section on research studies inspires you to get out there and help advance knowledge toward helping other people, and you.

A FINAL WORD

It is natural for people faced with a medical condition to want scientists to come up with a pill that can return you to the way you were before. We and other professionals, however, are doubtful that a single pill will ever be developed that can cure or prevent any form of dementia or MCI. Alzheimer's disease and likely most of the other forms of dementia are extremely complex diseases that have many different underlying biological mechanisms that together lead to the disease state. Thus, there is unlikely to ever be a single "magic pill" to treat any form of dementia. Even the authors who reviewed the many drugs in various stages of development to fight Alzhiemer's disease shown in Box 7.2 warned against the traditional one disease–one drug model of disease treatment. More likely, a multipronged approach of two or more drugs will be needed to treat dementia, and even then those drug combinations will probably be most effective when the people taking them also make healthy lifestyle changes and have proper support from their family members and supportive health-care professionals such as counselors and social workers. We advocate strongly for a more holistic approach to your health care, one combining the amazing promise of pharmaceutical interventions with the hard work of learning better cognitive habits and making positive lifestyle changes that will help you maximize your brain health and enjoy the most from life.

RECOMMENDED READINGS

www.clinicaltrials.gov and www.controlled-trials.com/isrctn/ are registries of clinical trials for all types of conditions, including MCI and various forms of dementia. There you will find information on ongoing and completed trials of drugs, supplements, and psycho-educational interventions occurring in your region.

The site http://www.alz.co.uk/associations lists Alzheimer's associations in many countries from around the world.

8

The Personal Impact of Mild Cognitive Impairment

Mild cognitive impairment (MCI) is truly a family affair. By now you are familiar with how memory and thinking skills are affected in people with MCI. It is important to have a sense of what these changes really mean in the everyday lives of individuals, both from the perspective of the person experiencing MCI as well as their close family and friends. We will not single out the objective effects on memory function, because we have spent some time characterizing this in previous chapters. We will, however, talk about the consequences of mild memory decline on daily life.

OVERVIEW OF THE EFFECTS OF MCI

We have repeatedly emphasized in previous chapters that, by definition, MCI does not significantly compromise a person's ability to manage their day-to-day responsibilities. The key word here is "significantly" because the cognitive decline characterizing MCI can have subtle impacts on level of independence, particularly when it comes to complex thinking tasks that rely on memory. This may include tasks such as financial management, event planning, and navigating less familiar routes. Further, more people with MCI experience negative mood changes, mild sensory loss such as reduced hearing acuity, and sometimes poorer quality of sleep, as compared to peers experiencing changes associated with normal aging (see chapter 2 for review of normal age-related cognitive change). In short, there are cognitive and noncognitive consequences associated with MCI, some of which we have previously referred to in the context of risk factors for dementia (see chapter 5).

In this chapter we will discuss the impact of these changes on the individual with MCI, and we will also explore how close family members are impacted by their relative's MCI. Yes the changes are mild, but even mild changes in a person affect those around them. Indeed, there is a growing body of research showing that close family members are vulnerable to developing symptoms associated with depressed and anxious mood and exhibit poorer overall physical health status when compared with peers who are not living with a relative experiencing MCI.

IMPACT ON THE PERSON WITH MCI

There are several ways in which having MCI can affect your life. It can influence how you manage tasks, your mood, how you feel about yourself, how you engage with others, and possibly even how well you sleep and hear. We will address each of these influences in turn.

Instrumental Activities of Daily Living

As discussed in chapter 1, one of the classification criteria for MCI is that there must be no or minimal impact on one's ability to perform complex daily tasks. These instrumental activities of daily living— sometimes abbreviated as IADLs—include tasks such as managing your own schedule, household, travel plans, banking, shopping, and getting around town on your own. We told you in chapter 6 that, in evaluating MCI, the doctor gathers information about your everyday activities in order to make a judgement about whether there is any compromise in how well you manage your responsibilities. If there is some compromise, then the doctor tries to gauge the degree of impairment. Unfortunately, even if you and your close family members think everything is fine, if one really digs deep, some chinks in the armor may emerge, so to speak. This was demonstrated very convincingly by a group of researchers in Massachusetts who showed that even for people with MCI, for whom no problems in everyday activities were identified on detailed questionnaire, there is a decline in how effectively they can manage novel or less familiar tasks of a "real-world" nature. These researchers measured how effectively older adults with and without MCI could manage less routine types of real-life tasks such as planning a vacation or looking up and dialing the telephone number of a tradesperson to deal with a mock maintenance issue. Sure people with MCI can take on these kinds of tasks, but as a group they often left out steps, such as forgetting some items for the vacation, and as a result they just didn't do as well overall at managing these tasks as their same-aged peers who were not experiencing MCI.

Driving

You may recall in chapter 6 we told you that having MCI normally does not significantly impact your ability to drive safely. Thus, you should not allow uneasiness about the potential impact on your driving privileges to stop you from having your memory concerns investigated. Now we would like to clarify a few things about this very sensitive topic. There is, indeed, a growing body of research out there that shows MCI does influence driving skills. For example, one study examined driving maneuvers, such as lane changes, in various on-the-road driving situations, and compared older adults with MCI to those without MCI. What they found was that, although there were no serious driving impairments in people with MCI, the MCI group did not score as well overall when compared to older adults without MCI. What this means is that driving safety should be monitored, particularly because there is the possibility that cognitive decline could progress. In chapter 10, we discuss in detail how you can take steps to evaluate your driving safety, what might prompt you to consider retiring from driving, and how you could effectively maintain your lifestyle if you did retire from driving.

Mood and Personality Changes

Not everyone with MCI experiences mood problems and/or changes in their personality; however, more do than is typical of their age group. Doctors and researchers refer to this as the presence of *neuropsy-chiatric symptoms* because the symptoms identified, such as increased worrying, are attributed to the brain changes associated with MCI. These symptoms are generally not severe; in other words, people with MCI would not typically manifest symptoms significant enough to warrant diagnosis of a psychiatric disorder. Nonetheless, although not meeting criteria for clinical depression or anxiety, for example, people with MCI do report more symptoms associated with these types of negative mood changes. Further, close family members regularly iden-tify changes in mood and personality in their MCI relative.

A recent *meta-analysis* (a statistical technique for combining find-ings from several independent studies) provides us with information about the types of neuropsychiatric symptoms seen in MCI. The most common symptoms associated with MCI were depression, *apathy* (lack of interest or emotion), anxiety, and irritability. Of course, these research outcomes are influenced by the nature of the survey ques-tions used. However, these symptoms are commonly found across studies, and seem pretty consistent across cultures and continents.

It is hard to get a handle on the prevalence of neuropsychiatric symptoms, but many studies seem to consistently indicate that these changes affect at least half or possibly more than half of the MCI pop-ulation. The "glass-half-full interpretation" here is about half of the folks with MCI are not exhibiting big changes in mood and personal-ity. Still it is something to be aware of, because there is also evidence that the presence of mood disturbance in MCI increases the risk of progression to dementia. This has been shown for depression, apathy, and anxiety. If you are experiencing problems with your mood, it is important to do something about it. Tell your doctor about these problems and get them checked out and treated.

Influence on Views of Oneself and Relationship with Others

It is one thing to acknowledge that there may be some small impacts of having MCI on level of effectiveness managing com-plex life tasks, and that there may be some impact on how the per-son with MCI seems in terms of their demeanor—but how does this really affect the person with MCI? Well, one way to figure it out is to ask them. There are rare reports of this approach, which is called a focus group, and it simply involves getting together a group of individuals experiencing MCI, asking them some open-ended questions, and seeing what types of common *themes* (ideas or topics) emerge from the discussion.

In collaboration with others, we recently conducted some focus groups with the aim of finding out how people with MCI feel the cognitive decline they are experiencing impacts their everyday lives. Two of the themes emerging from these focus groups were report of reduced confidence in oneself and decreased participation in *leisure activities* (recreational activities people do for fun like golf, going to a party, playing tennis, or reading a good book). We found these two themes, regarding decreased self-confidence and decreased engagement in leisure activities, rang particularly true in light of things people with MCI have told us about themselves in the memory programs

---

Box 8.1 How Having MCI Affects People (Part 1)

- *Antoinetta, aged 69 years, former school teacher, and diagnosed with MCI two years ago.* "I just don't talk anymore. I stay quiet when I am in a group, I just listen."

- *Abdullah, aged 72 years, still working part-time as an attorney, and diagnosed with MCI last year.* "I've always loved telling jokes, but on a few recent occasions I've been told by the person I'm telling the joke to that I'd already told them that joke. It's so embarrassing. I've stopped telling jokes, and I really miss that, it was part of who I was."

- *Pierre, aged 70, retired accountant, and diagnosed with MCI four years ago.* "My wife and I decided she would give me a hand signal when I repeated a question. At first I thought it was a good idea, but now I just find it rude and hurtful."

- *Consuela, aged 80, homemaker, and diagnosed with MCI a few months ago.* "My level of competitive bridge play is not what it used to be. I am having trouble keeping track of what's going on, and I don't want to let my partner down. I am thinking of quitting, it's stressful, and it's not fun being faced with my shortcomings like that."

we have been running for them and their family members since 2003. Box 8.1 contains some related examples of how people with MCI in our programs have expressed the impact of memory decline on their relationships with others. We have changed their names, but the dialogue is genuine.

It is clear from the comments in Box 8.1 that experiencing memory decline really can have an impact on how you feel about yourself, your interactions with others, and about the kinds of pastimes you engage in. Given our particular interest in providing an effective behavior-based treatment for MCI, we were very much struck by our finding that the people with MCI in our focus group report decreased participation in leisure activities. This is because research shows that greater participation in leisure activities can actually reduce dementia risk, so taking part less often in leisure activities is the exact opposite of what you should be doing if you have MCI! In the third section of this book, you will read about more research demonstrating the positive impact a variety of different leisure activities can have on our brain health and in reducing dementia risk.

We have taken the knowledge we have gained from our focus groups and directly applied it to how we deliver our behavioral intervention program for MCI (the details of which you read about in chapter 7). Specifically, in our program content we have placed more emphasis on the importance of leisure activities to health and well-being. We explore barriers and provide "how to" information for identifying and accessing opportunities to engage in pastimes that are personally meaningful and enjoyable. (This is further explored in chapter 10.) Here again, we have learned much from the attitudes and experiences of our program participants, for, although having MCI can have negative influences, there are also positive influences that are related to the attitudes and perspectives of the people who are experiencing MCI. In Box 8.2 we have included some comments from people demonstrating there are situations in which folks seem to feel MCI has had positive effects on their lives.

The examples in Box 8.2 make us think of the saying "when the going gets tough, the tough get going." In chapter 9 we will expand on the influence that perspective and attitude can have on our ability to live effectively with MCI.

Box 8.2 How Having MCI Affects People (Part 2)

- *Richard, aged 61 years, contractor, and diagnosed with MCI six months ago.* "It's made me reflect on what's important in life. I appreciate my family more, my wife....I am now diligent about scheduling and tracking stuff into my phone (referring to his cell phone which is equipped with an electronic organizer). I'm more on top of what's happening at work than I've ever been and the guys know it...they're always coming to me to verify the next steps because they know I am on top of it."

- *Lee, aged 78 years, retired dairy farmer, diagnosed with MCI two-and-a-half years ago.* "I love reading, but I couldn't remember everything that had happened in earlier chapters and reading just wasn't fun anymore. I switched to short stories. They are immensely satisfying, all this talent I never knew about. You can read one in an afternoon, it's just a treat each time."

- *Stephano, aged 70, retired physicist, and diagnosed with MCI four years ago.* "Finding out I had MCI improved my marriage. No really, I wasn't pulling my weight with walking the dog. Now I am, because I know daily exercise can help me stay healthy and I am healthy, and my wife's happy with me, the dog, too, for that matter. What more could a guy want?"

Sensory Changes

It is well established that people in the early stages of Alzheimer's disease can experience a reduced sense of smell and also hearing problems. Taste can also be affected a bit, secondary to the reduced sense of smell, but basic vision, tactile (touch) and temperature sensation remain relatively well preserved in the early stages of this disease. There are now some studies showing that hearing loss is more prevalent among people with MCI as compared to same-age peers without MCI—though, to our knowledge, there is no evidence of meaningful compromise to any of the other senses. Indeed, a very recent study of people with MCI found that those with hearing loss progressed to dementia more quickly than did those with intact hearing.

Changes in hearing, even subtle ones, mean your ability to participate in social situations suffers at least three blows. First, it is well established that people who are hard of hearing have greater difficulty distinguishing speech in a noisy environment, such as at a party for example, or even when trying to converse over the sound of the radio or TV. Second, if you cannot properly hear what has been said, then you have a pretty limited chance of accurately remembering it. Finally, people with MCI are already finding it more effortful to remember. Compound that with having to divert some of that effort toward just trying to properly make out what has been said and you can get a sense of the hurdles some individuals with MCI face day to day

You may have experienced the need to shut off the radio or to tune out of the conversation for a second when you are trying to figure out directions while driving. You may also find you now prefer to do complex thinking tasks, such as your taxes, in a quiet environment. Just making these allowances for yourself may give you some glimmer about how difficult it is to have the added burden of even some mild hearing loss. Now, perhaps, you can see how hearing loss can make socializing more difficult, but did you also know that, even in the most quiet of places, older adults with hearing loss as a group do poorer on tests of learning and memory compared to their peers who are not experiencing such sensory loss? This is true even in ideal hearing conditions in which one can verify the information was accurately heard. The idea is that taking auditory information in is more demanding of attention for people with hearing loss, and so they have less attention resources to put into learning and remembering the information. We hope this section motivates you to have your hearing checked and to follow your audiologist's advice about how to best improve your hearing (for example, getting fitted with a hearing aid if hearing loss is discovered); doing so may have beneficial effects for your memory and enjoyment when participating in social situations.

Sleep-Behavior Changes and Sleep Apnea

As we age, there are changes to our sleep cycle. A typical sleep cycle includes stages of light and deep sleep and the amount of time spent within each stage is sometimes referred to as your sleep architecture.

As we age we experience more fragmented sleep and reduced total sleep (referred to as reduced sleep continuity), as well as changes in the amount of time we spend in each of the sleep stages (sleep architecture), and to the timing of our sleep within the day-night cycle. Sleep continuity and sleep architecture are altered more extensively by dementia due to Alzheimer's disease (meaning sleep is even more fragmented and more reduced overall as compared to normal aging). Recent research shows that sleep changes are also evident in people with MCI, but at a stage that is in-between normal aging and dementia. Not surprisingly then perhaps, symptoms related to sleep problems are commonly reported by people with MCI.

You may recall from chapter 2 that getting proper sleep is very important for memory. This is because, as we sleep, the memories we have formed during the day actually become *consolidated* (a neurochemical process whereby a memory trace is made more permanent). Poor sleep can disrupt this process, and the result is that we cannot remember the specifics of recently acquired information as well as we should. We also have trouble keeping track of and re-organizing information, and learning new information. If you are already experiencing memory problems due to MCI, you certainly do not want sleeping difficulties to make the problem even worse. The good news is there are things you can do to help improve your ability to get a quality sleep, and these are reviewed next, in chapter 9. The other good news is that, unlike mood and hearing problems, which are associated with dementia risk, sleep behavior problems are not. The same cannot be said of sleep disorders, however.

As we age, we also become more prone to sleep disorders. One of these is *sleep apnea,* a sleep disorder in which you exhibit abnormal breathing during sleep, either by stopping breathing for a few seconds or minutes or by breathing very little. This means you are not getting the right amount of oxygen during sleep, and this disrupts your sleep cycle, even if you are not aware of the problem. Sleep apnea is a treatable problem, and often people can make effective uses of devices that can help them breathe properly during sleep. If you feel fatigued during the day, it is possible it could be related to breathing problems at night. If so, it is very important to speak to your doctor about this, especially if you have MCI, because you want to do all you can to minimize the influence of any other health conditions in further compromising your memory or other thinking skills.

IMPACT ON FAMILY MEMBERS

The behavioral changes associated with MCI, such as slight changes in how easily the finances are managed or observations of low mood, are much more subtle than those associated with dementia. Nonetheless, these changes can have an impact on family members, most particularly the person closest to the individual experiencing MCI.

Shifting Roles and Changes in the Relationship Dynamic

Family members of people with MCI are not caregivers in the same sense as those caring for a relative with dementia. The family member closest to the individual with MCI does, however, experience some shift in his or her role in the relationship dynamic. It could be as innocuous as just covertly checking over the shoulder of their loved one or maybe taking a more forward approach by verifying schedules and whether prescription medications have been refilled on time.

In the early years of our MCI program, we offered informal sessions for family members with MCI relatives to provide them with an opportunity to discuss their concerns within a group sharing a common experience. In collaboration with others, we conducted a qualitative analysis of these informal family sessions and discovered several themes. These included new roles (for example, helping with finances); uncertainty about the future; desire for knowledge about MCI, memory systems, and age-related changes; difficulty coping with mood changes in their spouse with MCI (for example, irritability) and their own frustrations over their spouses' memory slips; sense of loss for the way things used to be; and desire for emotional support. Regarding emotional support, they were looking for coping strategies and the opportunity to share experiences and solutions. These themes were closely similar to those identified by other researchers examining the needs of family members of individuals with MCI. Based on this work, we have now developed a more formal program of intervention for our family members. This program includes specific education about memory and aging, as well as training on how to identify and effectively manage problems associated with having a relative with MCI. The aim of the program is to proactively address identified problems, and participants' emotional responses to living with the changes in their MCI relative, with the purpose of preventing future negative health consequences in these family members. In Box 8.3 we provide examples of some of the most commonly cited problems reported by family in coping with the personal impact of their relative's MCI.

We are also concerned with helping family members identify the positive aspects associated with having a loved one who is experiencing MCI. It is important to recognize these positive aspects as well as our perceptions of "problems," because this can be critical in promoting our satisfaction with our lives and our confidence that we have a role to play that can make a positive impact for ourselves and our loved ones. Some positive outcomes family members have reported

---

Box 8.3 How Family Members Are Impacted by Their Relative's MCI

- I feel frustrated when my mother asks me the same question.
- It makes me worried when my husband makes a memory mistake; I worry about things getting worse and how we will manage.
- My wife gets really down on herself when she forgets something and it makes me feel sad to see her this way, but I am not sure how to help.
- I want to be able to discuss my concerns with my Dad, but I don't want to upset him.
- I am resentful of having to take on more responsibilities; my wife used to always take care of the bills, and now she wants me to do it, even though she can do it.
- Sometimes my husband takes the wrong turn when driving, he figures his way in the end, but I worry about him getting lost or being late for things.
- I get impatient when my sister forgets to follow through on something she agreed to do. I don't know if she really did forget or it just wasn't important enough to her to remember.

to us relate to learning to be more patient and valuing their relative with MCI more. We are currently researching the effectiveness of our program in helping our family participants deal more effectively with the impact of their relative's MCI on their own lives.

Symptoms of Caregiver Burden

Again, we want to emphasize that family members of relatives with MCI are not "caregivers." This is because, by definition, people with MCI are still managing their day-to-day responsibilities with a high degree of independence. However, as you now know, there are some subtle changes in level of proficiency at managing these daily tasks that families take note of and that can affect them. We are using the term *caregiver* only to refer to a family member who is assisting a relative with dementia. Importantly, there are some common impacts of living with a relative experiencing cognitive decline that are shared between family members living with a relative who has MCI and family members (who are caregivers) living with a relative who has dementia.

Negative impacts on mood, stress level, and cognition

There are now a number of studies showing that family members of people with MCI experience poorer health and/or elevated symptoms of depression and anxiety associated with providing increased functional support to their relative with MCI. Similarly, it is well known that family caregivers of individuals with dementia show evidence of decreased mental and physical health, including elevated rates of anxiety and clinical depression. In chapter 2 we described how negative mood and stress can impact cognition, and research does show that dementia caregivers can experience some decline in their own cognition, though we are not aware of any research demonstrating this among family members of relatives with MCI. In Box 8.4 we demonstrate how memory changes can cause increased stress and worry in the spouse of a person with MCI.

Increased health issues

It is well documented that stress can have a negative impact on your health. We talked a little bit about how stress influences memory in

---

Box 8.4 The Unpredictability of Memory and Its Effects on the Spouse of a Person with MCI

Lily is a 58-year-old woman who has been married to Ted for 30 years. Ted, who is 67, was diagnosed with MCI 2 years ago. She described her experiences as follows: "It is the unpredictability of the memory slips that is particularly worrying for me. I am not sure when to step in, how much to step in, and feel I just cannot count on him to come through. It might be something as unimportant as remembering to pick up the milk on the way home or more important such as remembering to pay the credit card bill on time. I always have to double check or I remind him, which then annoys him, either because he has remembered or because he's upset about forgetting. Talk about being between a rock and a hard place. It's just these little things, on a day-to-day basis, that are very wearing. I always have this nagging worry."

---

chapter 2. Stress can also have negative effects on your blood pressure and your sleep. Given the impacts on mood and stress reported by family members with MCI (reviewed previously), it is very possible these effects could have impacts on physical health. Certainly, it is well documented that family caregivers of relatives with dementia show increased health problems related to immune-system function, blood pressure, and even premature mortality. This is why it is also critical to target the close relative of the person with MCI for early intervention. Again, the purpose is to prevent medical conditions and promote health.

SUPPORT FOR FAMILY MEMBERS

In chapter 7 we described the MCI Program developed at Baycrest in Toronto Ontario as including a component directed specifically at addressing the needs of the loved ones of people with MCI. The importance of providing intervention for close family members is being increasingly recognized. We know from past research that the mental and physical health of family caregivers of persons with dementia can start to fail and this places added burden on the health-care system and society, not to mention the affected individual! Knowing this is a wake-up call to all of us. Addressing the needs of close relatives of people with MCI is an opportunity to provide support early to these family members with the aim of preventing health problems.

There is some evidence suggesting positive mood outcomes for family members who participate together with their MCI relative in intervention programs. Our own preliminary investigations into the effectiveness of the Baycrest program for family members are also consistent with positive outcome. For example, family members report being satisfied with their ability to manage the problems they had identified at the outset of their program participation. They also report feeling less worried about the future and feeling more capable of dealing with their current and future life circumstances as they relate to living with someone who has MCI. These outcomes indicate that even earlier intervention for family members with MCI relatives at high risk of dementia may serve to equip family with the skills, support, and resource knowledge to prevent the onset of the more serious negative health outcomes experienced by people who are caring for a loved one with dementia. This is a realistic impact, given research demonstrating that interventions for dementia caregivers help them manage to care for their relative with dementia for longer than those who do not receive this support and, most importantly, without associated declines in the primary family caregiver's own health.

A FINAL WORD

How to deal with the effects of MCI on your life is now going to be the focus of the remainder of this book. At this point in the book you have a gained a very thorough understanding of what MCI is, what causes it, how it is diagnosed and currently treated, and how it affects people's lives. In the next two chapters of this section of the book, we will extend this journey of discovery to include information specific to how to proactively manage the impact of living with MCI.

Now that you are aware of some of the health issues that can affect people living with MCI, you can take steps to head off these issues. Awareness is the first step. Next is action. We hope that you were encouraged by the positive results of behavioral interventions for both people with MCI and for their loved ones (described previously in this chapter and in chapter 7). We have mentioned before that there is no "magic pill." It takes work, but it's worth it.

The good news is that you have choices. There are ways you can choose to take effective action to minimize any negative impacts of MCI on your life and hinder the ability of these impacts to influence disease progression. In the remainder of the book we will demonstrate how you can take control of MCI.

Box 8.5 Questions to Ask Your Doctor if MCI Is Suspected or Confirmed in Yourself or in Your Family Member

1. If you or your partner have noted any unusual sleep problems, such as difficulty getting to sleep, staying asleep, or excessive snoring that wakes you or your partner up, then tell your doctor about these problems. Ask your doctor whether your sleep problems should be investigated further.

2. If you or your partner suspect you may not be seeing or hearing well, ask your doctor whether you should have an eye examination and a hearing test.

3. If you feel that you need more emotional support to deal with how MCI is impacting your life, ask your doctor or health care professional about counseling services or support groups available in your community. This would apply to both the person with MCI and their loved ones.

4. If you are unable to achieve a positive mood, tell your doctor and ask about treatment options.

RECOMMENDED READING

Greenberger, D & Padesky, C.A. (1995). *Mind over mood: Change how you feel by changing the way you think*. New York: The Guilford Press.

Silberman, S.A (2010). *The insomnia workbook: A Comprehesive guide to getting the sleep you need*. Oakland, CA: New Harbinger Publications.

Please also see recommended readings at the end of chapter 9.

9

Living Effectively with Mild Cognitive Impairment

Living effectively with mild cognitive impairment (MCI) is about making choices or changes that will promote your continued physical, emotional, and cognitive health. In chapter 8 we described the personal impact MCI can have on individuals and the persons closest to them. In this chapter we will focus on your well-being, that is, your capacity to feel reasonably satisfied with your existence in terms of your level of happiness, health, and ability to exert control over what's happening in your life. Being able to deal effectively with what causes you stress in life is where we will start. Then, we will move on to talk about managing your feelings, the influence of a good night's sleep, and the importance of developing good memory routines. In addressing each of these topics, we will point out how you can use this information to build in a "buffer" to help promote your health and memory even in the face of life's challenges.

STRESS

In chapter 2 and again in chapter 5 we told you that stress can have a negative impact on your memory. Stress is experienced when you lack a sense of control over a situation or event. How many *stressors* (the situations that are causing you stress) you are dealing with, whether they are of a short or prolonged duration, and whether they are positive (accepting an award) or negative (getting a root canal) are all irrelevant. The key to understanding why stress can have a negative impact on your health and wellness lies in the *stress response*, in other words, how your body responds to stress.

The stress response is a natural coping mechanism that becomes activated automatically whenever we encounter a stressor. Its function is to deal with the stressor by releasing hormones (such as cortisol) and glucose into the bloodstream to provide extra energy and alertness so that we can respond adaptively to it. Once the stressor is dealt with successfully, the stress response is turned off and our body returns to a relative state of balance. If we fail to deal with the stressor successfully or are exposed to too many stressors, then it is harder for the body to achieve the relatively constant internal environment it needs to function efficiently. We can liken the number of stressors we have to deal with at any given time to the burden our body has to bear. When the load remains high, the result is "wear and tear" on our physical health, and illness sets in, adding to the burden. Our inability to effectively manage our emotional response to the stressors in our lives also contributes to the load.

Stanford University biologist Raymond Sapolsky has an interesting analogy using a zebra and a lion to explain adaptive and maladaptive responses to stress. This is explained in detail in his book *Why Zebra's Don't Get Ulcers* (one of the recommended readings at the end of this chapter), and we'll summarize it here. The reason that zebras don't get ulcers is that when a lion threatens, they turn on the jets (in other words, the stress response is activated), and they get the heck out of there. If they manage to escape the lion and the lion is no longer around, they stop thinking about it. Their stress response is turned off. That's adaptive. Unfortunately, people are not like zebras. We would likely be worrying about the next time the lion would show up. Our worry is psychological—there is no lion, no threat—but because we are worrying, our stress response stays on. That's maladaptive.

Acute Versus Chronic Effects of Stress

An acute response to stress is adaptive, but a chronic response, when we keep the stress response turned on by fretting and worrying, for example, is maladaptive. Why? What does it mean to our health? High levels of cortisol, which is the primary stress hormone, contributes to the development of stress-related disorders, which include both physical and mental-health problems. Some examples of physical problems related to chronic stress are high blood pressure, heart disease, cancer, arthritis, diabetes, ulcers, colitis, and headache. Some examples of mental- health problems related to chronic stress are depression, anxiety, panic attacks, and *posttraumatic stress disorder* (significant and sustained anxiety in response to the past experience of a traumatic event, such as a car accident).

Cortisol can also have direct effects on the structure and function of the brain, and in particular on memory structures. We want to point out that this hormone is critical when it comes to helping us martial our energies for any activity, whether it is getting out of bed in the morning or going for a jog. Cortisol only exerts negative effects on our brain health when it is chronically elevated. The reason cortisol impacts our memory function under these conditions is because the hippocampus, the most important brain structure for memory, has many nerve cells with an affinity for cortisol. When there is too much cortisol in the system for a prolonged period, these cells are flooded and cannot properly perform their functions in supporting memory processes. Too much cortisol also interferes with the development of new cells in the hippocampus and causes shrinkage of existing cells. People with chronically elevated levels of circulating cortisol have smaller hippocampi and do poorer on memory tests compared to people who do not have these conditions.

Given the influence of chronically elevated cortisol on memory and the hippocampus, you may not be surprised to learn that older adults with Alzheimer's disease have higher circulating levels of cortisol compared to healthy older adults. What this means is that there is a change in how their bodies are able to balance hormones, yet another example of the many complexities of this disease. So far, research indicates that people with MCI do not show this type of elevation in circulating cortisol, though some would say the evidence is inconclusive. Further study is being done.

Methods for Regulating the Influence of Stress on our Health and Well-Being

It's all about perspective

Sometimes we keep the stress response "turned on" because of our propensity to dwell on what is bothering us and our failure to allow ourselves the opportunity to take steps to better manage our stressors. In other words, psychological factors, like our mindset, can influence the physiological stress response. The same identical stressor may elicit a larger or smaller stress response, depending on how it is appraised. Imagine another driver changing lanes too close in front of you and cutting you off. Most of us would have the same "behavioral" reaction to this sudden danger. That is, we would make a defensive driving maneuver to avoid a collision. Our recovery from that stressor, however, will be influenced by how we feel about what just happened. As noted in Box 9.1 we may not all have the same "psychological" reaction to this situation.

The impact of exercise on stress

Medical health conditions like high blood pressure, high cholesterol, and diabetes are considered *stress-related disorders*, meaning stress can cause or worsen them. You will read extensively in chapter 12 about how exercise positively affects physical health by preventing or helping you better control these medical conditions. Exercise also positively impacts your mood, such that it reduces any experience of symptoms associated with feeling worried or down. Essentially, physical activity can act as a buffer that prevents the negative consequences of chronic stress on our physical and emotional health. For example, people who are more physically active show a faster recovery

---

Box 9.1 Psychological Responses Influence Stress Recovery

Situation: Another driver cuts you off on the highway.

Response A: Yell "What a jerk! I can't believe you have a license!" Shake your fist. Imagine confronting the driver and telling the person off. Fume over what happened for the entire drive. Get to destination in a grumpy mood. [Stress response recovery is delayed = maladaptive].

Response B: Yell "Whoa!" Wonder to yourself what on earth the driver could be thinking of to drive that way. Hope no one else is bothered and feel thankful you averted a collision. Don't think on it further. Get to destination in good spirits. [Stress response recovery is on time = adaptive].

time with respect to their heart rate returning to normal for example following a stressor than people who are not physically active. This is similar in many ways to how having a positive attitude or a particular "perspective" can help you recover faster from your experience of a negative event, such as being cut off by another driver.

Formal and informal relaxation techniques

There are formal relaxation techniques such as meditation and breathing exercises and informal techniques that involve simply engaging in activities you find relaxing. The formal techniques require a little practice. Meditation is a form of "conscious relaxation" during which you choose to be still, to focus on your breathing, and to try to achieve a calm inner state. Prayer can be a form of meditation because it can also help you achieve a sense of inner peace through doing quiet reflective thinking. There are ways of relaxing that are solely focused on breathing (see Box 9.2). Activities, such as yoga and Tai Chi, that incorporate both breathing and slow and controlled body movements together are excellent at helping achieve a state of relaxation.

The reason relaxation techniques reduce stress is because of the way your body responds to them. Your body cannot feel relaxed and stressed at the same time. When you are feeling stressed, your body responds by increasing your heart rate, your blood pressure, your respiration rate (breathing), and the release of stress hormones. The exact opposite occurs when you are feeling relaxed. Your body responds by decreasing your heart rate, your blood pressure, your respiration rate, and the release of stress hormones. If some "psychological stressor," some problem, is bothering you, you may not be able to make the problem go away with a relaxation technique, but you can change how your body is responding to it. For example, relaxation won't heal a sick relative that you are worried about, but it can help you cope with that event in a healthier way. By changing the way your body is responding, you can change the way your mind is responding. For example, if you are nervous about getting into the dentist's chair, engaging in a deep breathing relaxation technique while you are in the waiting room might help you calm down.

In Box 9.2 we describe a great little "on-the-spot" deep breathing technique you can try. Closing your eyes can be helpful to focus your attention on your breathing when you try this technique. If you don't want to close your eyes, you can just lower your eyes and soften your gaze as you engage in the deep breathing. Following the steps below will normally lead to a feeling of relaxation fairly quickly. If it doesn't happen for you, it may be because your body needs more practice with this relaxation technique, so keep at it. It really does work and it's a great little technique to have in your back pocket, so to speak. You can do it anywhere, while you're sitting in the waiting room at the doctor's office, waiting to give a speech, or are just feeling tense for no particular reason.

We use the breathing technique just described in our MCI Program at Baycrest and, generally, get very positive feedback from participants. Most people report feeling more relaxed after engaging in the breathing exercise. We've even had the occasional person fall asleep on us! After they learn to do the deep breathing, some people use it to fall asleep at night. People have even told us it helps them with aches and pains. The latter is not surprising, given that relaxation techniques are commonly used as a method of pain management.

You do not have to be still, quiet, or alone to relax. Examples of relaxing activities could be reading, listening to or playing music,

---

Box 9.2 On-the-Spot Deep Breathing Relaxation Technique

- Pay attention to how you are breathing (your breathing pace or rate).
- Gradually start to breathe more slowly and deeply.
- As you inhale a deep and long breath, try to push your stomach out.
- Slowly exhale as though you were blowing on a spoonful of hot soup.
- As you exhale, let your shoulders and jaw drop.
- Continue this for a few minutes.

Some Tips

- If you feel light-headed or dizzy, stop and breathe normally for a few minutes before resuming deep breathing.
- If your thoughts wander, that's normal. Just bring your focus back to the breathing by paying attention to the pause between inhaling and exhaling and by counting as you inhale and then counting to the same number as you exhale.

going for a walk, or spending time with someone you feel very much at ease with. The important thing about relaxing is that we make the time to do it. It's okay; you can give yourself permission to relax. Even if it's only for a few minutes in your day, it can make a positive impact. The benefits of relaxation on your health can be best realized if the activity or activities become part of your daily routine. For example, most of us can find a few minutes to engage in deep breathing as a means of giving our body and minds a break. Because you don't need any special equipment or environment to do this, you can relax with deep breathing whenever and wherever you have a few minutes. We would encourage you to take a few minutes to do the deep breathing exercise described in Box 9.2 each day.

If you are interested in learning more about the kinds of relaxation activities we have described here, we would suggest you begin by making enquiries at your local library, place of worship, community center, or fitness club to find out if they offer meditation groups or other forms of relaxation exercises. In Box 9.3 we tell you about some characteristics and habits of people who are considered to be good at coping with stress that are consistent with the writings of Pelletier. You will see that engaging in daily relaxation is one of the habits. So, too, is having a positive attitude (described next).

PAY ATTENTION TO YOUR FEELINGS

Paying attention to your feelings can help you to address more promptly situations that are bothering you. Sometimes you may not have the control to change a situation, but you can take steps to help better manage your feelings about the situation. In chapters 2, 5, and 8 we talked about negative mood symptoms like depression and anxiety, how these symptoms are more prevalent in people with MCI, how they can affect memory, and how they can promote progression to dementia. If negative mood symptoms can cause all these problems for you, then what can the positive attitudes do?

What a positive attitude can do for you

Many studies have been conducted attesting to the benefits of a positive attitude on your cognition. In particular, a positive attitude

---

Box 9.3 Some Habits of People Who Cope Well with Stress

They:

- Anticipate stressors and plan how to manage them.
- Believe they can exert influence over events and their responses to events (self-efficacy).
- Engage in daily relaxation.
- Keep up their health promoting buffers (such as good sleep habits, physical exercise, healthy diet, and social relationships).
- Develop and foster a sense of purpose and meaning in their lives.
- Contribute to the well-being of others.
- Make use of in-the-moment tension-relief techniques (such as deep breathing or stretching).

---

promotes your ability to pay attention to happenings in your environment. It can also have a beneficial impact on your ability to deal more effectively with adverse situations. As mentioned earlier, having a positive attitude can even speed your body's recovery following a stressful event such that your heart and respiration rate return to normal faster. In fact there is strong evidence that having positive feelings has many health benefits, such as promoting heart health, immune-system function, cancer survival, and longevity.

We are not suggesting that you need to feel happy all the time to realize the health and wellness benefits of a positive attitude. We are suggesting that you pay attention to any negative thoughts and emotions and deal with them. Don't just wait for them to go away. Take action to engage in activities that you find enjoyable and that make you feel good about yourself. Next, we will tell you about some specific things that are known to help improve mood. Some of these are a good idea for everyone, because we all experience ups and downs in our moods. Other approaches can help deal with the more persistent negative moods that are associated with mental-health disorders.

Activities You Can Do to Promote a Positive Attitude

There are many activities you can do to try to help yourself achieve a more positive attitude. These fall into three broad categories; doing things that are personally meaningful (for example, activities that give you a sense of purpose or accomplishment), doing things that are sociable, and exercise.

Doing activities you find personally meaningful can exert a positive influence on your sense of well-being and may even prevent dementia! For example, The Rush Memory and Aging Project based in Chicago followed 900 community-dwelling older adults over 7 years and looked at a specific aspect of what contributes to a positive attitude, namely a *purpose in life.* This refers to having goals and intentions that guide your behavior and being able to derive meaning from your life's experiences. They found that people who scored higher on a "purpose-in-life" measure of well-being had a significantly lower risk of Alzheimer's disease.

These ideas about having a purpose in life are closely similar to the notion of *self-efficacy,* which is your belief in your ability to accomplish something. Having a sense of a purpose in life and self-efficacy are both associated with having a positive attitude. So, too, is the ability to adopt a healthy perspective in your interpretation of events and happenings, such as in the example provided earlier (Box 9.1, response B to being cut off by another driver).

Activities that involve interacting with other people also seem to foster a positive attitude. Some people may be able to achieve benefits from socializing through how they choose to act toward others and by the nature of the activities they engage in with others. It often makes people feel good when they help another person by doing them a favor, or when they work together with others toward a common cause, such as when participating in food drives or a neighborhood cleanup. It can also make people feel good when they enjoy the company of their friends (you will read more about how social activities can promote a positive mood and reduce stress in chapter 14).

Finally, activities that involve being physically active have been shown to promote a positive attitude. Indeed, exercise can have a tremendously beneficial impact on your mood, the ability to manage stress, and to reduce your risk of dementia. As mentioned earlier, you will read about just how exercise exerts all these beneficial influences to your health in chapter 12.

It might not be easy at first to identify activities to try to achieve a positive attitude. Here we would advise you to observe those around you. Are there things other folks are doing that seem interesting to you? Is there an activity you used to be interested in that you never had the opportunity to pursue (e.g., learn ballroom dancing) or an activity you used to do but gave up because of lack of time or resources (e.g., playing tennis)? Maybe you love children and would like to volunteer as a teacher's helper in a school. There are a tremendous number of possibilities, and we would encourage you to take the time to investigate and think about what kinds of activities you would find rewarding.

As mentioned earlier, it is normal to have ups and downs in life, and we don't always have control over a situation or event. We do have control over ourselves though, and how we choose to react to life's downs. If engaging in activities to promote a positive attitude does not work for you, and your negative thoughts and feelings persist, then you may want to talk to your doctor about this and explore more formal treatment options.

Formal treatment options

Sometimes counseling or a more formal form of talk therapy can help improve your mood. Medication is also an option you can discuss with your doctor, as well as some combination of both talk therapy and medication. Talk-therapy approaches can be delivered one-on-one or in a group of people experiencing similar symptoms.

One particularly effective form of talk therapy for treating people experiencing anxiety, depression, or some combination of both is called *cognitive behavioral therapy*. This type of therapy involves enabling people to identify their unhelpful ways of behaving and thinking in response to problems, situations, and events in their lives. For example, you decide not to invite a new friend to your home for dinner because you don't know what she would like, and deep down you believe she probably wouldn't like your cooking anyway. Through cognitive behavioral therapy, you would learn ways to stop that type of negative thought pattern and come up with a solution that would make you feel comfortable. For example, you might ask your friend what her favorite take-out meal is and invite her to join you for an informal dinner. Although cognitive behavioral therapy doesn't work for everyone, it is successful for a high percentage of people for whom this type of therapy is considered appropriate. What this means is that, for some people, their moods can be effectively managed without medication. As we mentioned in chapter 8, a recent study using group cognitive behavior therapy for people with MCI showed some preliminary evidence for the effectiveness of this approach in achieving positive outcomes, specifically an increased level of acceptance and marital satisfaction among participants.

In chapter 5 we discussed drug treatment of depression. Other kinds of mood problems that may be treated with medications include *anxiety* (worry) and *apathy* (lack of emotion or interest). In terms of treatment for depression among older adults, medication and talk-therapy approaches, alone or in combination can be highly effective at improving mood. The important thing here is to work together with your doctor to explore what treatment options are right for you.

SLEEP

Getting a good night's sleep is also very important to your ability to feel more positive. In chapter 8 we told you that sleep patterns shift as we age and that people with MCI often report experiencing difficulty either falling asleep, staying asleep during the night, or waking up too early. We also pointed out that sleep is a critical component to your physical and emotional health and to your memory functioning.

Given the importance of sleep to health and well-being, we wanted to make sure you knew about some simple things that can help improve your ability to sleep at night. See Box 9.4 for guidelines to improve your sleep habits or *sleep hygiene, as well as the recommended reading by Silberman listed in chapter 8.* These involve controlling aspects of your environment and your behavior that can impact your sleep. In order for these techniques to work, you have to be disciplined about doing them; you can't just do them when they are convenient. If you are committed to making these simple changes, though, you should soon find that you are sleeping better at night and waking up feeling more refreshed.

It is recommended that adults get at least seven hours of sleep per night, though some individuals may need more and others can

---

Box 9.4 The Dos and Don'ts of Good Sleep Habits

- Do eat a light snack before bedtime *if* you would otherwise be hungry, but don't eat a large meal just before bedtime.
- Don't drink alcohol right before bedtime. Alcohol may induce sleep, but it will disrupt sleep later in the night.
- Do exercise regularly, but don't exercise within a couple of hours of bedtime.
- Don't keep your bedroom at an extremely warm or cool temperature.
- Do keep your bedroom quiet and dark during sleep time.
- If you're a smoker, then don't smoke in the hour or so before bedtime, and don't smoke if you wake up in the middle of the night.
- Don't consume caffeine late in the day. In particular, avoid having that coffee with your evening meal if you are someone who has trouble sleeping.
- Do, as much as possible, keep to a regular sleep schedule in terms of when you typically go to bed and when you typically rise in the morning.

---

manage with a bit less. You may ask yourself, What can a good night's sleep really do for me? A lot. When you are asleep your body is engaged in many restorative functions that include producing proteins that repair cell damage and producing chemicals. Examples of these chemicals are *melatonin* (a hormone involved in sleep-cycle regulation and immune-system function among other things) and *serotonin* (a hormone with many functions, most importantly enabling communication between nerve cells, but also regulating your mood state, with low levels of serotonin being associated with depressed mood). If you don't get enough sleep, then your body is stressed (it has to carry an increased burden) because it doesn't have enough time to take care of all the daily wear and tear. When your body is stressed due to lack of sleep, more stress hormones are released, like cortisol. As a consequence, regulation of your blood pressure and cholesterol, your mood, and how effective you are at responding to stress, is not as efficient. We told you in chapter 8 that your memory also doesn't function as efficiently when you haven't had enough sleep.

Lack of sleep reduces your body's effectiveness at performing all the restorative functions, and this can make you more prone to medical conditions like heart disease and stroke and to mood problems like depression and anxiety. In short, sleep acts like a buffer to help your body and mind function optimally regardless of what the day throws your way.

DEVELOPING GOOD EVERYDAY MEMORY HABITS

Having good memory habits is yet another step you can take to effectively manage life's challenges. The great thing about a habit is that it can be relied upon. When you go into the bathroom to brush your teeth, you can be certain your toothbrush will be there. It does not matter whether you're having a bad day or a good day; your toothbrush is waiting. Why? Because, that's where you always keep it. It's a logical location, and because of your habit of keeping it there, you *know* where it is without having to think about it. The other good thing about a habit is that, once it is established, it is easy to maintain. Keep the toothbrush analogy in mind as you contemplate the potential for your ability to develop and reap the benefits of good memory habits. In chapter 15 we will provide specific information on practical strategies for remembering that you can incorporate into your everyday life.

People with MCI are capable of acquiring practical memory techniques

In chapter 7 we told you about our own research showing that participants in the Baycrest MCI Program were able to learn a lot about different memory strategies and put that knowledge into practice. Importantly, we are not the only researchers who have shown that people with MCI can learn and use new memory skills. This should not be surprising, because mild cognitive changes do not mean that you are unable to learn new information; it just means your development of new skills may take a little more effort.

The idea here is that, if you are consistently using effective memory strategies of the type that we describe in detail in chapter 15, then you should notice a reduction in the number of memory slips you make.

Box 9.5 Case Vignette of a Lady Who Conquered Her Memory Slip Related to Traveling on the Subway

---

Rose, a 73-year-old lady who was recently diagnosed with MCI, consistently found herself on the wrong side of the subway platform, heading west instead of east. This happened a lot. Each time it happened, she felt very distressed. It was not the extra trip up the escalator and over to the other side that bothered her. Rather, it was the fact that it happened, again and again, that really bothered her. We taught her a very simple strategy to help her remember her intention to get on the east platform. Before leaving the house to catch the subway, she had to stop, see herself in her mind's eye looking up at the platform sign marked east, and say to herself "I am going to the east platform." This little strategy is called "see it and say it" and it really can help you focus on and remember your intentions. It sure worked for Rose. She tried it with great success and consistently uses the strategy. She has not made that particular mistake since.

As a little preview to what you will learn in chapter 15, we have provided in Box 9.5 a true story of how the application of a new memory skill can really help with a bothersome everyday memory slip.

We are telling you about Rose because having some success with implementing a memory strategy can be a real confidence booster. Once you learn how to use a memory strategy to succeed with a particular memory situation, you can more easily apply it to other situations.

Self-efficacy and changing memory behavior

As we described earlier in this chapter, self-efficacy is your belief in your ability to accomplish something. There is a large field of study focusing on the power of self-efficacy to promote your success at accomplishing tasks at hand. It is commonly accepted in the field of cognitive rehabilitation that a key ingredient to someone changing their behavior (by using a particular memory strategy, for example) is an awareness of the problem. When it comes to having MCI, however, a recent research study showed that having a greater awareness of one's memory shortcomings was not a motivator in getting people with MCI to use cognitive strategies. In our view, it is a person's belief that there is a realistic possibility of success and a person's experience of success that are the critical ingredients here. In other words, the combination of believing a strategy will work and implementing a strategy that does work together constitute the important motivator for behavior change in people with or without MCI when it comes to using a memory strategy. In Box 9.6, Rose learned a strategy, experienced success, and now has a sense of self-efficacy when navigating the subway platform. A little change in approach to a task really can make a difference.

Memory routines can also act like a buffer to the impact that daily hassles, like a particularly busy day or having to deal with something unpleasant, can have on your mood and perceived stress level. Implementing a good strategy will minimize the chances you will make a memory slip even if you are having a bad day, because you're tired, worried, in a bad mood, or whatever. A good memory routine is like a good friend. You can count on it.

Box 9.6 Evaluating the Benefits and Costs of Making a behavior Change

---

Write down what behavior you are considering changing (be specific):

I'm not very physically active, and I'd like to change that because I've read about the many benefits of exercise to health.

	Changing	Not Changing
Benefits	*My heart health will be better and I will likely feel and look better. Losing a little weight would be good also.*	*I will have extra time in my day to do activities I like better than exercise, such as reading the newspaper.*
Costs	*It takes time away from other activities. I'll probably feel grumpy about doing it sometimes.*	*My blood pressure is on the verge of needing medication. If I don't exercise more regularly I may develop high blood pressure.*

A FINAL WORD

If changing behavior was easy, then we would all be perfect. It's not easy to make a change and then sustain it. That does not mean it is outside our reach, though. We would encourage you to think about the personal consequences of changing and of not changing. It can be overwhelming if you try to tackle too many changes at once, so just pick one thing you feel would benefit your health and well-being. What you would like to focus on may become even clearer when you read section three of this book, which addresses how to improve prognosis in MCI. Use the table in Box 9.6 (the basis of which is borrowed from the literature on motivational interviewing) as a tool to help you reflect on the benefits and costs associated with change. You may want to change your behavior as it relates to your sleep habits, coping style, diet practices, or leisure activities. If you find the risks associated with change to be preferable to the risks associated with not changing, then it is our hope that this chapter and the remainder of this book will motivate and guide you toward achieving your optimal health.

Box 9.7 Questions to Ask Your Doctor

---

1. If you have concerns about your mood or level of stress, ask if your doctor can conduct a screen to see if any follow-up is recommended.
2. As recommended in chapter 8, if you are unable to achieve a positive mood, ask about treatment options.
3. Are there any community resources for reducing stress via exercise, meditation, or support groups?

RECOMMENDED READINGS

Edwards, P., Lhotsky, M., & Turner, J. (1999). *The healthy boomer: A no-nonsense midlife health guide for women and men.* Toronto, Canada: McClelland & Stewart.

Sapolsky, Robert M. (2004). *Why zebras don't get ulcers* (3rd ed.). New York: Henry Holt and Company.

Davis, M., Eshelman, E. R., & Fanning, P. (2008). *The relaxation and stress reduction workbook* (6th ed.). Oakland, CA: New Harbinger Publications.

Please also see the recommended readings listed at the end of chapter 8,

10

Taking Charge of Mild Cognitive Impairment

"Hope for the best, but prepare for the worst," they say. As a person living with mild cognitive impairment (MCI) what could the future hold for you? In chapter 4 we discussed the three possible outcomes for someone diagnosed with MCI: for some people, their MCI reverts back to normal aging, for others their symptoms stay stable, and for others their MCI progresses to dementia. It is not possible to predict what the future holds for you, but that does not mean you have to sit idly by and let it happen. You can be an active participant and take charge of MCI to maintain your health and wellness for as long as possible as you continue to age. This chapter covers ways in which you can take charge of your future. To help you do this we have chosen to focus on the following four topics: the potential impact of MCI on driving; considerations of current and future levels of support and how these considerations may influence how and where you live; legal matters; and approaches for getting the information you need to make decisions about these issues. Although this is not an exhaustive list of all the things you may want to consider as you plan for the future, we hope it provides you with a good foundation to start. Although most people tend not to concern themselves with such matters when they are younger, the content of this chapter is really applicable to *all* adults, not just to those living with MCI.

DRIVING

In chapter 8 we told you that most people with MCI are safe to drive. Having MCI, however, does mean that you should pay attention to your driving behaviors, because many people with MCI exhibit subtle changes that show their skills are just not as "optimal" as they once were. Knowing the rules of the road and how to operate a motor vehicle are not what is at issue here, because those things are unlikely to change with MCI. Rather, it is whether there has been cognitive change in terms of how good you are at keeping track of and responding to multiple sources of information. These skills are required in situations such as the following: (a) being able to quickly respond to unpredictable changes and track movements of other vehicles, cyclists, and pedestrians; (b) being able to effectively pay attention to driving while following directions at the same time; and, (c) being able to override automatic responses when necessary—for example, not driving through a green light when a pedestrian is crossing illegally, when a road crew is present, or when an emergency vehicle is approaching the intersection.

You may not be the best judge of your own driving skills for two reasons First, if being able to drive is really important to you, then it is probably hard to imagine life without driving and the loss of independence and freedom you might experience if you stopped. As a result, even if you did notice some changes in your cognitive skills that are required to drive safely, you may not pursue having your driving evaluated. Perhaps because you are unsure how to go about doing this or maybe you are too busy. Second, if you are experiencing some cognitive decline, you may not be completely aware of changes that affect driving such as those described in the previous paragraph. You may also not remember how often you experience some of the warning signs (described later in this section) that indicate your driving skills have declined. It can be helpful to ask someone close to you whether they have any concerns about your driving and about being a passenger in your car. If they express concerns, then we recommend you discuss the warning signs outlined in Box 10.1 with this person or with others who know you well, and we recommend that you seriously consider having your driving formally evaluated.

Evaluating Whether to Retire from Driving

Warning signs

We need to be aware of changes in ourselves that might indicate we need to make some adjustments to our driving habits. One of the most robust and striking cognitive differences between younger and older adults is reaction speed. As we age we are just not as fast to react to situations, but that does not necessarily make us poorer drivers. In addition to our reaction speed, there are other common changes as we age that can impact our driving ability. You might also find you need glasses to see in the distance or that the head-lights from oncoming cars bother your eyes. Adjusting to these changes is important and demonstrates our awareness of the need to modify our driving habits. An excellent Web site to help older adults evaluate their driving skills is http://www.mto.gov.on.ca/eng-lish/pubs/seniors-guide/part2.shtml, from the Ontario Ministry of Transportation. Box 10.1 includes the checklist of driving warning signs adapted from this Web site.

If you find that you are answering yes to any of the questions in Box 10.1, then you should consider discussing this with someone you trust and determine what actions you need to take in order to keep driving safely. These actions might include restricting your driving a bit, perhaps to familiar routes or to certain times of day (for example, off peak times or during daylight hours) or taking a driving course to renew good driving habits. There are driver improvement programs for older adults and defensive driving programs for adults of any age. Later on in this chapter, we will talk about approaches to accessing resources in your community. Another option is to sched-ule a formal driving evaluation to reassure yourself (and others) that you are safe to drive. This is not about knowing the rules of the road; passing a written exam about the rules of the road does not mean you are safe to drive. If you believe that you may not be able to pass a road test, then maybe you should consider voluntarily retiring from driving on your own terms without pursuing a formal evaluation.

Formal driving evaluation

Depending on where you live, you can have your driving evaluated by a government agency or by a privately run company. Evaluating

---

Box 10.1 Warning Signs That You Should Consider Retiring from Driving.

- Am I in an increasing number of near collisions?

- Have I been directly involved in minor collisions?

- Do I have difficulty driving through intersections, judging distance, or seeing pedestrians, road signs, or other vehicles?

- Do I have difficulty concentrating while driving?

- Am I getting lost or disoriented on familiar roads?

- Do I have difficulty coordinating hand and foot movements?

- Do I have vision problems, especially at night?

- Am I nervous behind the wheel?

- Are other motorists frequently honking at me?

- Do family members express concern about my driving ability?

Adapted with permission http://www.mto.gov.on.ca/english/pubs/seniors-guide/part2.shtml.

---

driving skills used to be the sole domain of the provincial or state government agency granting drivers' licenses, such as a Ministry of Transportation or Division of Motor Vehicles. However, there are now many private companies providing assessments of driving skills for people who have a medical condition that may compromise their ability to safely drive. Many of these companies have formal agreements with the government agencies requiring them to report to the government agency any problems identified with your driving. If the company evaluating you has an agreement like this, you are supposed to be informed about it. Ask if you are not clear on the possible outcomes associated with the evaluation.

You can expect these formal evaluations to include a vision test, possibly some tests examining visual attention using a computer screen (no computer skills are required), and a road test on either a closed course or a public roadway. There may be two people in the car with you during this road test, the driving examiner and an *occupational therapist* (a health-care professional whose training encompasses the evaluation of how medical conditions affect day-to-day living skills such as driving). The occupational therapist can ensure that supports are in place to optimize your ability to physically operate the test vehicle.

If you are feeling really anxious about taking a driving evaluation, then it is a good idea to prepare with a lesson or two to restore your confidence. Some of these private companies may offer driving lessons, and they may also allow you to practice the driving route and to practice in the car that will be used for the test if it is not your own.

Cost of driving

If you are undecided about whether you are ready to retire from driving, you may want to look at some of the other factors that could influence this decision. You may find that when you consider what it costs you to own and operate a car, it might make financial sense for you to give up driving. In Box 10.2 we break down the average yearly cost of owning and operating a small sedan based on driving it about 15,000 miles or 18,000 kilometres per year. These numbers are estimates, of course, and your exact expenses may be higher or lower, depending on the cost and fuel efficiency of your car and how much you drive it. When you see this, you may find that you could get around using some combination of taxi, public transit, and rides from family and friends, and save a lot of money.

Alternative resources for transportation

If you have hung up the keys to the car, then you need to figure out how else you're going to get around. You do not want this change to prevent you from participating in the activities you normally do. Here are some things you might consider in evaluating your options. First, examine your former driving habits and make a list of all the places you would typically drive to over the course of a week and how often you went to each place. Note the distance to each place and also try and figure out how often you really need to be able to travel to each of these places. Work out whether you could make a set routine or schedule for some of your activities (such as grocery day, movie night, going to an exercise class, the racetrack, or a book club). Having a routine

Box 10.2 Costs of Driving a Small Sedan Based on 2011 Statistics from the American Automotive Association (AAA) and the Canadian Automotive Association (CAA).[1]

Yearly Driving Cost	AAA (15, 000 miles)	CAA (18, 000 kilometres)
Gasoline (taxes added if in Canada)	$1,508	$1,818
Maintenance & Tires	$717	$828
Insurance	$951	$1,913
Licence & Registration (taxes added if in USA)	$438	$112
Loan Finance Charges	$584	$699
Depreciation	$2,560	$3,515
Total	$6,758	$8,885

1 Estimates based on information from the Web sites of the American Automotive Association and the Canadian Automotive Association. Retrieved on November 14, 2011 from www.aaa.com and www.caa.ca

might make it easier for you to organize some regular transportation by taxi or bus or maybe by getting a ride with family or friends with whom you could do the activity. In some communities, there are driving services for older adults to take them to medical appointments and other appointments for a small fee or free of charge. Ask at your local senior's center, community center, or library about whether any of these services are available where you live. If a bad-weather day makes you uncomfortable about taking public transit, then consider allowing yourself a taxi on those days so that you don't miss out on your planned activity. You may also find that you can get some things such as groceries or medications delivered in your community. Finally, you may also want to consider whether you would want to or could move to a location with more amenities within a shorter distance from your home, perhaps even within walking distance.

Giving up your driver's licence

For many older adults the loss of their licence is a devastating blow. This can be particularly true when this decision has been imposed on them through actions taken by their family, their doctor, or because they failed a formal driving evaluation. It can still be a blow, even when the decision is voluntary. Even if other transportation options are readily available or if some money will be saved, for some, nothing can really compensate for this change in independence. People need to have this change and their feelings about it acknowledged, and they need to be able to grieve this loss. If you are having trouble dealing with your feelings about losing your driver's license, you may wish to talk to your doctor, who may be able to help you or refer you to someone who can. You could also speak with others who have experienced this and find out how they have managed to cope with the change. The final section in this chapter will provide you with recommendations on how to access resources that might enable you to do this.

PLANNING FOR CURRENT AND FUTURE SUPPORT NEEDS

If you or your family member has been diagnosed with MCI, what does this mean in terms of planning for the future? Sometimes it's easier to envision how a physical-health problem requires support, such as a bad back leading to hiring a snow-removal or lawn-care service or help with home maintenance. As illustrated in Box 10.3 and also in Box 10.4, it can sometimes be less obvious how the cognitive changes experienced in MCI require support.

A little bit of support when it comes to cognitive changes due to MCI can make a big difference to your ability to maintain your independence. Often, it is not about needing support all the time, but just once in awhile so you can get a bit of a breather to carry on with those daily activities that require some planning, such as in the example presented in Box 10.4.

Optimizing Your Living Arrangements

The environment in which one chooses to live—whether this is in one's own house or apartment or in a more supportive living environment, such as a retirement residence—has a direct impact on effectively living with MCI. This is because different housing options

---

Box 10.3 Case Vignette of a Couple Who Turn Over Management
of Their Tax Returns

Asmita is a 68-year-old retired chartered accountant who was diagnosed with MCI last year. She loves math, loves budgets, and has
always managed her immediate and extended family's tax returns.
When she retired, she gently extricated herself from managing her
extended family's taxes, but she continued to do her own and her
husband's and those of their two sons. Her husband Harilos has
doubts about whether she should be doing this anymore, particularly because they all have very complex tax returns. He noticed his
wife is taking longer than usual to sort everything out each year and
that it is stressing her out, even though she would never admit it. She
has not made any mistakes that he knows of, but he would rather
she turned things over to another professional. Harilos expressed his
concerns to Asmita and, fortunately, she readily agreed. She even
seemed relieved. Although they recognized that doing activities to
keep mentally active was important, they also knew that these should
be fun rather than stressful, and there shouldn't be any "high stakes"
for errors. Now, neither of them is stressed at tax time because they
have hired a professional accountant to take care of their taxes.

---

offer different opportunities and possibly challenges to engaging in
activities that can improve prognosis, such as eating healthy food and
participating in physical and social activities.

Aging in Place

You may have heard the phrase "aging in place." This phrase is generally thought to mean staying in your own home for as long as possible, irrespective of the level of support you might require. The idea is
to support people remaining in their homes for as long as possible by
bringing in necessary supports, such as community home care and
nursing supports, until such time as nursing home care (long-term
care) is the best or only option. There have been programs in some
parts of Canada and the United States promoting aging-in-place ini-
tiatives with mixed results in terms of whether such promotions are
effectively addressing the needs of older adults. The politics of this is

---

Box 10.4 Case Vignette of a Mother with MCI and Her Daughter

Aga, who is 83 years old, was identified as having MCI a couple of years ago. She lives in a spacious condo, and four years ago her 60-year-old divorced daughter Eada came to live with her. Unlike her mother, Eada has never been much of a cook. Aga loves to cook and has always prepared the evening meal, but she finds the whole process of planning and executing a meal to her former gourmet standards more of an effort than it used to be. Eada noticed her mom was struggling, and together they came up with some solutions. Every Sunday they plan the meals for the week, and Aga cooks three meals, Eada cooks one, and the remaining three meals are designated take-out nights. They also organize the meal schedule so that Aga never has to cook two nights in a row. Aga now has more time and is free from the burden of planning and making all the meals. Having the extra time has renewed her interest in cooking and she signed up for an Italian cooking class at the local community centre. She enjoys the meal planning with Eada and has hopes now of making something of a cook of her daughter.

---

not something we will get into in this book. We would like to be clear, however, that when we discuss aging in place, we are referring to living arrangements that promote living as independently as possible in the community, that is, outside a nursing home. This means you can age in place even if you move from your own home to a more supportive living environment.

The important consideration is whether your living environment promotes your ability to engage in behaviors that could potentially improve prognosis. In other words, does it promote your safety, access to medical treatment, your ability to eat well, and to participate in leisure activities that are important for your cognitive and physical health? In evaluating this, you need to think of several factors, such as what is important to you, your values, what supports your family and friends can provide, what supports are available in your community, what you can afford, and how much time you have before you need to start making some decisions.

Staying put or moving

For now, you may choose to stay where you are and continue living your current lifestyle. For your memory, there are some benefits
to staying put, because a familiar environment supports remembering where things are and how to carry out daily tasks. For example,
you know where the coffee is and how to make the coffee using your
own coffee maker, but figuring out how to make the coffee at your
daughter's place may be more difficult. (This is because a familiar
environment promotes our ability to remember how to do things).
Regardless of whether you stay put or make a move, you may also
choose to make a few changes to your current living environment
such as adapting your home in ways to make it safer. For example,
you might reduce your risk of falling by removing small rugs/mats on
the floor that pose tripping hazards or by installing grab bars in the
bathroom. If you are unsure of how you could make your home safer,
an occupational therapist can do an evaluation of the living environment and make recommendations in relation to your needs.

People may choose to move for many reasons. Sometimes it is to
downsize from a house to an apartment or condo to reduce home-
maintenance responsibilities. Often folks move because they want to
be closer to amenities or family, or to belong to a community that
affords opportunity to meet others with similar interests. As a person
with MCI, as time goes by you may require more help with organizing a move and adjusting to a new living environment. Thus, if living
in a different place is something you have already considered for your
future, you may want to do this early on in the course of your MCI,
before any possible future declines make such a move more difficult
to manage.

Living with Assistance

Whether you are staying put or moving to a different residence, it is
a prudent idea to plan for what you would do if you required more
support. You need to figure out what's available that is acceptable to
you and within your budget. It is good, too, to have discussions with
close family or friends so that they may better understand your opinions on the subject and perhaps can assist you in troubleshooting

some acceptable solutions in the short term and in the long term. Some of these needs can be anticipated in advance, such as needing help arranging transportation, cooking, managing appointments, paying bills, or taking medications. Think about whether you are starting to experience the need for some assistance with the activities just described. Think also about what could be changed about your current living situation that would enable you to better meet these kinds of challenges.

Domestic/personal care supports in the home

One way to receive needed support is to consider having others come to your home to assist you with more complex or challenging activities. Sometimes family or friends may pitch in to help you with shopping, meals, and medication and schedule management. This type of assistance may also be available through services in your community or from private sources, such as a private companion. For example, you may have a personal support worker from the community come to your home to help you with bathing if you have difficulty getting into or out of the tub. You may hire someone to help you with house cleaning or meal preparation. Often, people feel more secure about living alone if they have an emergency response system that they can activate to send emergency services to their door if the need arises. These types of supports may also be included in supportive living environments (described next).

Supportive living environments

Supportive living environments range from retirement residences, which are paid for by the occupants, to long-term care facilities, which typically have some government funding and oversight (often in addition to occupant fees) and are utilized when community services can no longer support "aging in place" (described earlier in this chapter). Many retirement residences offer a spectrum of services and living arrangements that can be modified with the changing needs of the resident. For example, accommodations can range from apartment units to shared rooms. Furthermore, people can opt in for various levels of services related to meals, housekeeping, laundry, assistance with managing medication, and personal care. The level of support can be low, such as reminders to refill prescriptions, or higher, such as providing assistance with dispensing medications. Indeed some retirement residences have long-term care facilities (nursing home) on the same site, which means residents do not have to make a big move if they eventually require more care. This can also make a big difference to spouses being able to continue to remain together even when one requires more significant nursing care.

Likely, none of us would consider a nursing home to be a desirable way in which to spend our remaining years, regardless of whether we could afford the best that money could buy, unless it became absolutely necessary. Generally, people who require 24-hour nursing care do so because they have significant physical and/or cognitive difficulties that require specialized nursing care and daily personal care. Just because you are aging and are dealing with MCI does not mean there is a nursing home in your future. It is important, though, to start making plans, and this advice applies to all adults, regardless of whether you have MCI. If it became difficult for you to manage all the decision-making associated with your health or finances, then it is wise to take steps to ensure that any decisions made on your behalf best reflect your own wishes.

LEGAL MATTERS

Putting your affairs in order is not something reserved for older adults. Rather, it is something all adults should attend to regardless of their age or their health status. Often, though, we put this sort of thing off, and then, when faced with health problems or memory changes, we realize that we should make some decisions about how we would like someone else to make choices on our behalf if we became unable to do so in the future. A good start is to discuss your finances and potential health needs as an aging adult with a trusted family member or friend. We will present you with some very basic information. We encourage you to seek professional legal advice if you decide to pursue assigning a "power of attorney" or making a "will," which are explained next. Facing these issues when you are capable of directing your affairs will ensure adherence to your decisions and wishes, which also takes the pressure off close family and friends.

Power of Attorney

Your power of attorney (POA) is a person you designate to make decisions on your behalf if you are unable to do so. This person could be required to make decisions about your medical care, safety, and living arrangements (personal care) or about what to do with your property and finances. Depending on your jurisdiction (province or state), you may be able to assign more than one person to these types of roles. In other words, you can assign one person to make decisions about your personal care and a different person to make decisions about your property and finances. For example, you might decide your sister knows your wishes best about your personal care, but your cousin is better able to deal with decisions related to your property and finances. If your jurisdiction permits and you do split up the POA duties, then it is important that those you assign are able to work together. It is also not a bad idea to designate some back-up people should your first choice or choices for POA themselves become unable to carry out this role for you for some reason. People often worry that assigning certain persons to these roles may create conflict within the family. In efforts to avoid conflict, it may be helpful to explain the reasons for your choices to family, to assign more than one person to the role, to assign someone who is not a family member, or to specify that all family members must be kept informed and provided with the details associated with any decisions made on your behalf by your POA.

Personal care

Your power of attorney (POA) for personal care should be a person or persons with whom you have a trusting relationship. Again, you may assign more than one person to this task, in which case they would work together on your behalf. Although difficult, it is very important to have a discussion about your wishes in any personal care situation in which you cannot make decisions for yourself. These personal care situations may involve decisions about medical treatment, what type of care facility or location you would want to be in, and what type of personal assistance you would prefer if you required help with your mobility, with eating, or any personal grooming activity, such as bathing and dressing.

One example regarding medical treatment might be your wishes in the event you were gravely ill with no hope of recovery. Would you want every effort to be made to resuscitate you if you stopped breathing? Would you want to be put on life support? You may wish to be cared for in your own home for as long as your finances allow this to be a safe option for you. If you do need to go to a care facility, then you may want one that meets certain standards of care, possibly has extra care options, is in a particular location, or serves a particular type of patient. For example, you may want a location that is as close as possible to your relatives. You may want to live in a care facility where the other residents are similar in age to yourself. If you were reasonably independent in terms of your mobility (walking on your own or with the assistance of a walker or able to drive or wheel your own wheelchair) then you might not want to be in a care facility in which most of the other patients could not get around on their own.

Decisions around personal assistance may relate to such things as food, hygiene, clothing, and even recreational activities, for example, what you like to wear, how you like your hair cut, your favorite foods, music and past times. Making your preferences known is critical to providing you with the best quality environment during your illness. This will help ensure that your power of attorney for personal care can advocate for you and make decisions on your behalf that are closely aligned to what you would have chosen for yourself.

Property and finances

Your power of attorney (POA) for property and finances may be the same person or persons you assigned for your personal care or it may be someone else. You will want to assign someone you can trust to act in your best interests, to act responsibly, protect your privacy, and to be capable of handling financial matters. Like the POA for personal care, this role, too, can require a lot of work, and you will want to ensure those responsible are willing to put time into the role should it become necessary for them to do so. For example, this person would need to manage your bank accounts, pay your bills, make sure your taxes were prepared and filed, and be required to make decisions about whether to buy or sell property on your behalf. You would want to choose someone you were certain would not abuse this trust, particularly given it is your property resources that will likely be used to provide for your living arrangements and care. You want to make certain this person can do a good job so your property and financial possessions can support you for as long as you need. Some banking institutions have their own forms they want to have filled in to allow access to your bank account, and you may wish to inquire about this to facilitate the ability of your POA to do his or her job should it become necessary for them to do so in the future.

A Legal Will

A will is a legal record of your wishes to be carried out in the event of your death. Generally your will includes instructions about to whom your money and property (personal possessions and land) are to be divided, the name or names of people who are to care for any of your dependents (children or other persons for whom you are responsible), and the name of the person you appoint as your executor. Your executor ensures the instructions left in your will are properly carried out. This person could be a family member, your lawyer, or your financial advisor for example. You may also draft something called a *living will*, which is a document that contains information about your wishes concerning your personal care should you become ill and no longer able to make these decisions for yourself. A living will may or may not contain specific information about whom you would name as your power of attorney for your personal care. A living will and power of attorney apply only when you are alive and your will applies only when you die. In Box 10.5 we provide a brief review of the general definitions of each of these legal terms.

Resources for Designating Power of Attorney and Making a Will

To designate a power of attorney or to create your will, most people will turn to a lawyer, who has the expertise to know all the steps that

Box. 10.5 General Definitions of Legal Terms Related to Power of Attorney and Wills.

Power of Attorney (POA): Person or persons who make decisions on your behalf because illness or absence makes you unable to do so.

1. *POA for personal care*: makes decision on your behalf regarding your medical treatment, safe living arrangements (place of care), and any personal assistance you require (food, clothing, leisure activities, hygiene).
2. *POA for property and finances*: makes decisions on your behalf regarding your finances and property (personal possessions and land).

A situation not involving illness, but rather your absence, is also one in which you might appoint a POA.

Will: a legal document that comes into effect on your death and specifies how your money and property (personal possessions and land) are to be divided among the recipients you designate, how anyone dependent on you for care will be provided for, and it names the person who will carry out your instructions.

Living will: a legal document that comes into effect while you are living and no longer capable of making decisions about your personal care. It contains instructions from you about how you would like to be cared for.

are needed. In order to prepare for a meeting with a lawyer, your first step might be to gather more information. You can search the Internet for information, and we would encourage you to sample several different Web sites as you gather knowledge and information. Just because the information is on the Internet does not mean it is always accurate or applicable to the legal jurisdiction in which you live. You may also wish to look for information at your local library, in bookstores, or through provincial or state government agencies. This is all good preparation so that you will know what questions to ask if you take the next step of getting a lawyer to prepare official documents for you. Some people prefer to skip the legal fees and prepare these documents themselves, despite the fact that they may miss some steps or leave something less complete. Forms to work from to create these documents are available from the information sources just listed (e.g., bookstores, government agencies, and the Internet); however, we would advocate for getting advice from a legal professional, who knows the rules and regulations of law for your province or state, to ensure nothing important has been missed. It is always helpful to ask friends and family about whether they know of a good lawyer in your community. Those close to us may also be willing to share their own experiences in dealing with the issues of assigning a power of attorney and crafting a will and can tell you about what considerations helped guide their decisions. If you are concerned that someone may challenge your decisions in designating your power of attorney or in making your will, then you could ask for a report, possibly obtained through your doctor, confirming your capacity to make these decisions.

HOW TO ACCESS INFORMATION AND RESOURCES

Throughout this chapter and all the chapters in this book we have included recommendations about where to find resources for further information about the topic or topics being discussed. We hope you find this helpful; however, we recognize that it's one thing to know *where* to access information and it's a totally different thing to know *how* to access information. In the final section of this chapter you will be provided with some practical information about how to identify what it is you want to know, how to find the information, and then how to take action. The idea is for you to be able to come back to this section and use it as a guide to help you navigate around getting the resource you need. In Box 10.6 we provide you with some examples to illustrate what we mean.

Identifying and Finding What You Want to Know

As you can see from the examples in Box 10.6, it is helpful if you begin your search for resources by being specific about what it is you want

Box 10.6 Examples of How to Be Specific about What You Want to Know, How to Find Out, and How to Take Action to Get Access to the Resource You Need.

What you want to know	How to find out	How to take action
You want to find out how to better control your blood sugars because your doctor says you are at risk of getting diabetes.	You remember you have a friend with diabetes so you ask them. Your friend tells you about a free program for seniors at the local hospital for people who want to prevent or better manage their diabetes.	You call the hospital, ask about the diabetes program for seniors, and enrol in the program. Now, you've take the first step toward achieving your goal of preventing diabetes.
You are concerned about your driving because you just had a fender bender and it was your fault.	You think you may be overreacting and ask your daughter for advice. She thinks you should get a professional opinion and helps you look up a reputable driving instructor who can give you some lessons to improve.	You call the driving instructor your daughter helped you find and book two lessons. Now you've taken the first step in finding out if your driving habits can be improved.
You need help organizing your move to a smaller home because you are feeling overwhelmed about trying to decide what to keep and what to give away.	You go to the library and ask the librarian if there are any books on the subject. She helps you find a book called *Downsizing: Tips from the Pros* and you learn that many moving companies offer services to help people make these organizational decisions.	You call a few moving companies listed in your phone directory and find out which ones offer the services of a moving organizer and their rates. Now, you've taken the first step toward finding an organizer. Next, you pick one and book their services.

(*continued*)

Box 10.6 (Continued)

What you want to know	How to find out	How to take action
You decide you want to make a will because you watched a TV program about how much distress it can cause families when someone passes away without leaving instructions for those who inherit their estate.	You decide to ask your neighbor who is a real estate agent and may know someone. Your neighbor tells you about three firms in town that she has heard are reputable.	You write down the names of the firms in your notebook. Now, you've taken the first step toward finding a lawyer. You decide to look up each firm, call, and ask their rates. You've already decided to go with the firm with the best rate, because you know they are reputable.

to know and why you want to know about it. This will help you figure out how to look for the information you need. Keep these examples in mind when you review our breakdown of the steps involved in locating the resources you need by helping you specify what it is you want to look for and providing you with some tips about how to find it (see Box 10.7). We would suggest that you keep a notebook to jot down what you want to know, why you want to know it, and track the results of your searching until you find all the information you require to act on what you have learned.

How to Act on What You Have Learned

We previously provided you with four examples in Box 10.6 to illustrate how you might go about taking action to access the resources you have identified. It may seem relatively straightforward when you review the examples; however, there could be barriers to your ability to access the resource or service you have discovered. For example, if the language the service is provided in is not your first language, this could be a problem for you when trying to understand all your options, such as when making a legal will. Another barrier could be that you find that the resource you would like to access is just too costly, or maybe it is difficult for you to find transportation to the resource. These barriers may require you to go back and repeat the process outlined in Box 10.7. Consider the first example presented in Box 10.6 about wanting to control your blood sugars better. What if you were having trouble arranging transportation to the hospital program for diabetes? Perhaps you want to find transportation to the hospital that does not involve taking the bus, because the bus route is long and the times inconvenient, and that doesn't involve you driving, because the parking cost is really high. How do you find transportation? You ask at your local seniors' center and find out there is

---

Box 10.7 Finding Resources by Identifying What to Look for and How to Look for It.

Identify What to Look For

- Write down exactly what you want to know and be specific.
- Write down why you want to know the information and be specific.
- Think about what category the information you want falls into (e.g., legal, health, transportation). If unsure, pick something close, because this can help you get started.

Know How to Look

- Ask family and friends.
- Go ask at your local library or community center.
- Look up services in the phone directory.
- Surf the Internet for directory information and Web sites, but be cautious about what you find.
- Gather printed materials such as newspaper, magazines, pamphlets, and community guides.
- Ask one of your health-care providers such as your doctor, community nurse, or social worker.
- Goverment agencies—municipal, provincial, and so forth, which you may be listed in the telephone book and also on the Internet.

a service that will drive seniors to health appointments for a small fee. Now you've found a solution to the transportation barrier and can access the resource, which is the program on diabetes. What if the solution isn't so neat, though, and you must chose between the costly parking, the lengthy bus ride, or simply not going? In exploring your options, you could consider attending the first day and ask about whether you could strategically miss some sessions, given your transportation situation, and about how you could acquire reading material in order to keep up with the other program participants with respect to the sessions you miss. Don't give up if you believe the resource is important to you. Revisit Box 10.7 as a guideline to help you determine next steps and enlist the help of others in finding a solution.

A FINAL WORD

Now you know about the future issues you might possibly face with respect to retiring from driving, living where you are happy and safe, and planning for your health in the long-term. You also know how to identify and access information that could be helpful to you in tackling these issues. You are in a good position to take action to better manage your health and your future as a person living with MCI, and we hope this chapter provides some practical guidance. In the final section of our book we are going to outline in detail the lifestyle choices you can consider in your efforts to prevent or delay progression of your symptoms of cognitive decline.

Box 10.8 Questions to Ask your Doctor

---

1. What do you look for in evaluating driving safety in your patients?
2. What should I be looking out for as signs that I should be concerned about my own driving safety?
3. If my MCI gets worse, how will we know if or when it is time to hang up my car keys?

(continued)

Box 10.8 (Continued)

---

4. Are there any organizations in the community where I can have a driving assessment or brush up on my driving skills?

5. Do you have access to resources that would help evaluate my safety at home?

6. What are the signs I should be looking for that would suggest I should make the move to a more supportive living environment?

7. Who should I consider appointing as my power of attorney (if your doctor knows you well)?

RECOMMENDED READING

Collins, J., & Warner, J. (2009). *Next steps: A practical guide to planning the best half of your life.* Fresno, CA: Linden Publishing Inc.

Driscoll, M. (2002). *The complete idiot's guide to long term care planning.* New York: Penguin Group (USA) Inc.

WHAT CAN BE DONE TO IMPROVE PROGNOSIS?

11

Healthy Diet: Feed Your Body, Fuel Your Brain

"You are what you eat" is a saying many of us have heard, but perhaps have failed to fully appreciate. In this chapter, we will tell you about how your diet can directly and indirectly influence your cognitive health. If we've done a good job, then you should finish this chapter with the realization that healthy eating is; (a) a means of controlling the risk factors for cardiovascular disease and dementia, (b) a way to optimize your cognitive functioning, and (c) not rocket science; in other words, it's achievable. You will also understand how diet has both direct and indirect (via improved physical health) effects on your cognitive health, as shown in Box 11.1.

Box 11.1 The Direct and Indirect Influences of Diet on Cognitive Health

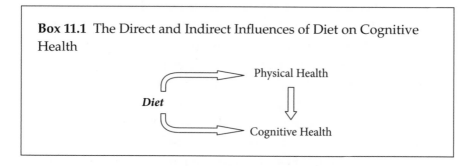

It is important from the outset to realize that, in using the term *diet*, we are referring to what you eat and not being *on a diet or dieting* for the specific purpose of influencing body weight. Healthy eating

does not mean "dieting"; it means eating good food that benefits heart health and, by association, brain health.

DIET PRACTICES AND DEMENTIA RISK IN OLDER ADULTS

In recent years a large number of epidemiological studies examining the influence of dietary practices on cognition and dementia risk in older adults have emerged. These studies examining the influence of dietary practice are either *prospective*, studying the same groups over time, or *cross-sectional*, comparing data from different groups across ages, who are distinguished primarily by differences in diet. The consensus, based on the results of these studies, is diets that are high in fruits, vegetables, and whole grains and low in saturated fats are associated with a number of cognitive benefits. These include better cognitive performance, lower rates of cognitive decline, and reduced risk of dementia among older adults. The limitations of these studies have to do with the fact that they are observational, and often it is difficult to control for other potential influential factors, such as level of physical activity and level of social and cognitive engagement. As you will read in subsequent chapters, these other factors are also independently associated with reduced dementia risk.

The cognitive benefits of a healthy diet, as opposed to an unhealthy diet, are supported by research studies. A healthy diet, also referred to as a *prudent diet, is a* diet high in fruits, vegetables, and whole grains; low in saturated fats; and including consumption of fish. A healthy or prudent diet can be described in many ways; it just means eating in a way that is consistent with diet patterns considered to be healthy. You may have heard about the Mediterranean diet (see Box 11.2 for a description), and this is one example of a healthy diet. It is one of many ways to follow the food-guide recommendations you will read about later on in this chapter. An unhealthy diet, often referred to as the *Western diet*, is a diet high in saturated fat, primarily from meat and packaged foods such as pastries and cookies, and low in intake of fruits and vegetables. In animal studies, a healthy diet has been associated with better learning of food locations in a maze and less *neuronal* (brain cell) damage. Unlike people, nonhuman animals can be randomly assigned to different diet conditions (healthy versus nonhealthy), which allows scientists

---

Box 11.2 The Mediterranean Diet is an Example of a Healthy Diet

---

- High consumption of a variety of plant-based foods such as vegetables, fruits, legumes, and whole grains (good source of protein, fiber, and complex carbohydrates)
- Olive oil (good source of monounsaturated fats).
- Fish (good source of omega-3 fatty acids).
- Wine (in moderation).
- Limited red meat and dairy (source of saturated fats).

---

to isolate the influence of the factor in question (in this case what is eaten) on the outcome measure being studied. This has prompted scientists to begin investigating the use of a healthy diet as a method of providing effective intervention and ultimately prevention of cognitive decline and dementia with age.

There are still only a handful of studies looking at the effects of diet on cognition in people, but a recent prospective study, involving individuals with mild cognitive impairment (MCI) who were followed over time, revealed reduced risk of progression from MCI to Alzheimer's type dementia among individuals who followed one type of healthy diet practice, the Mediterranean diet (see Box 11.2). This is a strong indication that diet can impact prognosis for people with MCI. In the next sections, we will try to explain just how diet can affect our cognitive health and provide you with the knowledge and tools to assist you in establishing, maintaining, or improving good dietary habits.

THE INFLUENCE OF DIET ON PHYSICAL HEALTH

There are several medical conditions, alone or in combination, that can be caused by or exacerbated by poor dietary practices. As part of the aging process, our bodies can become more susceptible to medical conditions, such as high cholesterol for example, and our diet can influence whether these conditions become severe enough alone or in combination to cause negative effects on our physical health. It is important to visit your doctor annually to assess for the presence of medical conditions such as high blood pressure, high cholesterol, and diabetes, because these conditions can often be "silent" and go undetected for some time, thereby increasing the possibility of serious health consequences.

Link between Diet and Heart Health

Cardiovascular disease, also called heart disease, increases your risk of heart attack and stroke. This condition is caused by *atherosclerosis*, a narrowing of the blood vessels (arteries and veins) due to build up of fatty substances in the blood. Research shows that diet can help you prevent, better manage, or even reverse conditions that lead to heart disease, namely high cholesterol (*hyperlipidemia*), high blood pressure (*hypertension*), and high blood sugar (*hyperglycemia*). Atherosclerosis makes it harder for the heart to circulate blood throughout the body, putting a strain on the circulatory system. This, in turn, affects optimal functioning of organs including the brain, due to inefficient transfer of glucose (food energy for cells) and oxygen necessary for optimal cell function. As mentioned in Chapter 4, this can lead to subtle ischemic brain changes (damage to brain cells resulting from inefficient blood flow) that may evolve into a vascular dementia or make Alzheimer's disease worse. In a more extreme form, if the blood vessels become severely or totally blocked, a heart attack or stroke can result.

The upside of healthy eating is that it allows you to control the risk factors for heart disease that you can change such as obesity, high blood pressure, high cholesterol, and high blood sugars. When at least three of these medical conditions or risk factors occur together, it is called *metabolic syndrome* (see Box 11.3 for details). Medication alone is not sufficient to optimally manage these risk factors. What we eat can work in conjunction with medications, and in some cases reduce the need for medication altogether, to significantly lower risk of heart attack or stroke.

Link between Diet and Diabetes

High blood sugar levels resulting from the inability of the body to either make or utilize the hormone insulin cause diabetes mellitus, or diabetes for short. As just indicated in Box 11.3, insulin regulates

---

Box 11.3 Metabolic Syndrome

Metabolic syndrome refers to a constellation of three or more of the medical conditions listed below. Recent research suggests that metabolic syndrome may be a better predictor of heart disease (and dementia risk) than any one of these medical conditions in isolation.

- *Hyperglycemia* (high blood sugars, fasting sugar at or greater than 100 milligrams/decilitre)
- *Dyslipidemia* (combination of fat content in the blood involving low good cholesterol, high bad cholesterol and high trigylcerides)
- *Hypertension* (high blood pressure, at or greater than 130/85)
- *Central obesity* (waist circumference greater than 100 cm or 40 inches for men and 88 cm or about 35 inches for women)
- *Insulin resistance* (condition in which insulin becomes less efficient at lowering blood sugars)

---

blood sugar levels. There are different types of diabetes, and the one of relevance for this chapter is called "type 2 diabetes." This is the type with adult onset, and poor diet and sedentary lifestyle contribute significantly to its development. Obesity is a common consequence of poor diet and inactivity. People with type 2 diabetes often have other risk factors for heart disease. For example, it is estimated that two out of three people with type 2 diabetes also have hypertension.

Type 2 diabetes is also strongly associated with cognitive decline and increased risk of Alzheimer's disease in older adults. Most importantly, evidence suggests that individuals with MCI and type 2 diabetes show increased risk for progression to dementia. The reason for this increased risk is that problems regulating insulin lead to amyloid accumulation in the brain (a marker of Alzheimer's type neuropathology reviewed in earlier chapters), *neuroinflammation* (a maladaptive inflammation of brain cells, described in more detail later), and *ischemia* (the blockage of blood vessels leading to stroke).

The good news is that it has been shown that improving dietary habits in older adults with type 2 diabetes can improve cognitive performance. Thus, healthy diet practices could be very important in reducing the risk of progression of MCI to dementia by preventing the development of type 2 diabetes or by promoting the management of this form of diabetes.

Link between Diet and Brain-Cell Function

Diet can also have a more direct influence on your cognitive health by virtue of the fact that what you eat can affect your brain's physiology. It is well established in the scientific literature that vitamins, minerals, and certain fatty acids are crucial to brain health. These nutrients perform critical functions related to neuronal development, repair, and communication.

In addition, these nutrients promote circulation and impede neuroinflammation. The role of nutrients in preventing neuroinflammation is particularly important because this is a process believed to trigger the development of neurodegenerative diseases like Alzheimer's disease. Inflammation of cells is an adaptive response to infection but can become chronic if the response is not properly controlled. Unnecessary inflammation occurs due to an imbalance in the transfer of oxygen between cells. Basically there are more oxygen-receiving (*oxidant*) and fewer oxygen-reducing (*antioxidant*) transfers going on, thus causing cell damage through oxidative stress. Antioxidants function to reduce oxidative stress or damage caused by *free radicals*, which are the metabolic waste products of cells in the body. They do this by adding an extra electron to the free radicals, neutralizing their oxidative properties, thereby preventing oxidative damage. This is an important function because oxidative damage in the body contributes to many health problems such as diabetes, heart disease, macular degeneration, cancer, and neurodegenerative diseases causing dementia, just to name a few. Our bodies produce some antioxidants and we can also get them from the foods we eat. You may have read or heard about foods that are rich in antioxidants or have anti-inflammatory properties, and we will tell you more about how to identify these kinds of foods as you read further on in the chapter.

Given the impact nutrients can have on brain health, it is not much of a leap to expect that they may impact cognition. Indeed there is a wealth of research attesting to cognitive deficiencies directly related to nutrient deficiencies. The link between low vitamin B (B12 in particular) and reduced memory ability, described as a reversible cause of memory decline in chapter 4, is a well-known example.

EVIDENCE LINKING SPECIFIC NUTRIENTS TO ENHANCED COGNITION

In the previous section, we mentioned that nutrient deficiencies have been linked to cognitive problems such as reduced thinking speed and poorer memory. However, to date there is no definitive evidence that supplementing one's otherwise normal diet with any one particular nutrient or even a certain combination of nutrients exerts a significant benefit on cognition. There have been a number of randomized control trials, in which participants are randomly assigned to receive either a particular nutrient pill or to receive a placebo pill that has no active ingredient. The two groups are then followed over time to see if one group shows an advantage over the other on the outcome measure (for example, a cognitive measure of thinking speed or memory ability). Although some of these trials have produced positive results, careful review of the literature indicates there is no one wonder nutrient. Indeed, in some studies extra intake of a particular nutrient that was believed to be beneficial actually had negative effects on health status! Rather than one particular nutrient pill, what is important seems to be the way that different nutrients act in combination in the variety of foods we eat. Eating a variety of foods containing combinations of nutrients is considered the best way to receive the benefits a healthy diet can have on physical and cognitive health.

Cause or Effect: The Relationship between Good Diet Practices and Cognitive Health

Does a healthy diet truly benefit cognition or is it the case that people with better cognitive abilities tend to eat a healthier diet? Scientists have tried to answer this question in several ways. One way is by trying to use statistics to control for potentially influential factors such as age, education, income, and activity level, before examining the impact of adherence to a healthy diet on cognition. Another way is to study dietary interventions and examine whether this has a positive impact on cognition. Unfortunately there are very few intervention studies to date in humans. It is much easier to control all these factors in mice or rats that live in a laboratory, and the bulk of the intervention research has been done with these types of animals. In these studies, random assignment to a healthy or unhealthy diet can be made and other living-experience variables can be strictly controlled. Results from these studies can be investigated to infer causality if they appear to support findings from studies with people looking at the impact of dietary practices. Overall, in human and nonhuman animals, the studies find that when all other factors are controlled, such as age, physical health, and educational experience, a healthy diet has a proven impact on enhancing cognitive performance and on reducing cognitive decline and dementia risk in older adults.

Healthy Diet versus Physical Activity

People who eat well tend to be more physically active. How, then, can one isolate which is the most important driving force in improving or maintaining heart health and cognitive health? Turns out they both seem to be major contenders in reducing cardiovascular disease and dementia risk with age. Researchers from Columbia University studied almost 2,000 older adults over a period of 14 years. They found that when all other lifestyle and demographic factors (such as age and education) are controlled for, both healthy diet and physical activity were found to independently reduce risk of Alzheimer's disease. What was really neat about their findings was the interaction between physical activity and healthy diet. People who engaged in high amounts of physical activity and strictly adhered to a healthy diet were the least likely to develop Alzheimer's disease, those who were sedentary and consistently ate unhealthy diets were the most likely to develop this disease, and people who either engaged in physical activity *or* adhered to a healthy diet (but not both) had an intermediate risk of developing Alzheimer's disease. Thus, it is better to do both—exercise and eat well—than either one alone.

There seems to be some other important interactions between diet and exercise. We give you two examples here. First, Dr. Carol

Greenwood and her colleagues recently reported an interaction between exercise and salt intake in healthy older adults: high salt intakes were associated with an increased risk of cognitive decline only if the older adults were sedentary. This suggests that physical fitness can help buffer some of the ill effects of a poor diet, although, from the example reviewed in the previous paragraph, we nevertheless recommend that you eat well and exercise. The second example demonstrates an interaction between dietary fat and exercise. Eating a diet that is low in saturated fat helps to prevent atherosclerosis, but so, too, does exercising, because physical activity helps metabolize fat. Indeed, recent research sheds light on how physical activity might be equally protective as a healthy diet by counteracting the negative influence of a meal that is high in fat. Researchers examined blood fat levels in two groups of middle-aged men who were relatively inactive and overweight. One group engaged in regular walking exercise as part of the study, and the other group did not. Both groups were given a pure fat cocktail to drink, and the researchers found the exercise group metabolized the fat better and had lower blood fat levels as compared to the nonexercise group. The take-home message is a brisk walk (or other form of exercise) before thanksgiving dinner or that pregame football party described in Box 11.4 might help you reduce the ill effects of a high fat meal.

MAKING SENSE OF THE DIET BUZZ

We often read or hear about particular foods or vitamins that have some sort of wonder properties that can prevent a particular disease or diseases and promote health. It can be difficult to feel confident about food choices in this climate. However, as reviewed earlier in this chapter, there is no evidence that one particular food, vitamin, or mineral is a cure or a cure-all. Focusing on one dietary element or choice too much could mean that you end up missing out on other important nutrients. In fact, taking more than the recommended dietary allowance of a particular vitamin or mineral can have deleterious effects on your health. A good rule of thumb is "everything in moderation including moderation" (a saying with origins in ancient philosophy but attributed to many famous people, including Oscar

Box 11.4 Case Vignette Describing a Success Story in Adopting a Healthier Diet

Lucia is a 56-year-old native of Green Bay Wisconsin who works as a mining engineer in Sault Ste Marie, Ontario. No surprise here, she is crazy about American football, and specifically her hometown team, the Green Bay Packers. Every time the Packers play, there is a pregame tailgate party. People park as close as they can to the football stadium and set-up for cooking outdoors right out of the backs of their vehicles. People take these parties seriously and walk about sampling each other's food and compete to attract passersby to their tailgate. So what are they cooking up? Deep-fried cheese, sausages, chili, ribs…did we mention the deep fried cheese? Fresh produce doesn't figure big on the menu. Although not exactly healthy fare, it is certainly tasty to many.

When Lucia travels home to attend a weekend game, she knows she will be sorely tempted to dig right into the food. However, in the back of her mind is the stern talking-to she had from her doctor last month about her weight, particularly increased girth around the middle, and blood-test results indicating she is borderline for requiring medication to control her cholesterol and blood sugars. She took this to heart (no pun intended) and has been making efforts to make better food choices and increase her physical activity level. However, she loves deep-fried cheese, and how will she manage when she goes to the pregame party? All the yummy smells! Who could resist?

To help stiffen her resolve, she makes an appointment to see her doctor the Friday before she heads home. To her shock and amazement here is what he told her: Cheat. He was impressed with her efforts to maintain a healthy diet and considered that if Lucia felt deprived it could hamper her efforts to keep on with the overall changes she had made. If she craves the deep-fried cheese, he figured she should have it, but only every now and then. It appears his attitude was wise, because Lucia, who had been on her way to a diagnosis of metabolic syndrome, kept up with her lifestyle changes. After about eight months, she achieved a healthy weight and was able to effectively control her blood sugars with diet and exercise. She did need to go on medication for cholesterol, but between the medicine, her overall healthy diet (with the occasional cheat), and some brisk walking a few times a week, her good cholesterol is high and her bad cholesterol is low. This success has reduced her risk of heart disease and associated cognitive decline.

Wilde and Julia Child). Later on in this chapter, we will talk about how to make sure you include a variety of different foods in your diet, with an emphasis on fruits and vegetables and whole grains, so that you can maximize your intake of vitamins and minerals. First, though, we will go over some of the most important building blocks of nutrition that are related to cognition—antioxidants, vitamins, and fats—and tell you why they are so crucial for your health.

Antioxidants: Evidence for Benefits and Food Sources

Some nutrients (vitamins, minerals, and enzymes) in our foods are considered antioxidants because they act to prevent cell damage by reducing oxidative stress, which you now know contributes to many health problems such as heart disease, diabetes, cancer, and Alzheimer's disease. Our bodies make some antioxidants, but there are many others that come from our diets in the form of essential vitamins (like C and E), selenium (a mineral), and various kinds of compounds called *flavonoids,* which have antioxidant properties. Foods rich in antioxidants are brightly colored fruits and vegetables like blueberries, raspberries, tomatoes, carrots to name a few. Foods with the most flavonoids are those of darker colors, in particular, *cruciferous* (Latin for cross-bearing) vegetables. These vegetables are named so because their flowers form a cross, and include broccoli, cauliflower, bok choy, arugula, cabbage, kale, and brussels sprouts to name a few.

Vitamins and Minerals: Evidence for Benefits and Food Sources

There are specific daily intake recommendations for many different kinds of nutrients. We are going to provide you with the specifics about two nutrients, vitamin D and the mineral calcium for two reasons. First, these nutrients combat age-related decline in bone health that leads to *osteoporosis* (thinning of the bones) that is associated with bone fractures. Second, it can be difficult, even with healthy diet practices, to achieve the recommended intake for these nutrients. Other vitamins and minerals, such as the B vitamins, vitamin C, and selenium, for example, are just as critical to your health. However, if you are following a healthy diet that includes the recommended number of servings from among the four food groups (described in the section on "Maintaining a Healthy Diet" later in this chapter), then you most definitely will be getting plenty of these other nutrients. At the start of this chapter, we promised that healthy eating would not be "rocket science." Worrying about how many milligrams of vitamin C are in the orange you are eating and exactly how much more of a particular something you have to eat to achieve your recommended daily allowance of vitamin C is just not necessary if you are eating a well-balanced diet.

Recommended Vitamin D and Calcium Intake for People over 50

Vitamin D and the mineral calcium are important to bone health and also appear to have some disease fighting properties. For example, vitamin D is thought to impede neuroinflammation, and insufficient vitamin D is associated with increased risk of cancer and diabetes. Vitamin D also helps the body absorb calcium, which promotes bone, heart, and colon health and helps to control blood pressure and obesity. The recommended daily intake for vitamin D is 800 international units (IU) and the recommended daily intake of calcium is 1200 milligrams (mg) for people over 50. The body can only absorb 500 mg of calcium at one time so spread consumption out over the day in order to obtain the recommended intake.

Often, these two nutrients are found in the same food source. For example, many dairy products are good sources of vitamin D and calcium, such as milk, yogurt, and even ice cream. Salmon with bones and sardines with bones—like what you get out of canned fish—are also good sources, although eating fish bones may not be everyone's cup of tea. Almonds and baked beans are also considered good sources of calcium. Eggs, salmon, tuna, and fortified cereals are particularly good sources of vitamin D.

The other natural source of vitamin D is the sun, as ultraviolet rays from the sun trigger our body to synthesize vitamin D. However, sun exposure is a recognized risk factor for skin cancer, and people living in Northern climates and/or people with darker skin absorb fewer ultraviolet rays when in the sun. That is why it is recommended that we obtain our vitamin D from natural food sources and, in some cases as described next, from supplements.

Health Canada recommends that, in addition to healthy diet practices, everyone over the age of 50 also take a daily vitamin D supplement of 400 IU. It is important not to try and exceed vitamin D requirements because this can have harmful health effects, such as nausea or muscle weakness. In Box 11.5 we provide you with more specific information about good food sources and amounts of vitamin D and calcium nutrients contained in a serving. Remember that your goal is to take in at least 1200 mg of calcium and 800 IU of vitamin D every day. You will see from Box 11.5 that this would be pretty hard to do with respect to vitamin D, which is why a supplement is recommended.

Intake of Other Types of Vitamins and Minerals

Plant-based foods (vegetables, fruits, and whole grains) are good sources for many other important nutrients, such as vitamins C, E, K, and the B vitamins, minerals such as selenium, and *polyphenol compounds* (the compounds found in plant-based foods, with previously discussed flavonoids being an example). These nutrients are rich in antioxidants and occur together in plant-based foods and seem to work together to promote their uptake into the body. The more darkly coloured plant-based foods contain the most antioxidants, a point alluded to in our discussion of antioxidant food sources, and one we shall return to a few times in this chapter.

As previously mentioned, rather than focusing on the recommended daily requirements, we emphasize simply eating a well-balanced diet, because this will ensure you are getting sufficient quantity and variety of these nutrients, many of which are also derived from plant sources. Nonetheless, it is important to acknowledge that it is sometimes difficult to manage to consume the recommended daily servings from among the four food groups, which you will read about in detail later in the section titled "Maintaining a Healthy Diet." If this is the case for you, then you may wish to consider taking a multivitamin supplement, because many multivitamin supplements are designed to deliver the recommended daily allowances for many of the nutrients we have discussed. Vitamin supplements are also very important for people who take medications that influence how well the body can absorb certain vitamins,

Box 11.5 Examples of Good Food Sources for Calcium and Vitamin D (with approximate amounts of nutrient contained in a serving).

Good Sources of Calcium in Foods (amounts in mg)

Milk	1 cup = ~300 mg
Buttermilk	1 cup = ~300 mg
Soy Beverage, fortified	1 cup = ~310 mg
Orange juice, fortified	1 cup = ~300 mg
Yogurt	1 cup = ~250 mg
Cheese	2 oz. or 50 g = ~350 mg
Cottage cheese	1 cup = ~150 mg
Sour cream	1 cup = ~150 mg
Ice cream	1 cup = ~180 mg
Sardines, with bones	2.5 oz. = ~280 mg
Salmon, canned with bones	2.5 oz. = ~190 mg
Pudding or custard	1 cup = ~200 mg
Almonds	1/2 cup = ~200 mg
Baked beans	1 cup = ~125 mg
Dark green vegetables (collards, spinach, turnip greens, and kale)	½ cup = ~50 to 100 mg

Good Sources of vitamin D (amounts in IU, see text for explanation of IU measure)

Eggs	2 large = ~58 IU
Sardines	2.5 oz. = ~140 IU
Salmon	2.5 oz. = ~350 IU
Tuna	2.5 oz = ~80 IU
Margarine (choose non-hydrogenated)	1 tsp. = ~25 IU
Milk	1 cup = ~100 IU
Yogurt, fortified	¾ cup = ~60 IU
Orange juice, fortified	½ cup = ~50 IU
Cereals, fortified	2/3 cup = anywhere from 29 to 300 IU

Notes: 1. Check product labels when 'fortified', as the amount of vitamin D and calcium added may vary. 2. Table content are gross estimated amounts that can vary and are based in part on review of information from http://www.healthlinkbc.ca/healthfiles/hfile68e.stm and http://ods.od.nih.gov/factsheets/VitaminD and http://ods.od.nih.gov/factsheets/Caclium.

or for individuals who are attempting to loose weight and, as a consequence, are eating less food.

We strongly encourage you to ask your pharmacist whether any medications you are taking can promote nutrient deficiencies and whether any vitamin supplements you are taking could compromise the effectiveness of any of your medications. It is also a good idea to consult with your family doctor about these same kinds of questions. As much as possible, we would encourage you to try and get your nutrients through a healthy diet, because science shows that the way nutrients interact and are contained within a food source optimizes their ability to exercise their disease-fighting properties.

Omega-3 Fatty Acids: Evidence for Benefits and Food Sources

Omega-3 fatty acids are considered an essential fat to have in our diets because our bodies cannot produce this type of fat. Research shows Omega-3 prevents heart disease by slowing atherosclerosis and lowering lousy cholesterol (low-density lipoprotein). They also have antioxidant properties so that they reduce neuroinflammation and protect nerve cell membranes. Omega-3 eggs and oily fish such as salmon, mackerel, char, sardines, herring, rainbow trout, and fresh water white fish, to name a few, are particularly good sources of omega-3 fatty acids. Fish digest seaweed to make omega-3 fatty acids, and humans cannot extract these acids in seaweed, walnuts, and flaxseed in quite the same fashion. Canada's food guide recommends that people have at least two servings of fish each week. True to the maxim of "everything in moderation," however, experts also agree that we should try to limit our exposure to mercury, which is high in some types of fish (see www.healthcanada.gc.ca for more information).

As reviewed in chapter 7, omega-3 fatty acids have been investigated as a treatment for Alzheimer's disease. To date there is no definitive evidence that these nutrients have any significant influence on the disease or its progression. On the other hand, there is some limited evidence that these fatty acids may prevent cognitive decline in older adults who are not apolipoprotein e4 allele carriers (a genetic risk factor for Alzheimer's disease, see Chapter 5). One thing scientists agree on is that these particular fatty acids still warrant further study as having a possible role in preventing or slowing disease progression.

THE TRUTH ABOUT FAT: THE GOOD, THE BAD, AND THE REALLY BAD

Many essential nutrients in our diet come in foods that contain fat, and fat helps us absorb these nutrients. Not all fats are created equal, however, and we need to consider this as we balance our necessary intake of protein, vitamins, and minerals with our food choices.

THE GOOD: Unsaturated Fat

These are plant fats and can be in liquid or solid forms. There are two types of unsaturated fats, mono-unsaturated and poly-unsaturated. The mono and the poly just refer to the number of bonds between carbon and hydrogen in the fat, with mono having one and poly having two or more, and with both types being good. Sources of mono-unsaturated fats include oils like olive, canola, and peanut, as well as avocado and many different kinds of nuts such as cashews, almonds, and peanuts to name a few. Sources of poly-unsaturated fats include oils like corn, sunflower, safflower, cottonseed and soybean, as well as fish and flaxseed oils, either extracted or from whole fish and flaxseed.

What's so great about these unsaturated fats? Well for one they make salads and other foods taste good, but most importantly, these fats help us metabolize the fabulous vitamins contained within the vegetables comprising our salad, because vitamins like A, D, E, and K are fat soluble. Indeed when researchers from the Chicago Health and Aging Project discovered that the consumption of vegetables, but not fruit, appeared to be associated with slower rates of cognitive decline with aging, it was speculated that unsaturated fats had something to do with it. Vegetables are more likely to be eaten with a salad dressing than fruits, so vitamins from vegetable consumption get metabolized better. Perhaps most important, though, is how these fats affect cholesterol in the blood stream. They have a good influence on cholesterol because, like omega-3 fatty acids, they reduce the "bad" kind of cholesterol. This leads us to our next topic: the BAD fats.

THE BAD: Saturated Fat

Saturated fats are typically solid at room temperature and primarily involve animal fat. Examples of foods high in saturated fat include dairy (whole milk, butter, cheese, ice cream), red meat, shortening and lard (derived from animal fat and often used in baked goods), and coconuts (including coconut milk and coconut oil). You might be thinking, "Hey dairy products are good sources of calcium and vitamin D and meat has protein. So, now you're telling me not to eat these things?" Of course not! Some saturated fat in your diet is good for you, depending on the source. Just watch your number of daily and weekly servings and portion sizes. Think about drinking lower fat milk, and consider choosing leaner and smaller portions of meat. Also, opt for fish once or twice a week instead of meat, because fish is also an excellent source of protein and has the bonus of containing the good fat with omega-3 fatty acids.

THE REALLY BAD: Transfats

Transfats are a type of saturated fat that come in two varieties: naturally occurring and manufactured. It is the manufactured transfats that you should especially keep away from. Some transfats are naturally occurring in the meat and whole dairy products of *ruminants*, which are grass fed animals like cows, goats, and sheep. Although it is important to limit foods high in saturated fat, naturally occurring transfats like *conjugated linoleic acid*, which is found in red meat and dairy products, are the exception. These transfats have been shown by researchers to be good for bone health, to have fat burning qualities, and even to have anticancer properties.

Importantly, a naturally occurring transfat typically only comprises 2– 5% of the saturated fat content in food, whereas manufactured transfats comprise 50– 60% of the fat content. Manufactured transfats are anything that says "hydrogenated" or "partially hydrogenated" on the label. Transfats are manufactured by injecting hydrogens into plant-based oils, hence the term *hydrogenated oil*, so that it becomes a solid at room temperature. Food sources high in transfat include palm oil, hydrogenated and partially hydrogenated vegetable oils, most margarine (although nonhydrogenated margarines are now available), vegetable shortening, and most fast-food and commercially baked goods, especially cookies! Transfats are considered the most harmful types of fats because of how they influence our cholesterol levels, as described in the next section. Look at the ingredient label on the foods you buy for the word *hydrogenated*, because the U.S. Food and Drug Administration will allow manufacturers to advertise products as "transfat free" if the transfat content on the nutrition-facts label is less than 0.5g. This is a good example of a food-packaging health claim and the nutrition-facts label differing, and we refer to this later in this chapter in the section on "Tips for Grocery Shopping."

How Dietary Fat Influences Cholesterol and Heart Health

Cholesterol is a type of fatty substance in the blood that is produced primarily by the liver, naturally occurs in all parts of the body, and functions to protect nerves and to make cell tissue and even certain hormones. In a nutshell, unsaturated fats lower the lousy cholesterol and raise the healthy cholesterol, saturated fats raise both kinds, and those manufactured transfats raise the lousy and lower the healthy (that's why they are really bad).

The lousy cholesterol is low-density lipoprotein (LDL), which is the main transporter of fatty substances in the blood. It's considered lousy because too much of it causes atherosclerosis and increases risk of heart disease. The healthy cholesterol is high-density lipoprotein (HDL). This form is considered healthy because it picks up the extra fat circulating in the blood and returns it to the liver thereby reducing the risk of atherosclerosis. Sometimes blood-test results report the number for the total blood cholesterol level (HDL + LDL, which should be less than 200 milligrams per decilitre of blood in total) and the HDL number. If these are the two numbers you get from your blood tests, then do the math and subtract the HDL from your total to get an index of your LDL. It is the LDL number that will

Box 11.6 Optimal Levels for Healthy (HDL) and Lousy (LDL) Blood Cholesterol.

	HDL	LDL
Excellent	> 60 mg/dL	< 100 mg/dL
Good to Fair	50–59 mg/dL	100–129 mg/dL
Poor	< 40 mg/dL in men; <50 mg/dL in women	130–159 mg/dL
Very Poor	—	> 160 mg/dL

Measured in milligrams per decilitre of blood (mg/dL).

help you best identify and appreciate the degree to which change in your diet may be warranted and could benefit your health. Box 11.6 details the optimal levels for the healthy and lousy types of blood cholesterol.

MAINTAINING A HEALTHY DIET

Maintaining a healthy diet will allow you to keep to a healthy body weight and better control conditions such as diabetes, high cholesterol, and high blood pressure if you have one or more these. It will also help prevent you from getting one of these medical conditions if you don't have one. In Canada and the United States, diabetes affects approximately 20%, high cholesterol approximately 50%, and high blood pressure approximately 50% of the population 50 years of age and over. In other words, these conditions are highly prevalent among middle-aged and older adults. As we reviewed in chapter 5, these conditions are considered important risk factors for dementia as we age. We cannot control the aging process or our genetic predispositions that might make these conditions have greater or lesser impact on our brain health, but we can control our diet to better manage this risk. Medications for managing these medical conditions are important but are not sufficient on their own. Healthy eating also has a role, as does physical activity, the topic of the next chapter.

Food Guide Recommendations and Resource Information

There are several resources available for information about food sources and food intake recommendations that can help you develop healthy diet practices. These resources include: Federal, provincial, and state government publications for seniors; local libraries, community centers and groups; and your family doctor. There is also, of course, the Internet. Two official government Web sites are from Health Canada (www.healthcanada.gc.ca) and from the United States Department of Agriculture Center for Nutrition Policy and Promotion (www.cnpp.usda.gov). Both are pretty fantastic for providing food-guide recommendations, information about food-product safety, how to read nutrition labeling, and so on. The information can be made available in multiple languages and also includes food-guide recommendations for different cultural groups. For additional guidance and information, we would also recommend a book by registered dietician Leslie Beck, which is referenced in the "recommended reading" section at the end of this chapter.

Self-Monitoring Daily Food Intake to Achieve Food Guide Recommendations

Food Groups and Recommended Serving Sizes

Basically we have to eat a particular number and size of servings from the four food groups per day to maintain a healthy diet. It seems to be particularly troublesome to figure out what constitutes a serving, and the number of servings varies by age and sex. Simply put, most of the time, a serving is either the size of a tennis-ball, like a medium-sized apple, or it's a cup or half a cup of something. Don't worry. Of course, we are going to give you the specifics, and for more information you can refer to the government Web sites we previously mentioned. The recently revamped national food guide (see www.cnpp.usda.gov) is particularly spectacular with a very simple and interactive dinner plate example (see Box 11.6) that helps you visualize roughly how much space each food group should be occupying on your plate.

It's important to eat good food and not too much food, so let's talk about the specific number and sizes of servings as they relate

Box 11.7 The MyPlate Icon from the USDA Center for Nutrition Policy and Promotion (CNPP): A Quick Reference to Guide Food Choices and Amounts. (Notice that "Fruits and Vegetables" takes up half the plate.)

to the four food groups. The four food groups are: (a) *Fruits and vegetables*—fresh, frozen, or canned, and, yes, juice counts, but it should be 100% juice. Serving size is a half-cup with the exception of raw leafy vegetables, in which case it's a whole cup. (b) *Grains*, such as bread, cereal, pasta, and rice,. Serving size is typically a half- cup of anything cooked, half a bagel, half a pita, half a tortilla, half the bread in your sandwich, so 1 slice of bread. (c) *Milk or milk alternatives* including canned or powdered milk, soy, (all 1 cup) yogurt, kefir (both serving size three-quarters of a cup or 175 g, which is typically the size of an individual container) and cheese, but only about a ping-pong-ball size serving, so 50 g or one-and- a-half ounces. Sorry, but butter and ice-cream generally don't make it as the top foods of choice for getting your recommended servings of dairy. (d) *Meat or meat alternatives* including animals on the land and in the sea (half a cup or no bigger than the size of your palm), legumes (half a cup of beans, lentils, chick peas, etc.), various types of nuts (one-quarter cup shelled), tofu (three-quarters of a cup), eggs (2 eggs), and peanut or other type of nut butter (2 tablespoons). So now you must be

Box 11.8 Daily Recommended Number of Servings and Serving

	Vegetables & Fruit	Grain Products
Food Group		
Serving Size	½ cup fresh, frozen or canned; 1 fruit whole; ½ cup juice	1 slice bread; ½ bagel, pita, or tortilla; ½ cup rice, bulgur, quinoa, cooked pasta; ½ to 1 cup cold cereal based on type or ¾ cup hot cereal
Daily Servings	7	6 for women 7 for men
Tick off the boxes to keep track of your servings on a given day		

Table content based on guidelines from Health Canada Consultation and Communications Branch, Health Canada. Adapted with permission.

Sizes by Food Group for Adults aged 50+

Milk & Alternatives	Meat & Alternatives
1 cup milk or soy beverage; ¾ cup yogurt; 1 ½ oz cheese	½ cup fish, poultry, lean meat; ¾ cup legumes/ beans/tofu; 2 eggs; 2 Tbsp peanut butter; ¼ cup nuts
3	2 for women 3 for men

(www.healthcanada.gc.ca/foodguide). From the Public Affairs, wondering how many servings from each of these groups you should eat per day. Given that the focus of our book is the older adult, we are going to keep the details to adults aged 50+. Please access the official government Web sites previously referenced for recommended daily intakes for younger adults and children.

Tracking Your Daily Progress in Eating a Well-Balanced Diet

Here we have provided you with an easy-to-use table to track your progress at achieving a well-balanced diet that adheres to the recommended number of servings from among the four food groups. The recommended number of servings for the grains and meat food groups is a little different for men and women, so pay attention to the number of daily servings specified for these food groups in the table below. You can also download printable versions of the table in Box 11.8 from www.baycrest.org/livingwithMCI if you want to stick it on your fridge to help track whether you are getting too much or too little of particular food group.

Recommendations for Grocery Shopping

Interpreting Packaging Information: Nutrition Labels and Health Claims

The three things you want to look at first on the nutrition facts label of a prepared food is the fat, sugar, and salt content. The percent of the daily value is relative to a 2000-calorie-per-day diet, which is kind of a ballpark figure suitable for the average sized adult who is moderately active. So you have to make a bit of general evaluation of this information if you are bigger or smaller than average or if you are more or less active than average or if you want to gain, lose, or maintain your current weight. Look for the "% daily value" column on the nutrition facts label. Anything less than 5 to 10% is considered low and anything 10 to 15% or higher is considered high. Use these values to help you watch out for foods for which most of the calories are derived from the fat and sugar content, because this means you're not getting much nutrition out of the calories consumed. You also want to make sure that the salt content is not too high with respect to your recommended daily intake. If you're interested in learning more, the Canadian and United States government's Web sites mentioned previously have great information to walk you through how to read these nutrition facts labels. The Canadian site even has an interactive quiz to teach you how to evaluate these labels.

In addition to the nutrition facts label, health claims on packaging also need to be evaluated especially since these are what tend to catch our eye and drive our purchasing. Packaging that claims "low in fat" may be high in salt or sugar content. Packaging that says "no transfats" could still be made with hydrogenated oil, if it was in low enough quantities. Don't be fooled, take time to look at the ingredients list.

Why We Should Watch the Salt and Sugar Content on Nutrition Labels

One of the reasons we should watch salt intake is because of the influence of salt on blood pressure. Salt (sodium) is a mineral that is essential to the body because it helps to transport nutrients into cells and waste products out of cells. We do not really need much salt in our diet to do this—less than 500 milligrams per day. The kidneys control our salt level by passing it into the urine if it gets high. When we have too much salt in our diet, then the kidneys have more trouble control-ing salt levels and some of it gets into the blood stream. Salt in the blood raises blood pressure by attracting extra water into the blood stream and thereby increasing the volume of the blood. Many herbs and spices, such as saffron, black pepper, oregano, cinnamon, and rose-mary to name just a few, are rich in antioxidants and are great alterna-tives to salt for adding flavor to food. Most of your added salt comes not from the table saltshaker, but from processed and packaged foods, which is why it is so important to check the nutrition facts label.

One of the reasons we should watch our sugar intake is because once we've exceeded the body's need, it is quickly converted to fat for storage. Refined sugars in sweets and in other foods you may not expect to find them in (hidden sugars)—like your salad dressing—are quickly converted to glucose in the blood stream and soon require insulin to restore the balance by promoting conversion of glucose to fat. A poor diet high in refined sugars (approximately greater than 40 grams per day) can result in prolonged elevation of insulin levels, thereby reducing the ability of insulin to adequately regulate blood sugars. This can lead to one or more of the medical conditions described as part of the metabolic syndrome earlier in this chapter. The calories we get from eating refined sugar are often referred to as "empty calories" because the sugary food is typically lacking in other nutrients and cannot satisfy the nutritional requirements of the body, causing us to eat more.

It is better for us to consume complex carbohydrates, such as those contained in whole grains, fruits, and vegetables, because these are converted more slowly into glucose and thus deliver a steady stream of energy. As a result, we don't feel the urge to eat more, conversion of glucose to excess fat is reduced, and there is a better balance of blood glucose and insulin levels in the blood stream. If you have a sweet tooth, it may be hard to stay within a limit of 40 grams per day of refined sugar. Being physically active can help offset the deleterious effect of that extra sugar intake to some degree, and you will read about this more in chapter 12.

Fresh, Frozen, or Canned Produce: Does It Make a Difference?

Not really. Canned produce has some minimal loss of nutrients, but it is still good. You just have to be aware of whether there has been too much salt and/or sugar added as preservative. Frozen is just as good or is better than fresh because frozen produce is picked when ready and immediately frozen, whereas fresh tends to be picked early so that it can ripen on route to the supermarket. Frozen is a great alternative if you find you have trouble eating some of the fresh produce you've bought before it spoils.

How to Identify Foods Rich in Vitamins and Minerals

This is easy. Go for brightly colored fruits and vegetables and choose grains that are not highly refined or processed (yep, that means brown bread, but make sure you look for "whole grain" on the label and try for as close to 100% as your taste buds allow). Regarding fruits and vegetables, the richer colors have the most flavonoids, which you now know are nutrients with antioxidant properties that act to prevent diseases like heart disease by removing plaque build-up in the arteries. Regarding the grains, it is best to go for those that are less refined, such as brown rice and whole-grain breads, oats, and flour, because these are the types that are the richest in vitamins and minerals (and fiber, which helps control blood cholesterol). If you really hate the taste of baked goods made with whole-wheat flour, you can always opt for the processed versions with the vitamins and minerals added back in. These packaged products are usually referred to as being enriched and would at least be considered second best.

A FINAL WORD

There is very compelling evidence that what we eat influences our cognition and our risk of cognitive decline as we age. There is no definitive evidence that a particular nutrient benefits cognition or treats dementia. The best advice is to eat a varied diet that is plant based, includes fish, and is low in saturated and transfats (and preferably contains no manufactured transfats). Having said that, eating does more than just perform the function of providing our body with the energy to live; it also influences how we feel physically and emotionally. What we choose to eat reflects our individual likes and dislikes, our heritage, and even our state of mind sometimes. It is an activity we often engage in with others; thus, it is associated with our friends, family, routines, and celebrations. In other words, "it's personal." However, it's also a myth that adhering to a healthy diet means you have to give up great tasting food that is enjoyable to eat. Here we've provided you with the tools to assist you in maintaining or adopting healthy diet practices. So give it a try. We would encourage you to further educate yourself about how to eat flavorful fun food that is also good for you. In addition to the content and resource information provided in this chapter, we have also included two recommended readings at the end of this chapter to further assist you in achieving these aims. Like the story we told you about Lucia, for most of us it is okay to indulge once in a while, especially if you do so in moderation. After all, chocolate, cheese, and red wine are just some of the food choices these authors would not want to have to live without!

Box 11.9 Questions to Ask Your Doctor

---

1. How is my weight, blood pressure, blood cholesterol, and blood sugar, and should I be doing anything to improve them? How severe is it?

2. Should I be concerned about developing diabetes, given what you know about my medical history?

3. Could you refer me to a dietician or nutritionist to help me with strategies to adopt a more healthy diet that will allow me to optimize my nutritional intake?

4. What vitamin supplements would you recommend, if any, that would be safe for me to take?

5. Given my dietary restrictions (for example, I can't have dairy or I don't eat meat), how can I make sure that I am still getting all of my nutritional requirements?

6. Could any of my medications cause a vitamin deficiency? If yes, what steps should I take with respect to my diet?

RECOMMENDED READINGS

Beck, L. (2010). *Leslie Beck's longevity diet: The power of food to slow aging and maintain optimal health and energy.* Toronto, Canada: Penguin.

Baycrest is preparing a cookbook called *Mindfull: Delicious recipes to support brain health,* written in conjunction with Dr. Carol E. Greenwood, a nutrition scientist who studies the relationship between nutrition and brain health in older adults. Check out our Web site www.baycrest.org/livingwithMCI for news about its release!

12

Exercise: Jog Your Memory

On October 16, 2011, Mr. Fauja Singh of London, England, earned his spot in the record books when he crossed the finish line of the Toronto Waterfront Marathon. It isn't his time that makes his race newsworthy—it took him over 8 hours to run the 42.2 km, and, in fact, he finished in 3845th place out of 3854 runners who crossed the finish line. What is remarkable is the fact that just three months earlier, Mr. Singh had celebrated his 100th birthday! Lesser mortals like ourselves are unlikely to cross a marathon finish line alive no matter what our age, but people like Mr. Singh can inspire us nevertheless to get off the couch and get moving. In this chapter, we review the many new discoveries that have been made in recent years about the power of exercise to promote brain health. The good news is that you don't have to run a marathon to reap the rewards of exercise!

WHAT IS EXERCISE AND HOW IS IT MEASURED?

We know it seems like a stupid question to ask what exercise is, but in reality, there is no strict dividing line between sedentary activities and physically challenging activities. Rather, as you will see soon, different activities vary along a continuum of physical demand.

There are many ways to measure how physically challenging an activity is. One way is to measure how many calories are burned when engaging in an activity for a particular amount of time. *Calorie expenditure* refers to the amount of energy metabolized during an activity. How many calories you burn depends on your body size, and on your *metabolic rate*, or the efficiency with which you burn energy, which varies with age and your level of physical fitness among other things. A second way to measure how physically challenging activities are for you is to keep track of your *heart rate* (the rate as which your heart beats). The harder you are working out, the faster your heart rate, although a given level of exercise intensity increases heart rate less in physically fit than sedentary people. A third way to measure the amount of physical activity expended is VO_2 max, which is a measure of the maximum amount of oxygen a person can use during a period of intense exercise, where V refers to the volume of oxygen over a given period of time, O_2 is the chemical symbol for oxygen, and max is short for maximum. To have it measured, you would be fitted with a mask through which oxygen would be supplied and the amount of oxygen versus carbon dioxide exhaled would be measured. You would then jog on a treadmill or ride a stationary bike, and the technologist would gradually have you increase the intensity of the exercise. VO_2 max is defined as the point at which oxygen consumption no longer increases despite increases in the intensity of the exercise (that is, when you have literally maxed yourself out!). Because people have to be pushed to their max, obtaining a VO_2 max can be risky, and so it is usually measured in a professional setting with close medical supervision when the person tested is an older adult.

Measuring VO_2 max is not feasible outside of a specialized laboratory, but in many research studies it is considered the gold standard measure of physical fitness; we will refer to this measure later on the chapter. You can, however, use calories expended or your heart rate to gauge whether you are getting adequate physical activity. Box 12.1 lists many activities along with something called a metabolic equivalent, or MET value. These values take into account the fact that how many calories you expend doing any one of these activities varies as a function of your weight. A MET value of 1 describes an activity in which you would burn 1 calorie per kilogram an hour. So, if you weigh 150 pounds, that is equivalent to about 68 kilograms, and so you would burn 68 calories doing that activity for an hour. Note that these are only rough estimates—the amount of calories that *you* burn engaging in these activities may be higher or lower, depending on a host of variables including your age and level of physical fitness.

The chart in Box 12.1 makes it clear that the question, "What is exercise?" isn't so stupid after all, because just about any activity puts

---

Box 12.1 Estimated Metabolic Equivalent of a Range of Activities

Sleeping	0.9
Sitting on couch	1.0
Standing in Line	1.3
Eating	1.5
Light Household Chores (for example, dusting or sweeping)	2.3
Putting Away Groceries	2.5
Driving	2.5
Moderate Household Chores (for example, vacuuming)	3.3
Playing Golf (with cart)	3.5
Bowling	3.8
Gardening	3.8
Walking (3.5 mph)	4.3
Ballroom Dancing	5.5
Mowing lawn (push mower)	5.5
Playing golf (walking)	4.3
Water Aerobics	5.5
Swimming	5.8
Shovelling Snow	6.0
Bicycling (fast)	7.5
Tennis (singles)	8.0
Jogging (5 mph)	8.3
Running (6 mph)	9.8
Jump Rope	12.3
Sprinting (12 mph)	19.0

Herrmann, Stephen, "The 2011 Compendium of Physical Activities: Tracking Guide," Retrieved from https://sites.google.com/site/compendiumofphysicalactivities/tracking-guide, November 7, 2011. Used with permission.

our bodies to work. Nevertheless, most people would agree that exercise refers to activities that are over and above our normal day-to-day activities such as sleeping and eating, and professionals define exercise as being activities that are done with the specific purpose of improving or maintaining health. The good news, however, is that a range of activities can provide you with opportunities to give your body a workout, from vacuuming, to bowling, to gardening, to water aerobics, whether you are trying to or not!

The second way to measure how hard you are working is to keep track of your heart rate when you are exercising. A simple calculation is to subtract your age (in years) from 220. For example, the maximum heart rate of an average 65-year old would be $220 - 65 = 155$. Whatever number you calculate, based on your age, is the rate that you should not exceed without potentially harming yourself. For a moderate-intensity work out, you want your heart rate to be between 50% and 70% of your maximum heart rate, and for a vigorous-intensity work out, you want your heart rate to be between 70% and 85% of your maximum heart rate. So if you are going for a moderate-intensity work out, aim to get your heart rate between $(220 - \text{age}) \times .50$ and $(220 - \text{age}) \times .70$. If you are going for a vigorous-intensity workout, aim to get your heart rate between $(220 - \text{age}) * \times 70$ and $(220 - \text{age}) \times .85$.

To use these formulas, you need to stop when you are exercising and take your pulse. Place your index and middle fingers of one hand on the inside edge of your wrist below your thumb. If you press lightly, you should feel the steady pulse of an artery. Start your count on the beat of your pulse, starting at 0, and count the number of pulse beats that occur in 60 seconds (or in 30 seconds and double that number). There are also heart rate monitors that you can wear around your chest or even built into special watches that can measure or give you a good estimate of your heart rate. Check out your local sporting goods store if you are interested in these products.

ON YOUR MARK, SET, GO?

It is extremely important that you exercise within the limits of your physical abilities. Certain underlying conditions, such as heart conditions and arthritis, and certain medications can impose limits on the types and amounts of physical activity you should engage in. To be safe, you should consult with your physician about these issues before embarking on new physical activities. She or he knows what conditions you have, what medications you are on, and how well you are managing your conditions, and then he or she can give you the best advice about what types and what amounts of exercise are right for you.

The Canadian Society for Exercise Physiology published a short questionnaire, called the Physical Activity Readiness Questionnaire (PAR-Q), for use in people aged 15–69. For adults over the age of 69, they recommend that you *not* rely on this questionnaire and instead consult with your doctor before adding exercise to your routine. For those of you who are between the ages of 15 and 69, there are seven questions, reproduced in Box 12.2, that help to guide you in your efforts to get into gear.

Box 12.2 The Physical Activities Readiness Questionnaire (PAR-Q) © 2002. Used with permission from the Canadian Society for Exercise Physiology www.csep.ca.

Please read the questions carefully and answer each one honestly. Check yes or no.

❑ Yes ❑ No   1. Has your doctor ever said that you have a heart condition *and* that you should only do physical activity recommended by a doctor?

❑ Yes ❑ No   2. Do you feel pain in your chest when you do physical activity?

❑ Yes ❑ No   3. In the past month, have you had chest pain when you were not doing physical activity?

❑ Yes ❑ No   4. Do you lose your balance because of dizziness or do you ever lose consciousness?

❑ Yes ❑ No   5. Do you have a bone or joint problem (for example, back, knee or hip) that could be made worse by a change in your physical activity?

(continued)

Box 12.2 (Continued)

❑ Yes ❑ No   6. Is your doctor currently prescribing drugs (for example, water pills) for your blood pressure or heart condition?

❑ Yes ❑ No   7. Do you know of *any other reason* why you should not do physical activity?

If you answered **YES to one or more question:**
Talk with your doctor by phone or in person BEFORE you start becoming much more physically active or BEFORE you have a fitness appraisal. Tell your doctor about the PAR-Q and which questions you answered YES.

- You may be able to do any activity you want—as long as you start slowly and build up gradually. Or, you may need to restrict your activities to those which are safe for you. Talk with your doctor about the kinds of activities you wish to participate in and follow his/her advice.
- Find out which community programs are safe and helpful for you.

If you answered **NO to all questions:**
If you answered NO honestly to *all* PAR-Q questions, you can be reasonably sure that you can:

- Start becoming much more physically active—begin slowly and build up gradually. This is the safest and easiest way to go.
- Take part in a fitness appraisal—this is an excellent way to determine your basic fitness so that you can plan the best way for you to live actively. It is also highly recommended that you have your blood pressure evaluated. If your reading is over 144/94, talk with your doctor before you start becoming much more physically active.

DELAY BECOMING MUCH MORE ACTIVE:

- If you are not feeling well because of a temporary illness such as a cold or fever—wait until you feel better; or
- If you are or may be pregnant—talk to your doctor before you start becoming more active.

Reproduced with permission of the Canadian Society for Exercise Physiology.

PHYSICAL AND COGNITIVE BENEFITS OF EXERCISE

When you think of exercise, you no doubt know about its positive effects on your muscles, your lungs, and your heart, but did you know that when you exercise you are also working out your brain? Well, you are, and in impressive ways as well. Perhaps the most impressive evidence has come out of the laboratory of Dr. Carl Cotman at the University of California, Irvine. He has shown that mice allowed to run voluntarily on a running wheel show improved memory for locations and increased *brain-derived neurotrophic factor*, a brain chemical that is associated with *neurogenesis*, or the growth of new neurons. What is really neat is that he has also shown this in mice with the ε4 allele of the apolipoprotein E gene that is associated with an increased risk of Alzheimer's disease in humans (for more on this gene, see chapter 5).

Before you get too skeptical about the degree to which we can generalize from mice to humans, you should know that greater physical fitness is associated with larger brain volumes, in both healthy older adults and even in people with mild Alzheimer's disease. As you might suspect, greater degrees of physical activity either in the recent past, in middle age, and even during your teenage years is associated with lower rates of mild cognitive impairment (MCI) and dementia later on.

One issue with these sorts of studies that follow people over many years is the famous chicken-and-egg problem. As you know from earlier chapters, dementia can be brewing for many years before it is detected, and so it is possible that people who were already experiencing the early brain pathology of dementia, or who were genetically predisposed to develop dementia, were less physically active in their younger years than were their healthier counterparts.

The best way to resolve the chicken-and-egg question is to conduct a randomized controlled trial, in which a larger group of people is randomly split into two groups, one of which is assigned to participate in an exercise intervention of some sort, and the other either does nothing or, better yet, engages in some kind of physical activity, but one that is much less vigorous. From an experimental design perspective, this latter, active control group is better than an inactive control group because people get together at the same intervals as the physically challenged group, and with a trainer, thus, both groups have the same level of professional and social interaction as the group of primary interest. This means that when comparing the two groups' changes from pre- to posttest, any group differences found favoring the exercise group can be attributed more directly to the exercise itself and not to meeting with professionals or interacting with peers.

Our favorite studies employing this sort of design come from the group led by Arthur Kramer, Stanley Colcombe, and Kirk Erickson of the Beckman Institute at the University of Illinois in Urbana, Illinois. They have taken groups of sedentary older adults, randomly assigned them to either join an aerobic fitness group or to a stretching and toning group for 6 or 12 months, depending on the study. Both groups met three days a week with a trainer, thus equating the level of social activity and professional attention. These researchers have found that older adults who engage in aerobic training show improvements in their VO_2 max, reflecting improved physical fitness levels. This boost in physical fitness was accompanied by improvements in memory and executive functioning. Moreover, these cognitive changes were related to increases in three key markers of better brain function: levels of brain-derived neurotrophic factor suggesting heightened growth of new neurons; use of the frontal lobes during tasks requiring that attention be paid to relevant information and suppressed from irrelevant information; and size of the frontal lobes and hippocampus, areas that are key to executive functioning and memory. These results were greater for those in the exercise group than in the group assigned to stretching and toning. It's not that stretching and toning are not important activities—they are, as you will see later in this chapter—but engaging *only* in stretching and toning is not the best recipe for better brain health. We talk about many of the effects just described in greater detail later because they help to explain how exercise promotes brain health, but the point here is that we find these results incredibly persuasive—just 6 or 12 months of exercising a few days a week can literally change the brains of older adults!

Our absolutely favorite thing about these studies is what the aerobic training condition was. It wasn't running marathons, or climbing mountains, or doing 12 Jane Fonda workout videos per session—it

was walking. Yes, walking! For only 10 minutes a day at the beginning, gradually increasing up to about 40 minutes a day as participants' stamina improved. It was brisk walking, the sort that raises
your heart rate to 50% to 70% of maximum, but still, when we tell
older adults that these great benefits to brain health can be achieved
by walking, we can see it in their faces—that encouraged look of
"I could do that!"! As inspiring as Mr. Singh is running marathons at
100 years of age, the work of Drs. Kramer, Colcombe, and Erickson
shows us that we don't have to make it to the Olympics, finish a marathon, or be a professional athlete to enjoy the health benefits of physical fitness. They have shown us that a group of otherwise ordinary
older adults can literally walk their way toward healthier brains. What
can be more motivating than that?

The relationship between physical fitness and cognitive ability
also exists in people with MCI. For example, evidence shows that the
faster people with MCI walk and get up from a chair, both of which
are measures of overall physical fitness, the better performance is on
tests of executive functioning. Another study randomly assigned people with MCI to either six months of high-intensity aerobics or to
six months of a stretching and toning control condition. They found
improvements in executive functioning only in the group who got the
intensive fitness program, and these effects were greater in women
with MCI than in males with MCI. These results might suggest that
hormones play a role in the link between exercise and brain health
when it comes to MCI, but this should be confirmed in future studies. Regardless, studies such as this are promising in that they show
that the brain health benefits of exercise that we see in research conducted with older adults are also evident in older adults with MCI.

HOW DOES IT WORK?

There is no single answer to the question, "how does exercise promote brain health?" Many mechanisms are at play for sure. Much
of the evidence comes from studies with nonhuman animals such
as mice. This is because scientists can examine the effects of exercise
on brain cells and brain chemicals directly in nonhuman animals,
whereas in humans we can only infer what is going on at that level.

Research with nonhuman animals also avoids confounds that often exist in studies with people, such as differences across people in how well they adhere to an exercise plan, how healthy their diet and other health habits are, and in their social circumstances. However, brain-imaging techniques are also providing a glimpse into how the brain is changed by exercise in people. In this section, we describe some of the many ways that the brain is changed by exercise that likely contribute to the improvements in cognitive abilities.

New brain cells

Probably the most consistent finding is that exercise leads to the growth and survival of new *neurons* (brain cells), particularly in the hippocampus, the area of the brain that is most important for memory. Brain cells need energy to work, and so they need nutrients that are delivered via the blood stream. This means that the brain responds to the growth of new neurons by increasing the presence of certain brain chemicals that trigger the growth of new *capillaries* (tiny blood vessels) to deliver the food the new neurons need. Three of these brain chemicals are vascular endothelial growth factor, insulin-like growth factor 1, and brain-derived neurotrophic factor. This last chemical has been shown to be directly related to improved memory. That is how exercise sets off the cascade of brain changes that ulti-mately leads to improved cognitive functioning.

Bigger brains

The new neurons developed in the hippocampus in response to exer-cise don't necessarily stay there—neurons can migrate from their birth place to somewhere else in the brain. Research using magnetic resonance imaging has shown increases in the size of the frontal and temporal lobes of the brain—regions that are involved in executive functioning and memory. The changes in the frontal lobe have been found both in the *grey matter*, or the outer layers of the brain that contain the brain cells, and in the *white matter*, or the inner parts of the brain that contain the long connections between brain cells in different parts of the brain. The expansion of both grey and white matter suggests that exercise improves not only the ability to hold on to and process information in the brain cells themselves, but also to transmit information between different brain regions.

Better brains

The beneficial effects of exercise on the cardiovascular system, in particular on reducing blood pressure, likely has positive consequences on the neurovascular system as well, helping to prevent the small infarcts (small strokes) in the white matter that are associated with vascular dementia and that have been shown to make Alzheimer's disease worse. In addition, while you are exercising, you are increasing the amount of oxygen supplied to your brain because your heart is pumping more rapidly. Our primary interest in this section, however, is on research that has shown that exercise changes *how* people use their brains.

Electroencephalograms (EEGs) can be used to examine the effects of exercise on how the brain works. EEGs measure the electrical activity of the brain: Many small electrodes are placed on the surface of your skull that record the tiny electrical currents that occur when your neurons fire. Scientists examine peaks of electrical activity at different times following presentation of a stimulus to infer how the brain is working. One consistent finding is that a particular peak that is associated with attention is stronger and faster in physically fit than sedentary people. Importantly, this change is measured when people are sitting, not exercising. This suggests that becoming physically fit alters your baseline brain activity, making you better able to pay attention even when you are not exercising.

Functional magnetic resonance imaging (fMRI) can also be used to measure brain activity. As mentioned earlier, Drs. Kramer, Colcombe, and Erickson have found that older adults who completed a 6- or 12-month walking program showed increased activity in the frontal lobes and hippocampus, increases that were not seen in people who did the same amount of stretching and toning classes.

Happier brains

Exercise interventions reduce rates of clinically diagnosed depression in older adults and lower self-reports of depression symptoms such as sadness and low energy in older adults who are not clinically depressed. Given that memory is negatively affected by depression (see chapter 5), alleviation of depressive symptoms by exercise can be one additional mechanism by which getting physically fit can help your cognitive abilities.

ON YOUR WAY TO BETTER BRAIN HEALTH

The previous section showed that exercise can improve cognitive functioning, increase the size and activity of your brain, and reduce dementia risk. So now that you are convinced and eager to lace up those running shoes, we want to give you some advice on the frequency and types of physical fitness activities you can and should engage in. How often should you aim to exercise, and what are some options to get you into gear?

How Much Is Enough?

Presuming that you have the green light to start exercising, what should you be aiming for? The World Health Organization (WHO) has set two recommended levels of activity for adults aged 65 and older with good mobility: (a) *at the bare minimum*: at least 150 minutes (that is, 2.5 hours) of moderate-intensity physical activity per week, or at least 75 minutes (that is, an hour and 15 minutes) of vigorous-intensity physical activity per week; (b) *for greater health benefits*: 300 minutes (that is, 5 hours) of moderate-intensity physical activity per week, or 150 minutes (that is, 1.5 hours) of vigorous-intensity activity, per week. These activities should be performed in bouts of at least 10 minutes duration (so it is okay to take a break, but you can't include your break time in your total minute counts!). Workouts should focus on muscle-strengthening activities at least 2 days a week. Older adults with poor mobility should focus on activities to enhance balance and prevent falls 3 or more days a week (see examples below). You can download these recommendations from http://www.who.int/dietphysicalactivity/physical-activity-recommendations-65years.pdf.

Anyone who is sedentary probably looks at numbers like 5 hours a week and gasps. This is understandable. If you are not currently getting much exercise, you do have a long way to go. However, there are two reasons not to panic. First, there are a variety of ways to get exercise other than hitting the gym. We give you lots of ideas at the end of this chapter. Second, rest assured, you can and *should* start slow. Start with 10 minutes a day, three times a week, and then gradually build up over months toward these targets. What will probably happen is that you will come to crave exercise and won't feel right if you miss a session. That is, once you start exercising regularly, it will become part of your normal lifestyle.

It is also important to listen to your body. Exercise shouldn't hurt, although your muscles may be mildly sore for a day or two after you add a new activity to your routine or step up its intensity or duration. Stop exercising if you feel dizzy, experience chest pain, or have shortness of breath, and call for help immediately. If your joints are swollen or sore, let them heal before you exercise again.

Any amount of exercise can feel like torture if you are doing things you don't enjoy or if you make a plan that has barriers to success (like signing up at a gym that has limited hours or that is on the other side of town and difficult to get to). In the next section, we give you a number of ideas to add physical activity to your everyday life.

Types of Exercise

Although the WHO guidelines focus primarily on aerobic activity for mobile older adults, there are actually four main types of exercise, and each provides a different benefit for your overall physical well-being. These are listed in Box 12.3. *Endurance*, or aerobic, exercises include things like running, swimming, riding a bike, and brisk walking, and this type of exercise has been most strongly linked to good brain health (neurogenesis, larger brains, better cognition). However, for whole body fitness, it is important that your physical regimen include the other forms of exercise as well. *Resistance*, or strengthening, exercises include lifting weights and using rubber resistance bands. Improving your strength will make many everyday activities easier, from getting up from a chair, to opening a bottle of spaghetti sauce, to climbing stairs. A 2010 study randomized a group of older adults to receive a year of resistance training once or twice a week or balance and toning training twice a week. They found that executive

---

Box 12.3 Four Main Types of Exercise and Benefits of Each

- **Endurance (aerobic) exercises:** Add stamina and promote good heart, lung, and brain health.
- **Resistance (strengthening) exercises:** Build muscle and promote good bone health.
- **Stretching exercises:** Make you limber and flexible.
- **Balance exercises:** Reduce the risk of falls.

---

functioning improved in those receiving the resistance training, but declined in those who did balance and toning exercises alone. Aim to work all your muscle groups. You can lift dumbbells to improve arm strength, lean over and lift your elbow above your back to strengthen your back muscles. Do sit-ups for your stomach muscles and leg lifts for your leg muscles. Most *stretching* exercises don't require any equipment at all. A number of examples to stretch different muscle groups can be found at http://www.nia.nih.gov/health/publication/ exercise-physical-activity-your-everyday-guide-national-institute-aging/sample-2. The key to stretching is to do it slow and steady. Gradually move into a stretch position (for example, turn your head toward the right) until you feel resistance, then hold that position for 10–30 seconds. Do not bounce (for example, don't jerk or push your head further to the right), as this might pull a muscle or tendon. Finally, *balance* exercises include standing on one foot (holding on to a countertop or chair if needed) for 10 seconds each leg, holding on to a counter or chair and raising one knee up to hip level, and walking heel-to-toe (placing the heel of one foot at the toe of the other, then alternating as you move forward). For more examples including pho- tographed demonstrations and specific instructions for all of these different types of exercises, see the Recommended Readings section at the end of this chapter.

To help you keep track of the frequency and type of your phys- ical activities, and to see how your level of activity measures up to the guidelines discussed here, you can use the worksheet printed at the end of chapter 14 in Box 14.4. You can also download this

Box 12.4 Case Vignette of Someone with MCI Benefiting from Exercise

Norman, a 76-year old retired bus driver, has recently been diagnosed with MCI. Norman never had been particularly fit. Throughout his middle and older adulthood, he has been about 50 pounds overweight. For 25 years, he smoked about a pack of cigarettes a day, but fortunately, he gave that up before he retired. Norman has high blood pressure and high cholesterol that are controlled by medication. Lately, he has felt tired much of the time, and his wife Rita is worried that Norman doesn't seem to do much other than read the paper and watch television. Rita wonders if Norman is depressed, and is trying to think of ways to get him living a more engaged life. While she was out shopping, she saw a flyer in the grocery store foyer for a new seniors center in their neighborhood. On her way home she stopped by and was intrigued to learn about a seniors walking group. Back home, she told Norman about the program, and they decided to give it a try.

The first day, they were a bit uneasy. They didn't know the other couples in the walking group, and were concerned that they couldn't keep up. Before they knew it though, they had walked two miles and met another nice couple that lives only a couple of blocks away from them. Norman and Rita started attending the walking group regularly and met even more new friends. After a few months, Norman noticed that he had lots more energy, and one day while at the seniors center waiting for the walking group to head out, he spotted a notice for another exercise group focusing on strength training, stretching, and balance, and decided to give it a shot.

A year after Norman and Rita started on this adventure, Norman had lost 20 pounds, and he was able to reduce the dosage of his blood pressure medication. Rita also noticed that she didn't need to remind Norman about upcoming events or things that needed to be done around the house as much, too. Most importantly, Norman seemed happier, and more interested in life.

worksheet at www.baycrest.org/livingwithMCI. Box 12.4 provides an illustration about how easy and rewarding adding physical activity can be.

Ideas to Fit Fitness in Your Everyday Life

There are many ways to increase your level of physical activity. Some are obvious, but many may surprise you. In Box 12.5 we list some of the many possible activities that could add greater physical activity to your life.

Box 12.5 Fitting Fitness in Your Everyday Life

Gear up

- Join an aerobic, yoga, swim fit, or spin (stationary bicycling) class or other such formal fitness program at your local fitness centre, Y, or senior center.
- Set a schedule with family members, neighbors, or friends to do morning or evening walks in your neighborhood.
- Hit the shopping malls—but to power walk before the stores open, not to leisurely browse!
- Purchase a treadmill, elliptical trainer (a machine that combines stair climbing and walking movements together with arm movements), or stationary bike so that bad weather is no longer an excuse.
- Sign up for a ballroom dance class.

Add umph to your chores

- Park in the back of the shopping-store parking lots to add extra walking time to your shopping trip.
- Carry reusable bags for smaller shopping trips, rather than pushing a cart, to add weight-bearing activity to your shopping errands.
- Vacuum, scrub the floors and tub, or clean the windows like you mean it—enough to increase your heart rate.
- Fire the neighborhood kid. Do your own leaf raking and snow shoveling (if your physical health permits).
- Take the stairs rather than the escalator or elevator.

(continued)

Box 12.5 (Continued)

- Offer to walk your grandchildren to school instead of having them taking the bus.
- Get a dog—evidence shows caring for a pet has mood-positive effects, and you have to take it for walks!

Play Games

- Purchase a step counter that counts how many steps you take in a day. Have family members and or friends purchase them, too, and start a competition to see who can walk the most. Aim to build up to 8000–10,000 steps a day.
- Play tag, throw or kick a ball, or have a snowball fight with your grandkids.
- Add a game of charades to your next evening party.
- Visit a park that you haven't been to and go for a hike.
- Play your grandkids' drum or bongo set.

A FINAL WORD

The chapter provided a lot of evidence that exercise makes your brain newer, bigger, better, and happier, which, in turn, helps you to think and remember better. The subtitle of our chapter is "Jog your Memory" because we liked the double-entendre, but we hope this chapter makes it clear that you can improve your memory and other thinking skills not only by jogging but by just about any physical activity. We gave you lots of ideas for how to add physical activity to your everyday life, and we provided tips for how to do so safely. For whatever reason, people find it harder to make changes around their physical activity than making changes around their cognitive or social activity, but when people ask us, "If I were to do only one thing to improve my brain, what would you recommend?" our first reply is "Exercise." This is because there is so much more direct evidence about the benefits of physical fitness for the brain than there is for cognitive or social fitness, if you will. Nevertheless, our second reply is always, "But we don't recommend that you do only one thing. It is also important to work out your brain through cognitive engagement and to enrich your social interactions, because these two have been shown to promote good brain health." The next two chapters provide the evidence regarding the effects of cognitive and social engagement, and we encourage you to enrich your live in all three ways to optimize your brain health.

Box 12.6 Questions to Ask Your Doctor

1. Can you do a health screen to tell me what type and level of exercise is safe for me?
2. Are there any types of exercise that I should avoid?
3. Are there any types of exercise I should focus on, for example, to help improve my balance?
4. What symptoms should I watch for to signal that I am overexerting myself?
5. Are there any community programs I could access to meet my specific exercise needs?

RECOMMENDED READINGS

The compendium of metabolic equivalent (MET) values for hundreds of activities can be found at http://sites.google.com/site/compendiumofphysicalactivities/home

For a great guide to help you achieve well-rounded physical activity that includes endurance, strengthening, stretching, and balance activities, download the following guides:

- U.S. National Institute of Aging: http://www.nia.nih.gov/health/publication/exercise-physical-activity-your-everyday-guide-national-institute-aging/
- Public Health Agency of Canada: http://www.phac-aspc.gc.ca/hp-ps/hl-mvs/pa-ap/08paap-eng.php

13

Cognitive Engagement: Getting Your Brain in Gear

In this section, we talk about proactive things you can do to maximize your brain health and your cognitive abilities. Fortunately, some of the most important things you can do in this regard can also be a lot of fun. Your leisure activities, for example, can provide you with opportunities for engaging your brain through critical thinking and new learning, and this has positive benefits for brain health. In this chapter, we'll talk about the idea of *cognitive engagement*, the types of activities that provide this, and why they are it is so important for your brain health.

WHAT IS COGNITIVE ENGAGEMENT?

Cognitive engagement is the process of getting your brain in gear and putting it to work. As we mentioned earlier in this book, *cognition* refers to the various processes of thought, such as intelligence, reasoning, judgment, learning, remembering, and other mental abilities. To be *engaged* in something means to be actively and effortfully involved in it. Cognitive engagement, then, refers to actively using your thinking skills in a way that requires effort. Other terms that share similarities with the term cognitive engagement include *mental stimulation, intellectual engagement*, and— less scientifically—*brain exercise*; all of these terms refer to the idea of actively using your thinking abilities.

Although you obviously use your brain all of the time, many activities involve only minimal cognitive engagement. It doesn't require a great deal of effort or thought to drive to familiar places, cook your usual meals, watch television, tidy the house, or make small talk with people you know well. These things can be done fairly automatically. On the other hand, you are more likely to do major thinking when you expose yourself to new and challenging activities, such as volunteering for a new organization, playing Scrabble, or helping your grandson with his algebra homework.

WHAT MAKES AN ACTIVITY "ENGAGING"?

The crucial ingredients in cognitive engagement are solving novel problems through logic or reasoning, and learning and remembering new information. Take the example of volunteering for an organization that is new to you. When you start the position, you are likely to encounter lots of new information, processes, and people that you will have to become familiar with. Depending on your role in the organization, you may also have to gather relevant information in order to solve problems or make decisions, and you may be asked to manage or train other people. All these processes are cognitively challenging—we normally have to work hard to do them well. These are the processes that define cognitively engaging activities. Any activity that requires new learning and problem solving provides you with cognitive engagement.

Clearly, of all the activities that you participate in from day to day, some are more cognitively engaging than others. Because engagement relates to *new* experiences, the level of engagement of any particular activity also varies from person to person and over time. If you want to figure out whether an activity is engaging to you, try this test: While you are doing the activity, see whether you can do another task at the same time, like carrying on a conversation or perusing the newspaper headlines. If you can do both tasks reasonably well, then the activity is not a cognitively challenging one for you.

A good example is driving. When you drive the same routes on a regular basis, such as to and from work or the grocery store, you can likely do so while doing other things like having a conversation, listening to an interesting radio program, or even daydreaming. You may have had the experience of arriving home with little recollection of the trip along the way. This is an indicator that the activity is an automatic one for you, requiring little effort on your part. Compare this experience to driving an unfamiliar rental car in a new city to a place that you have never been before. Likely, you will turn off the radio and kindly ask your passengers to stop talking to you so you can find the streets you are looking for. In this scenario, you need your full attention to focus on the task, take in new information, and figure things out. In other words, you are actively engaging your cognitive skills.

Cognitive engagement does not occur with the same tasks for everyone. It happens when you are involved in new and unfamiliar tasks and, as such, it is related to personal experience with that activity. You may find that learning to play *Für Elise* on the piano is challenging and engaging for you. In contrast, this same task would not be engaging for the piano teacher who has taught the piece to umpteen students over her career. Similarly, an activity that starts off as engaging can eventually become less challenging over time. Although your original learning of *Für Elise* may have been very engaging, after playing it several times a day for weeks on end, it will eventually become more automatic for you. This is when it's time to switch things up in order to re-engage your brain. Try learning a new piano piece, and consider some variety: Instead of more Beethoven, learn a jazz or new-age song that requires you to approach piano playing in a different way.

Another example of an engaging activity is doing crossword puzzles. Often, this is a great way to challenge your mind. Eventually, though, if you keep doing crossword puzzles by the same author, such as the one found in your local daily newspaper, you may start to notice similarities in the cues across puzzles. At this point, the task may become more automatic. After all, learning that a mine entrance is called an *adit* is only a learning experience once. When you get to this point, find new ways to keep it challenging, like timing yourself to see how quickly you can complete a crossword or moving on to more difficult puzzles.

BENEFITS OF COGNITIVE ENGAGEMENT

If you choose the right activities, cognitive engagement can be a lot of fun. Fortunately, there are also a number of benefits that go along with the fun of participating in these activities. There is a growing body of research looking at the effect of cognitive engagement on brain health. These studies point to benefits of cognitive engagement on your cognitive abilities over time, and a possible lowering of the risk of developing dementia.

We will discuss each of these benefits in more detail, by relating them to specific types of engagement activities. Most of our cognitive engagement comes from three broad categories of activities: leisure, educational, and occupational.

Leisure Activities

When we talk about leisure activities, we are referring to activities that are not part of our household, occupational, or educational responsibilities. Usually these activities are optional, and we choose to participate in them mainly because of the enjoyment they bring. Of course, not all leisure activities are cognitively engaging. Watching TV or relaxing by the pool is enjoyable, but these activities don't normally provide us with much cognitive engagement. Fortunately, many leisure activities do provide engagement. Some examples are playing board or card games, reading challenging books or news-papers, attending lectures, taking courses at a community center or library, visiting museums, playing a musical instrument, sewing, or woodworking.

Benefits of cognitive engagement through leisure activities

Research into the benefits of leisure activities generally takes the form of longitudinal studies that involve following the same individuals over time. In a typical study, a large group of individuals would be asked to fill out questionnaires to indicate whether or how often they currently participate in specific activities that are considered to be cog-nitively engaging, like reading, playing chess, or going to a museum. An overall "cognitive engagement" score would be calculated for each research participant, and participants might be classified as having either a high or low level of cognitive engagement. They would also be given tests of their memory and other cognitive abilities to determine their baseline ability level. Over the ensuing years, each participant would return to the lab, perhaps every 2 to 3 years, to repeat the memory and cognitive testing. Over time, the researchers can determine which individuals experience significant declines in their cognitive scores and whether anyone develops a cognitive disorder like dementia, and they can relate these changes to the original cognitive engagement score.

These studies show two important findings. First, individuals who have higher levels of cognitive engagement at the beginning of the study tend to experience less cognitive decline over the years. As we reviewed earlier in this book, aging is associated with some degree of decline in a number of areas of cognition, such as specific types of memory, as well as abilities like speed of thinking and abstract problem solving. The rate of decline, however, depends on a person's level of cognitive engagement, among other things. As illustrated in Box 13.1 individuals who are involved in a wider variety of activities and spend more time doing them tend to show less cognitive decline over the years in comparison to their peers who are not as cognitively engaged. Importantly, these studies control for important

---

Box 13.1 Change in Cognitive Ability over Time

The graph below shows how cognitive ability can change for older adults with a high level of cognitive engagement (solid line) and those with a low level of cognitive engagement (dashed line), as measured through leisure activities.

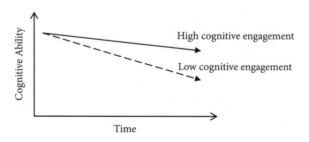

confounding variables that could complicate the interpretation of the findings. That is, the researchers have ensured that the two groups are equivalent in age, education, physical health, and other factors that could have an impact on cognitive abilities.

The second finding follows from the first, and relates to the development of cognitive disorders like Alzheimer's dementia. If a person's cognitive skills are stronger, it makes sense that they are less likely to meet criteria for a cognitive disorder. As time goes on, individuals with a higher level of cognitive engagement are less likely to develop dementia than those with a lower level of engagement.

The reason for the lower rate of dementia is not that cognitive engagement through leisure activities *prevents* dementia. Rather, dementia, when it does occur, tends to develop later in life for those individuals with more cognitive engagement than for those with less. That means that, instead of developing dementia in one's late 70s, for example, a person with a high level of cognitive engagement may instead develop dementia in his or her 80s. For some people, adding 4 or 5 cognitively healthy years to their life means living out their natural lifespan without ever developing dementia.

A word on "brain fitness" software

In recent years, as individuals have become more aware of the importance of brain health, a new consumer market has emerged that provides cognitive engagement through software programs. Although this is a relatively new market, it has been growing steadily. According to SharpBrains (www.sharpbrains.com), a market research firm that tracks the brain-fitness industry, the worldwide size of the brain-fitness software market was almost $300 million dollars in 2009. Many of the software programs claim to improve various cognitive skills, like memory, attention, problem solving, and processing speed, but the smart consumer should heed the warning, "let the buyer beware." Some products have no scientific validation of the claims that they make. Others have been evaluated more thoroughly, but this is a fairly new area of research, and the scientific evidence needed to back up these products is still in its infancy. Certainly, the long-term benefits of brain-fitness computer programs are unknown. If you decide you are interested in brain-fitness computer software, you should do some investigating to be sure you are choosing something that is most likely to be beneficial to you. Some issues to keep in mind are listed in Box 13.2.

If, in spite of these words of caution, you are particularly interested in computer programs, you can certainly build them into your overall strategy for increasing your level of cognitive engagement. Different software programs vary in terms of the activities that are involved. Many of these can provide opportunities for new learning and novel problem solving, and they can be challenging and interesting. These are the crucial ingredients that we have been talking about in this chapter for activities that provide cognitive engagement. If you decide to look into these programs, think of them as one of many activities that you do to provide cognitive engagement in your life.

Education

Another source of cognitive engagement is education. Education encompasses a variety of activities, and here we will focus on formal educational activities. This refers to your attendance in structured educational programs, such as elementary, middle, and high school, as well as college or university, where you work toward a degree or diploma. Research shows a clear association between level of formal

---

Box 13.2 What to Look for in a Brain-Fitness Software Program

---

Experts in the industry suggest that you should do some background research before making an investment in any particular brain fitness program. Look for software that has the following:

1. Backing by scientists or a scientific advisory board.
2. Research on the software program that has been published in peer-reviewed scientific journals.
3. Evidence in the research that there is an impact on users' everyday lives, not just that they get better at the program.
4. Activities that are novel to you.
5. Activities that continue to challenge and interest you, even as you become more and more familiar with the activities.

education and cognitive abilities. Overall, individuals who have more years of formal education tend to have stronger abilities in a range of cognitive areas, including memory, problem solving, and specific types of attention. Also, level of education is related to risk of developing dementia later in life. Specifically, individuals with a higher level of education are less likely to develop dementia than individuals with a lower level of education.

Our discussion so far may leave some readers gratified to know that their years of hard work in school will pay off in terms of cognitive health in their later years. If you did not continue on in school earlier in life, however, there is no need to resign yourself to a future of cognitive impairment. Recent research has shown that participation in cognitively engaging activities makes up for differences in memory related to formal education. In one study, individuals with fewer years of education but frequent participation in engaging activities had equivalent memory scores to individuals with more years of education. This means that the effect of education in childhood and young adulthood on cognition isn't necessarily life-long, and cognitive engagement can compensate for early differences in educational attainment.

Work

Work can also be a source of cognitive engagement. Over the course of our lives, many of us will spend a large portion of our waking hours at work. The nature of the activities that we engage in at work can impact our cognitive abilities. Researchers have looked at what is called "work complexity," which refers to the diversity encountered in work activities, and the number and level of difficulty of decisions that are required. Jobs that are straightforward and primarily involve following standard procedures would be considered low in complexity. Jobs that are constantly changing and require solving ill-defined or seemingly contradictory problems would be considered high in complexity.

Longitudinal research that has followed workers over many years has shown that work complexity increases a person's level of cognitive functioning over time, particularly for older workers. Specifically, older individuals who had more complex jobs during their working years tend to do better on tests measuring skills like problem solving, reasoning, flexibility of thinking, and new learning.

Work complexity is also associated with lower risk of dementia. That is, a person has a lower risk of dementia if he or she worked in a job that requires complex skills in working with people (for example, mentoring or negotiating with people) or working with data (such as analyzing and synthesizing data). Interestingly, this benefit of a highly complex job is seen even for individuals with low levels of formal education. In other words, the positive effects of a complex job can help make up for the negative effects of having fewer years of education, in terms of decreasing the overall risk of dementia in one's later years.

Volunteering

Closely related to work experience is volunteering. Around the time of retirement, many people seek out activities to fill their days, bring them fulfilment, and contribute to society. From the point of view of cognitive engagement, volunteering is one way that you can make up for the engagement you no longer get from your work activities after retiring.

Depending on the nature of the volunteer experience, you may reap a number of benefits from volunteering, such as being more physically active, having more social connections, and generally feeling more satisfied with your life. Of particular interest here is the relationship between volunteering and cognitive functioning. Although there is very little research to date on this, there are a few studies that have used rigorous experimental designs and have produced some very interesting findings. One volunteer program, *Experience Corps*, was designed and evaluated by researchers at Johns Hopkins University. They found that individuals who were randomly assigned to volunteer in an elementary school working with young students for up to one school year showed specific cognitive benefits relative to individuals assigned to a control group that had to wait for a year before volunteering. The cognitive benefits included improved performance on tests of memory and some types of attention. The take-home message here is that volunteering can provide cognitive engagement that may be of benefit to your cognitive health in the long run.

One of the authors of this book is currently conducting a study called Baycrest Research About Volunteering among Older adults, or BRAVO. We are looking at the effects of occupational complexity of older adults' volunteer roles on physical, cognitive, and psychosocial functioning. Volunteer roles vary in how complex or challenging they are, much in the same way that paid occupations are. Thus, the prediction is that volunteer roles that challenge older adults more should be more beneficial than less engaging volunteer roles. So far, the preliminary results are confirming this prediction, but readers can keep up to date with the study at www.baycrest.org/bravo.

Other Life Experiences

Another activity that provides cognitive engagement—whether it is part of your leisure activities or not—is speaking more than one language. As you might imagine, when you are fluent in more than one language (*bilingual*), and you use both languages on a regular basis, your mind is frequently switching back and forth between languages. Younger and older adults who have been bilingual most of their lives tend to do better on cognitive tests that measure things like flexibility of thinking and attention. (There can be a down side as well. Not surprisingly, it may take longer to pull up a specific word when a person has to sort through more than one language.)

Recent research has provided even more good news for bilingual folks. A team of researchers in Toronto found that, for those individuals who eventually develop dementia, those who are bilingual develop their first symptoms on average five years later than their counterparts who know only one language. Similar research that we have been involved in has also shown that individuals who are bilingual and who have been diagnosed with the type of mild cognitive impairment (MCI) that can lead to Alzheimer's disease tend to develop MCI four to five years later than individuals who are not bilingual. This delay in the development of cognitive impairment is similar to the effects of leisure activities that are cognitively engaging.

Somewhat similar to exposure to multiple languages from a young age is early (and sustained) musical training. There are a number of interesting differences between older adults who have had life-long musical training and those who have not. At a very fundamental level, musicians show fewer of the usual age-related changes in the overall volume of the brain as well as the size of specific brain structures. Following from this finding, it may not be surprising that individuals who frequently play a musical instrument are less likely to develop dementia than individuals who do not play an instrument.

Even if you did not learn a second language or take music lessons from a young age, there are benefits to learning later in life. A recent study from Sweden showed that individuals who received intensive language training also improved their ability to learn and remember other types of information, relative to matched individuals who did not receive language training. Similarly, older adults who agreed to take piano lessons for six months (and practiced regularly!) performed better on a variety of cognitive tests than similar older adults who did not take music lessons. The take-home message is that it is never too late to reap benefits from cognitive engagement. If you don't already know more than one language or play a musical instrument, consider learning one now. Or, if you used to speak another language or play an instrument, think about picking it back up again. There are a number of benefits to doing so.

HOW DOES IT WORK?

Cause and Effect

If you've been reading this chapter with a critical eye, it may have occurred to you that the direction of the relationship between engagement and cognitive abilities isn't clear. In other words, which one is the cause and which one is the effect? Perhaps participating in engaging activities improves one's cognitive abilities, or, just as believable, perhaps people with better cognitive abilities tend to participate in more of these activities. Both of these could explain the relationship between engagement and cognitive ability in studies in which the researcher simply looks at what people are naturally doing.

The true test of the cause-or-effect question is to use an *experimental* design where level of engagement is manipulated by the researchers, rather than simply observed. The research on the

---

Box 13.3 "Senior Odyssey": A Study of Cognitive Engagement

A team of researchers led by Dr. Elizabeth Stine-Morrow from the University of Illinois designed a study to look at the benefits of cognitive engagement by healthy adults ranging in age from their late 50s to early 90s. Participants were recruited from the community, and 181 eager and willing individuals were randomly assigned to an experimental Senior Odyssey condition or a control condition. The Senior Odyssey program was designed for this study and was based on Odyssey of the Mind (www.odysseyofthemind.com), which is an educational program that provides "creative problem-solving opportunities" for children and young adults. Senior Odyssey participants attended 20 weekly meetings in small teams of 5–7 individuals, and worked together to design, implement, and present solutions to problems such as building a structure from specific materials so that it will bear maximum weight or creating and presenting a musical performance that re-interprets an historical event. Teams also engaged in spontaneous problem solving on a weekly basis, completing tasks that required them to think on their feet by, for example, thinking of alternative uses of common objects or solving rebus (pictogram) puzzles. Participants in the control group and the Senior Odyssey group were given a battery of cognitive tests at the beginning and end of the study. The researchers found that, in comparison to the control group, the Senior Odyssey group improved more on a composite measure of "fluid ability" that included tests of thinking speed, inductive reasoning, visual-spatial analysis, and creative thinking. Studies such as this one show that real cognitive benefits can come through cognitive engagement.

---

volunteer program Experience Corps, mentioned earlier in this chapter, used this type of design. Another study using a program called Senior Odyssey is described in detail in Box 13.3 to illustrate this type of research. Generally in an experimental design, participants are randomly assigned to one of two groups: an intervention group that participates in a specific activity designed to increase cognitive engagement or a control group that does not participate in the activity or participates in a different "control" activity. The two groups would be compared before and after the intervention or control period in order to look at the specific effects of the intervention. A number of recent studies that use this type of design—some of which have already been reviewed in this chapter—have shown that individuals who participated in the training programs improved their scores on various types of cognitive tests, but individuals in the control group did not. This shows that increasing your level of engagement does, indeed, result in improved cognitive ability, and helps settle the question about cause and effect.

Although the studies described so far have involved older individuals with normal cognitive abilities, there is also some evidence that cognitive engagement is beneficial for individuals with cognitive impairment, including dementia. One type of program used with groups of individuals with dementia provides cognitive stimulation in the form of group discussions, reminiscence activities, and thinking games. Individuals who participate in these types of groups can show improvements in cognitive scores relative to similar individuals who do not participate. What this research tells us is that it is never too late to get involved in engaging activities. Regardless of a person's current level of cognitive ability, there are benefits to be had by participating in activities that are challenging and engaging.

The Idea of "Reserve"

To explain how things like education, leisure activities, and cognitive interventions can maximize memory and decrease the risk of dementia, theories of "reserve" have been suggested. The idea is that all the hard thinking that is associated with cognitive engagement increases the efficiency of brain structures and processes. Very early research with animals showed differences in the brains of rats that lived in enriched environments—that is, cages with a variety of toys and other rats—in comparison to rats living in less stimulating environments. The main brain difference was a greater number of connections between neurons in the brains of rats raised in the enriched environments. More connections mean that the brain can process information more efficiently. Not surprisingly, animals living in an enriched environment also tended to do better on tasks (like running through a maze, for example) that require them to learn and remember new information.

More recent research with animals has shown a role of new learning in the development (*neurogenesis*) and retention of new neurons in the hippocampus, a brain structure that is crucial for memory. Many new neurons are generated in the hippocampus every day, but most of these new neurons will not survive unless the animal is challenged to learn something new. The more engaging and challenging the new learning, the more new neurons will survive. These changes to the brain mean that, overall, it can work more efficiently, and this could explain how cognitive engagement results in stronger cognitive abilities over time.

These brain changes can also explain how cognitive engagement results in a lower risk of dementia. We raised this topic earlier, in chapter 5. Basically, the idea is that brains that are healthier and more efficient can likely tolerate the pathological changes associated with dementia for longer without showing cognitive changes that are symptoms of dementia. In effect, there is a "reserve" of brain cells and connections that provide a buffer against early brain changes. Once this buffer is depleted later in the dementia process, however, the benefits of prior cognitive engagement are not as obvious. In fact, cognitive decline can actually occur more rapidly in individuals with more cognitive reserve. Although this seems contradictory, remember that the brains of individuals with more cognitive reserve have a higher level of pathology once the clinical symptoms start. Thus, they are actually at a later stage in terms of the physical progress of the dementia, so the cognitive symptoms progress more quickly. The bulk of the benefit of cognitive reserve, then, is in maximizing cognitive abilities early on and in delaying the onset of cognitive impairment if dementia does indeed occur.

AN "ENGAGED" LIFESTYLE

As you think about developing a more engaged lifestyle, you may be wondering about exactly how you might do this. Unfortunately, there are no recognized standards for cognitive engagement as there are for diet and exercise, which we have discussed in previous chapters in this section. However, based on research that has been done in this area, we can give you some general guidelines to help you build cognitive engagement into your daily life. You can refer to Box 13.4 if you need some inspiration for new activities to take up. Keep in mind that you are aiming to improve your lifestyle, not looking for a quick fix. Spend some time thinking about how you will create a more engaged lifestyle in a way that is interesting, satisfying, and sustainable over the long run.

Box 13.4 Activities that Require Cognitive Engagement

There are countless ways to increase your level of cognitive engagement. Look for activities that are novel for you and that you would enjoy. In this box we list some of the many possible activities that could provide you with engagement.

Nurture your inner artist:

- Reconnect with a musical instrument that you used to play, or learn how to play a new one.
- Join a choir or start your own musical group.
- Sign up for a class to learn how to paint, draw, or sculpt.
- Join a local theater group and help put on a play.
- Read up on the art of photography, and see how you can improve your camera skills.
- Write a poem or essay, or start a journal.

Take up a new hobby:

- Build model airplanes and learn how to fly them.
- Join a knitting group and learn how to make that chunky wool sweater you've always wanted.
- Buy a scrapbook-making kit and organize all those new photos you've been taking.
- Learn how to make your own wine or beer.
- Play board or card games that require strategic thinking or memory, like chess, bridge, mah-jong, Scrabble, backgammon, or even poker.

Explore cultural activities:

- Visit a museum or historical site.
- Travel to new places and expose yourself to unfamiliar languages, customs, and people.

(continued)

Box 13.4 (Continued)

- Travel closer to home and discover local tourist attractions and popular hot spots.
- Go to the theater, symphony, ballet, or opera.

Do old activities in new ways:
- Buy a new cookbook or search the Internet for new recipes, then cook or bake something you've never made before.
- Look at a map and figure out alternate routes to get to familiar places, using back roads or streets you rarely use. Then walk or drive these different routes from time to time.

Learn something new, just for the fun of it:

- Buy an abacus or a slide rule, then research and learn how to use it. Once you have mastered the skill, make a point of using it from time to time.
- Learn how to play logic games like Sudoku if you haven't already. If regular Sudoku puzzles seem intimidating, start with simpler versions designed for youngsters. Once you master the basic puzzle, move on to variations like Kakuro, Killer Sudoku, and Hypersudoku so that you are continually learning and using new strategies.
- Play a sport that you have never played before. Take a class or ask a friend to teach you how to play squash, lawn bowling, curling, cricket, or something else that is unfamiliar to you.
- Pick up a self-study workbook at a bookstore and learn something new or re-acquaint yourself with one of your favorite subjects from school.
- Read up on the rules of a sport that is new to you. Then attend a game or match and see what you learn.
- Think of a topic that you're interested in knowing more about, and research it on the Internet.
- Attend a public lecture.

Take the ultimate learning challenge:

- Sign up for a course at your local library, community center, college, or university.

(continued)

Box 13.4 (Continued)

- Learn how to speak a new language, or brush up on a language you used to know. Find opportunities to use the new language whenever you can.
- Volunteer in a new organization, doing something you have never done before.

Variety of Activities

There is evidence for the importance of participating in a *variety* of engaging activities, as opposed to participating in only one or two. As you can imagine, different activities vary in the types of cognitive skills that are used. Playing chess requires visuo-spatial skills, strategy, and planning. Writing a poem uses verbal skills and artistic creativity. Taking up golf involves learning new rules and new motor skills. Participating in each of these activities helps you develop different cognitive skills and relies on different brain systems. Building variety into your activities, therefore, helps ensure that you are getting the maximum benefit of cognitive engagement, a "whole brain" workout.

How Often Should I Do Them?

In addition to variety, it is also important that you engage in these activities often. Playing the piano once in a while is good, but doing it two or three times a week is even better. There are no hard and fast guidelines for how many activities you should do, but some studies have looked at the relationship between the number of activities and the level of cognitive benefit derived. In a study published in the *New England Journal of Medicine*, activities were counted as the number of times a person participated in an engaging activity within a one-week period. For example, if, within a week, a person played a musical instrument on three different days, read the newspaper every weekday, attended a lecture, and played bridge once, his activity count would be 10. The greatest cognitive benefit was for individuals with activity counts of 12 or greater per week: They were 63% less likely to develop dementia over a 20-year period relative to individuals with the lowest activity counts. If you use this level of activity as a guideline, you would aim to participate in two cognitively engaging activities per day for most days of the week.

If you find that you need to increase your dose of cognitive engagement, you will want to think about how to do this in a sustainable way. You may not want to immerse yourself in nine new activities starting tomorrow, because this is a sure-fire way to burn out. Rather, spend some time thinking about your needs and interests, then start by adding just one or two new activities. After a few weeks, reevaluate where you are, and consider adding or changing a few activities, until you reach your goal.

To help you keep track of your activities, and to see how your level of activity measures up to the guidelines discussed here, you can use the worksheet printed at the end of chapter 14 in Box 14.4. You can also download this worksheet at www.baycrest.org/livingwithMCI.

A FINAL WORD

We will end this chapter by reminding you of the importance of fun. As you think about choosing activities that will provide you with cognitive engagement, be sure to choose those that are enjoyable to you. The reason for this should be obvious. It is important that you participate in these activities often, as part of an engaged lifestyle, and you are much more likely to stick with activities that you enjoy than activities that you don't. So, if you like doing crossword puzzles, keep doing them. On the other hand, if doing a crossword puzzle feels like taking medicine, then don't do it. You may be able to force yourself to do something you're not interested in a few times, but you are unlikely to keep at it. Find a variety of activities that are engaging and interesting to you, then participate in them frequently, and have some fun!

RECOMMENDED READING

Shors, T. J. (March 2009). Saving new brain cells. *Scientific American, 300*(3), 47–54.

14

Social Engagement: A Good Friend Is Good Medicine

Humans by nature are social beings. Many of our important cultural activities and institutions are based on social structures. We tend to gather and live together, raise families together, and look after each other. Education usually occurs in group settings, and many occupations depend on interacting with others. There are a number of benefits to being part of a social group, including increased safety, shared responsibility, and pooled economic support. Being with others is also known to improve mood and make us feel less stressed. Perhaps surprisingly, socializing can also provide cognitive benefits, and this is why the topic is relevant to your journey with mild cognitive impairment (MCI). In this chapter, we'll talk about the idea of *social engagement*, the types of relationships and activities that provide this, and why it is so important for your brain health.

WHAT IS SOCIAL ENGAGEMENT?

Broadly speaking, social engagement refers to interacting with other people. There are two important components of social engagement: social networks and social activities. Your *social network* consists of the individuals with whom you have regular contact, and they may include your family members, neighbors, and friends. *Social activities*, on the other hand, are the things you do that involve interacting with others. These might include working or volunteering with others, participating in a group like a book club or fitness class, or simply visiting with others in person or by telephone.

Research on the benefits of social engagement has indicated that both the *quantity* and *quality* of social interactions are important. *Quantity* (how many) is fairly easy to measure. Social networks can be quantified as the number of individuals with whom you interact. Social activities can be quantified as the frequency of social interactions that you have on a daily or weekly basis. *Quality* (how good) can also be measured, although this is obviously more subjective and usually more varied. One way of measuring quality of social interactions is in terms of social support. Generally, we feel supported when we have a friend or family member with whom we can share our feelings and who we feel is available to us when we are in need. Quality can also be measured by our sense of companionship. This is a feeling of fellowship or closeness to someone, and it is the opposite of feeling lonely. Some of the more common ways of measuring social engagement are provided in Box 14.1.

Although these different aspects of social engagement tend to go hand in hand, they are, in fact, distinct components that can be independent of each other. You may be a very sociable person with a large network of close friends and family that you meet regularly, or you may be more of a loner with few friends whom you rarely see. These are the extremes of social engagement. There are also variations in between these extremes that combine aspects of both. It is possible to have a large network of friends and family but not see them often if, for example, you have moved recently or have difficulty leaving the house. It is also possible to be around other people frequently, for example if you live in a busy retirement community, but still feel disconnected and alone. Just as possible, you may have a small number of friends but see them often and feel very close to them. As you will see, these different aspects of social engagement can provide independent benefits. So, what you lack in one area you may be able to make up in another in order to obtain the most benefit from your social life.

Box 14.1 Measure Your Own Level of Social Engagement

There are a number of ways to measure social engagement, with no single agreed-on standard. The following are some ways different aspects of social engagement can be measured. To compare your scores to those of others, see section in this chapter entitled "How much and how often?"

Social network size
In the grey space below, list the first names of any family members (such as spouse, children, siblings, etc.) or any friends that meet both of the following criteria: he or she is (a) someone with whom you feel close and can talk to about personal matters; and (b) someone you have contact with at least once per month.

Count the number of names listed above to calculate your social network size.

Social activities[1]
Read each activity listed below and decide how often you did each one *in the past year*. Circle the number next to the option that best describes how often you did the activity.

A. Went to restaurants or sporting events or played Bingo.

1. Once a year or less.
2. Several times a year.
3. Several times a month.
4. Several times a week.
5. Every day or nearly every day.

B. Went on day trips or overnight trips.

1. Once a year or less.
2. Several times a year.
3. Several times a month.

(continued)

Box 14.1 (Continued)

4. Several times a week.
5. Every day or nearly every day.

C. Did unpaid community or volunteer work.

1. Once a year or less.
2. Several times a year.
3. Several times a month.
4. Several times a week.
5. Every day or nearly every day.

D. Visited relatives' or friends' houses.

1. Once a year or less.
2. Several times a year.
3. Several times a month.
4. Several times a week.
5. Every day or nearly every day.

E. Participated in groups (such as at a senior's center, veteran's groups, Knights of Columbus, or something similar).

1. Once a year or less.
2. Several times a year.
3. Several times a month.
4. Several times a week.
5. Every day or nearly every day.

F. Attended church or religious services.

1. Once a year or less.
2. Several times a year.
3. Several times a month.
4. Several times a week.
5. Every day or nearly every day.

Add the six circled numbers to calculate your social activity score: ☐

Social support[2]
Read each of the statements below and decide how you feel about each one. After each statement, circle the number that best describes how you feel.

(*continued*)

Box 14.1 (Continued)

A. There is a special person who is around when I am in need.

1. Very strongly disagree.
2. Strongly disagree.
3. Mildly disagree.
4. Neutral.
5. Mildly agree.
6. Strongly agree.
7. Very strongly agree.

B. There is a special person with whom I can share my joys and sorrows.

1. Very strongly disagree.
2. Strongly disagree.
3. Mildly disagree.
4. Neutral.
5. Mildly agree.
6. Strongly agree.
7. Very strongly agree.

C. I have a special person who is a real source of comfort to me.

1. Very strongly disagree.
2. Strongly disagree.
3. Mildly disagree.
4. Neutral.
5. Mildly agree.
6. Strongly agree.
7. Very strongly agree.

D. There is a special person in my life who cares about my feelings.

1. Very strongly disagree.
2. Strongly disagree.
3. Mildly disagree.
4. Neutral.
5. Mildly agree.

(*continued*)

Box 14.1 (Continued)

6. Strongly agree.
7. Very strongly agree.

Add the four circled numbers to calculate your social support total
score. ☐

[1] Mendes de Leon et al., Social Engagement and Disability in a Community
Population of Older Adults: The New Haven EPESE, American Journal of
Epidemiology, 157: 7, 636, 2003, adapted with permission of Oxford University
Press; [2] Zimmet et al., The Multidimensional Scale of Perceived Social Support,
Journal of Personality Assessment, 1998, Taylor & Francis, Ltd., adapted with
permission of the publisher (Taylor & Francis Ltd., http://www.tandf.co.uk/
journals)

ACTIVITIES THAT PROVIDE SOCIAL ENGAGEMENT

There is a nearly endless number of ways to be socially engaged.
Similar to our advice regarding physical and cognitive activities, it is
important to find a variety of activities you enjoy doing, and participate in them often. Box 14.2 lists some of the many possible activities
that can be socially engaging.

As you think about these social activities, you may realize that
many of them also involve cognitive engagement or physical activity, or maybe even both. For example, playing bridge or learning
and using Skype involves social and cognitive engagement. Taking a
walk with a friend or playing with your grandkids in a playground
are activities that involve social engagement and physical exercise.
Playing golf or taking dance lessons provides social, cognitive, and
physical engagement. As we will review later, social activities that
are purely social are beneficial in and of themselves. However, there
are added benefits to choosing activities that also engage you physically or cognitively.

> **Box 14.2** Activities That Provide Opportunities for Social Engagement
> ___
>
> - Attending courses or groups at your local community recreation center, library, college, or university.
> - Attending religious services at your church, synagogue, or temple.
> - Singing in a choir or making music in a group.
> - Volunteering at not-for-profit or political organizations.
> - Participating in a neighborhood or community group.
> - Playing a group sport like lawn bowling, golf, or croquet.
> - Using Skype or other computer technology to communicate with family and friends from a distance.
> - Walking through your neighborhood and making a point of stopping to say hello to people you meet.
> - Baby sitting for your relatives or neighbors, or volunteering to help with a youngster's homework.
> - Having your friends or family over for a meal or—more simply— for coffee or tea.
> - Playing cards or board games with others.
> - Exercising with a friend by walking, swimming, or lifting weights at the gym.

BENEFITS OF SOCIAL ENGAGEMENT

Like cognitive engagement, we often seek out social engagement simply because it is enjoyable. However, there are also real benefits to be gained from socializing. We will start off by talking about general benefits of social engagement to health and mood, then focus more specifically on benefits to cognition and the brain.

General Benefits

Social engagement provides a number of general benefits to your health. The ultimate benefit is that social engagement is associated with lower mortality rates. That is, individuals with more social support have a decreased risk of death from any cause relative to individuals with less social support. This phenomenon has been studied most often among individuals with serious illnesses such as cardiovascular disease, cancer, and infectious disease. In these patient groups, individuals with greater social support live longer on average than those without such support. The remarkable thing is that the link between social engagement and mortality is present even after accounting for initial health problems. In other words, if you compare two individuals with the same level of heart disease, the individual with more social support is likely to live longer with the disease than an individual with less social support.

Research on the effects of social engagement has provided some insight into *why* this benefit is present. One explanation is that social support is known to be associated with healthier physiological reactions to stress. As you learned in chapter 9 of this book, under normal circumstances, our bodies respond to stress by increasing blood pressure and heart rate and increasing levels of the stress hormone cortisol. The mere presence of a familiar individual during a stressful event—such as visiting the doctor or giving a speech—can be associated with less of an increase in blood pressure and heart rate. Of course, this may not be the case 100% of the time. Surely you can think of an acquaintance or family member whose presence would increase rather than decrease your level of stress. However, when the other person is a source of support to you, then his or her presence can help buffer the physiological effects of stress. Because of this link between social engagement, blood pressure, and heart rate, it is not difficult to imagine that social engagement would also be related to better heart health and, in the long run, mortality.

In addition to these effects on the stress response, social engagement is also associated with a more robust immune system, especially in older adults. Your immune system is responsible for protecting your body from diseases by finding and killing harmful micro-organisms such as viruses and bacteria as well as tumor cells. Individuals with more social support show a greater level of activity of specific white-blood cells that help identify and fight tumors and viruses in the body. As a result, social support can have a positive effect on the body's response to some types of cancer, infectious diseases, and even the common cold.

Social engagement is also associated with mental health. It has long been known that social interactions have a positive effect on feelings of well-being. Similarly, a lack of social support can be associated with depression and other mental health issues. This connection between social engagement and mood has been used in some therapeutic approaches to the treatment of depression. Individuals who specifically work on building social connections and participating in more social activities can show significant improvements in mood.

Benefits to Cognition

The benefits of social engagement extend to cognition. There is a small but growing scientific literature on the link between social engagement and ability levels in specific cognitive areas. Because there are so many different ways to study social engagement as well as cognition, and because there are also numerous possible confounding factors to consider, the findings from different studies are not completely consistent. However, it is safe to say that the majority of studies point to a positive relationship between social engagement and cognitive abilities.

One line of evidence comes from observational studies of large groups of individuals. Researchers can take a measure of social engagement—such as social network size, number of social activities, and/or satisfaction with social relations—and see how it corresponds to a measure of cognition—such as a test of attention, memory, or a composite measure of several abilities. Because social engagement may also be related to important factors like age, sex, education, physical health, and hearing ability, these variables are usually controlled for, so that we can see the impact of social engagement on cognition, independent of these other factors. The general findings from these studies is that individuals with a higher level of social engagement tend to perform better on cognitive tests, even after controlling for important individual variables.

A similar finding is obtained when older adults are followed for several years to see how their cognitive abilities change over time. As we discussed in chapter 2, the normal aging process is associated with declines in some cognitive areas, even in the absence of dementia or MCI. There is considerable variation between individuals in rate of decline, however, with some individuals experiencing greater degrees of decline over time than others. Several studies have shown that those individuals with greater social engagement experience less cognitive decline over time than individuals with less social engagement.

Another way to look at the relationship between social engagement and cognition is to manipulate level of social engagement in the laboratory, as opposed to simply observing it in the real world. There are considerably fewer of these types of studies, but at least one deserves mention here. A recent study from the University of Michigan randomly assigned younger participants to engage in one of three activities just prior to cognitive testing. The activity was either social (i.e., having a conversation with another individual), intellectual (i.e., completing crossword and visual-spatial puzzles), or, as a control condition, neither social nor intellectual (i.e., watching a humorous video clip). After engaging in one of these activities for 10 minutes, participants were given tests to measure speed of thinking and memory over a short term. Perhaps you can guess the findings. People who spent time socializing before being tested tended to perform better on the subsequent cognitive tests relative to people in the control condition. The boost to cognitive performance from socializing was equivalent to the boost from engaging in thinking tasks. Although more research is needed in this area, this type of study provides evidence for an immediate benefit to socializing, and complements other findings from observational studies of more lasting effects of social engagement on cognition.

Benefits to Risk of Dementia

Given the effect of social engagement on general health and specifically on cognition, a natural extension of these findings is a link between social engagement and dementia. There is accumulating evidence that increased social engagement is associated with a lower risk of dementia in the general population. One factor that is highly related to social engagement is marital status: People who are married tend to spend more time interacting with others than do people who are not married. There are several studies showing a link between marital status and dementia. In general, individuals who have never been married are at a higher risk of developing dementia at some point in their lives than individuals who are currently married, widowed, or divorced.

A similar finding is that *quality* of social relationships is related to dementia risk. That is, individuals who are more satisfied with their social interactions are at lower risk of dementia than individuals who are less satisfied. In some studies, this is found to be true regardless of the frequency of the social interactions. In other words, participating in a few social activities that help you feel more connected and less alone is more important than participating in many social activities that do not provide this level of satisfaction. In this case, quality is better than quantity.

Another measure of social engagement, participation in leisure activities that involve social interactions, is also related to dementia risk. The effect of social activities can be tricky to study, because these activities are highly related to cognitive activities. For example, playing board games, attending cultural events, and taking courses—all activities that require cognitive engagement—are often done in a group setting. As such, it is important to tease out the effects of social and cognitive engagement on dementia risk. Although there are only a few studies on this topic, there is some evidence for a positive effect of social engagement on dementia risk, even after accounting for any effects of cognitive engagement.

Currently, there is no research on the effects of social engagement on risk or progression of MCI. However, we do know that vascular factors, stress, and depression are risk factors for MCI (as reviewed in chapter 5). Given that social engagement helps counteract these factors, it would follow that social engagement could reduce risk of MCI and/or progression of MCI to dementia. Although only further research will provide a definite answer to this question, the current and growing research findings certainly point in this direction.

HOW DOES IT WORK?

Cause or Effect

In chapter 13, we raised the chicken-and-egg question about whether cognitive engagement is a cause or an effect of better cognitive abilities and decreased risk of dementia. The same holds for the relationship between social engagement and cognitive ability. Is it true that being socially engaged provides a benefit to your cognition, or is it simply the case that individuals with better cognitive abilities (including individuals who are *not* in the earliest stages of dementia) tend to socialize more?

Undoubtedly, it is difficult to tease out these different explanations in observational studies. That is, when we simply look at what naturally occurs—by measuring social interactions and cognitive abilities in everyday life—we don't know what causes what. Several studies, however, have looked at the relationship between social engagement and cognition *after controlling for baseline level of cognition*, and find that the benefit remains. Similarly, other studies address this issue by excluding from the analyses any individuals who already have low levels of cognition or are in the earliest stages of cognitive decline. These precautions help minimize the chance that any reduction in social engagement is caused by declines in cognition.

Experimental studies are especially useful in addressing the cause-or-effect question, but these are much harder to come by. Recall the University of Michigan study we mentioned earlier in this chapter, where individuals were randomly assigned to participate in a social (or other) activity immediately prior to cognitive testing. In this case, socializing resulted in improved cognition, and the causal factor was clear. Other experimental studies described in chapter 13 regarding the effect of cognitive engagement on cognitive abilities are relevant here. Many of the interventions studied have a sizable social component. We described interventions that involved working in groups to engage in creative problem solving (Box 13.4) or to produce and perform theatrical plays. Reminiscence therapy used with individuals with dementia involves engaging in group discussion. The cognitive benefits obtained from these groups may be related in part to the social engagement that is inherent in the intervention. Clearly, more research is needed to determine the causal relationship between social engagement and improved cognition, but the evidence to date is consistent with positive effects of social interactions.

In the next sections, we will talk about the mechanisms that are thought to create this benefit of social engagement. As you will see, there are several possible explanations, and it may well be that a number of forces are at work.

Physical Health and Mood

Earlier in this chapter, we discussed the benefits of social engagement on physical health. Specifically, social engagement is known to impact the body's physiological response to stress by decreasing heart rate and blood pressure, factors that contribute to cardiovascular disease. Poor cardiovascular health is a risk factor for cognitive decline and dementia, as we reviewed in chapter 5. Thus, better cognition and lower rates of dementia may be related to the positive effects of social engagement on heart health and brain health.

Social engagement may benefit cognition via improvement in mood. As reviewed in chapter 5, depressed mood is a risk factor for dementia. There are many ways that depression can be prevented or treated, including increasing a person's social activities. Therefore, improved social engagement may increase your feelings of well-being, decrease your risk of depression, and thus improve cognition.

Cognitive Engagement

A related issue is the influence of social engagement on cognitive engagement. Social interactions make demands on a number of cognitive functions. Having even a simple conversation with another person requires you to pay attention to that person, maintain in your memory the content of the conversation, recall past events or information that are relevant to the topic of conversation, try to understand the thoughts or beliefs of the other person, and not let your mind wander or become distracted. These mental gymnastics certainly provide cognitive engagement, which is known to impact cognition and dementia risk, as we reviewed in chapter 13.

Another way that social networks can impact cognitive engagement is through social expectations or norms. When you are surrounded by friends and family, these individuals may encourage you to participate in other activities with them, such as having a meal together, visiting new places, or attending groups together. Thus, having friends around you may encourage you to get out and participate in life, and this, in turn, provides cognitive engagement that is crucial for maintaining optimal cognitive health.

It is clear that social engagement likely produces some of the benefits to cognition via indirect influences of physical health, mood, and cognitive engagement. Although this is part of the story, it is not the entire story. Research studies have looked at the independent influence of these factors, and have found that the effect of social engagement on cognition remains *even after controlling for* individual differences in stress and mood. Furthermore, when physical, cognitive, and social activities are considered together, there are independent effects of social engagement on cognition and dementia risk. So, there must be another factor that contributes to the effect of social engagement on cognitive health, above and beyond these factors. This leads us, once again, to the idea of brain reserve.

Brain Reserve

We talked about brain reserve earlier in this book when we reviewed risk factors for dementia and again when we discussed cognitive engagement. The idea is that some of the activities we do on a regular basis that use our brains cause our brains to become more efficient over time. This increased efficiency is due to the creation and retention of new neurons as well as improved connectivity between neurons. There is considerable research that links brain reserve to things like formal education, complexity of work, and cognitive engagement.

The idea that social engagement can contribute to brain reserve has been less well studied. A link was recently identified in a study conducted at Rush University Medical Center in Chicago. A group of older adults without any signs of cognitive impairment underwent cognitive testing and answered questions about their social networks, among other things. They also agreed to donate their brains to research after they died, so that the presence of any amyloid plaques and neurofibrillary tangles in their brains could be measured. You may recall from earlier chapters that plaques and tangles are abnormal neuropathological findings that are found in elevated numbers in the brains of individuals with Alzheimer's disease. Similar to many previous studies, this study found a correlation between cognitive performance and these types of Alzheimer's pathology, wherein individuals with lower cognitive skills had higher levels of pathology in their brains. Not surprising. The novel finding was that social-network size *moderated* (or affected the size of) the relationship between cognition and neuropathology. Although cognition and neuropathology were related for individuals with small social networks, these variables were not related for individuals with large social networks. In other words, individuals with more social connections can tolerate the presence of Alzheimer's pathology in their brains without showing signs of cognitive decline! In this study, the effect persisted after controlling for other factors that have been related to brain reserve, such as age, education, cognitive engagement, depression, and physical health. These findings were interpreted as evidence that social connectedness provides some type of reserve that reduces the harmful effects of Alzheimer's pathology on cognition.

BUILDING A MORE SOCIABLE LIFESTYLE

We hope that by now you are convinced of the many benefits that social engagement has on your health, your cognition, and your risk of dementia. We also hope that this realization has made you think about ways that you might increase your social networks, your social activities, and the quality of your relationships with others. In this section, we will give you some tips for doing just that. Box 14.3 provides an example of how one individual built more social engagement into her life.

How Much and How Often?

Unlike some lifestyle factors like diet and exercise, there are no hard and fast rules or guidelines for how much social engagement you should have in your life. There are also large differences between individuals: although some people may need many friends, others can get sufficient social support from having one or two good friends. Instead of giving specific guidelines here, what we can do is review what is known about the "average" person's social life. If you find that your social engagement is below this, you may want to consider ways to increase it. If you are the same as the average person, you are doing

---

Box 14.3 Case Vignette Illustrating Steps to Increase Social Engagement

---

Juanita is a recently widowed woman who moved to a condominium after realizing that she was having difficulty keeping up the house on her own. Without the regular companionship of her husband and her friends from the old neighborhood, she found herself feeling lonely and not getting as much enjoyment out of life. One of her daughters, with whom she keeps in regular telephone contact, suggested that she make a point of getting out and being with people more often. Juanita explored some of the activities in her condominium, and found a water aerobics class offered on site, and she also became interested in joining the condo association. Through these two activities, she made a number of friends who lived in the same building, and she quickly found that they had a lot in common.

True to the saying that "old friends are gold," Juanita made an extra effort to keep in touch with her friends from her old neighborhood. She started bi-weekly pot-luck lunches that rotated between her home and those of her friends. By making these efforts, she soon found that she felt re-connected with others and had more to look forward to on a day-to-day basis.

---

well, but you still may want to see if you can increase this a little more. Several studies looking at the relationship between social engagement and dementia risk show that the greatest protection against dementia occurs for those individuals who engage in more social activities and/or have larger social networks than the average person.

So what are these averages? A number of studies have indicated that the average social network size for older adults is about 7. The range is very large: a sizeable number of people have no close friends or family members, whereas others have upwards of 20. Check your own score (the first score in Box 14.1) to see how it compares to the average of 7.

Social activities and social support are measured in more varied ways, so there are not as many studies on any particular measure. In the studies that do use the scales and scoring systems we provide in

Box 14.1, the majority of older adults scored between 12 and 20 for social activity, and between 14 and 20 for social support. Compare these numbers with your own scores (the second and third scores in Box 14.1) to see if you have room for improvement.

We have created a worksheet to help you keep track of your social activities, as well as physical and cognitive activities discussed in previous chapters. The worksheet, printed in Box 14.4 at the end of this chapter and downloadable at www.baycrest.org/livingwithMCI can help you determine whether you need to add more activities of particular types in order to meet the general guidelines we have suggested.

Meeting People and Doing New Social Activities

If you decide you would like to increase your social network, one way to do this is by trying new social activities. Making new friends can be difficult if you haven't done it in awhile, so finding common interests through shared activities can help.

For practical advice about increasing your social network, you can refer to a free guide about making and keeping friendships that is published by the United States Department of Health and Human Services. The full reference is listed at the end of this chapter. Here, we will share some of the key suggestions from this guide. One obvious piece of information is that, in order to make new friends, you have to be in places or at events where other people are gathered. These could include support groups, sporting events, theatrical productions, concerts, art shows, poetry readings, book signings, civic groups, special interest groups, political meetings, and church services. Just hanging out in public places like a library or coffee shop sometimes leads to conversations with others who have common interests. Volunteering your time provides opportunities to make strong connections when you are working with others on projects of mutual interest. Some volunteer activities could include helping out at a soup kitchen or food bank, reading to children in a day care center, visiting people in a nursing home or hospital, or serving on political or social committees.

Once you meet new people, taking that extra step to develop a friendship requires some reaching out. You can get to know others better by inviting them for a coffee or to go for a walk, calling or

Box 14.4 Worksheet to Record Physical, Cognitive, and Social Activities

Use this form to record the activities you do that involve physical exercise, cognitive engagement, and social interaction. Record the date and the type of activity. For each activity, decide if it is physical, cognitive, and/or social. If it is a physical activity, record the amount of time that you spent doing it, placing your time in the appropriate column for moderate and vigorous activities (see Chapter 12). If it is cognitive or social, place an "x" in the appropriate box. At the end of the week, add up your totals to see how you compare with recommended activity levels. We provide a sample to show you how to fill out the form as well as a blank form for you to use.

Date	Activity	A physical activity? Record time spent		A cognitive activity?	A social activity?
		Moderate	**Vigorous**		
Monday	Went for a walk with a friend	1 hour			x
Monday	Played on-line Scrabble			x	
Tuesday	Went to choir practice			x	x
Tuesday	Went swimming		½ hour		
Tuesday	Wrote a letter to the editor			x	
Wednesday	Called an old friend				x
Thursday	Learned a new set of Tai Chi moves	1 hour		x	
Thursday	Practiced new choir piece			x	
Totals for the week		2 hour	½ hour	5	3

(continued)

Box 14.4 (Continued)

Date	Activity	A physical activity? Record time spent		A cognitive activity?	A social activity?
		Moderate	**Vigorous**		

Totals for the week

Note: Recommended activity levels per week are: 2 ½ hours of moderate physical activity, 75 minutes of vigorous physical activity, 12 cognitive activities, and 9 social activities.

e-mailing to share news that may be of interest to them, striking up a conversation on a topic of mutual interest, or offering to help with something they are working on.

Making Social Interactions More Satisfying

We mentioned earlier that the *quality* of your social activities, not just the quantity, is important. In other words, spending time interacting with a person or a group with whom you feel comfortable and connected is much more important than being around others but not feeling fully engaged. The Health and Human Services guide mentioned earlier includes a number of suggestions for how to strengthen friendships, old and new. We'll review some of them here.

First, it is important to communicate openly and honestly. Talk about what you need and want, and ask your friends what they need and want. Second, focus on listening and sharing. Pay close attention to what the other person is saying, and try to see things from his or her perspective. Let the person you are talking with know you are listening by making eye contact, inserting brief comments, and asking questions. Third, keeping personal information confidential is crucial for building trust. Assume that any personal information you learn about the other person is strictly confidential and not to be shared with others. Fourth, it is important to focus on fun. Laughter brings people together, so make a point of building fun activities into your interactions. Finally, stay in touch. Quality comes from quantity, so keep in touch regularly, even if only briefly. Have a plan for when you will meet next, and between visits, make a point of calling or sending a note or e-mail.

A FINAL WORD

Our parting advice is to have fun. The whole point of social engagement is to get to know others and share common interests. The health benefits that you get from your social interactions are a bonus. So, do what comes naturally, stretch yourself if you need to, and have fun. As you do this, you just may notice that you feel better, that you are less stressed, and perhaps even that you can remember things a bit better than you used to.

RECOMMENDED READING

U.S. Department of Health and Human Services, Substance Abuse and Mental Health Services Administration (2002). *Making and keeping friends—A self-help guide.* Publication ID SMA-3716. Downloaded from http://store.samhsa.gov.

15

Memory Strategies: Techniques to Improve Everyday Remembering

So far in this section, we have talked about things that you can do to improve your cognition through a healthy and active lifestyle. Now we will turn to a discussion of specific techniques you can use when you would like to remember something new, such as names of new people, important dates, and things you intend to do. Obviously, you are more likely to succeed with remembering new information when you make a deliberate effort to learn the name, but there are a number of strategies that can usually do a better job for you than simply trying hard. Our aim in this chapter is to provide you with practical information about various memory strategies that you can quickly learn and effectively apply to everyday memory situations.

SOME GENERAL INFORMATION ABOUT MEMORY STRATEGIES

Before talking about specific memory strategies, it is important to have a general understanding about why and when to use strategies, the different types of strategies, and how to fit them into your daily life.

Why Use Memory Strategies?

Memory strategies can serve a number of purposes. At the extreme, they have been used for pure entertainment. Some individuals practice the strategies so extensively that they can amaze their friends (or audiences) with an impressive ability to memorize long lists of words nearly instantly. This is accomplished using the formal mnemonic strategies described later in this chapter. For most of us, however, memory strategies are used for more practical purposes of ensuring that important information is available to us when we need it in our day-to-day lives. The types of information that many people describe as important to remember include, among other things, names of people, dates, phone numbers and PIN numbers, locations of household objects, things that need to be done, and medications. A variety of memory strategies can be used for remembering these types of information.

If you think about it, you'll realize that you don't necessarily need to have all of this information memorized. For some memory tasks—such as remembering what you need to do on a particular day—it is sufficient to have easy access to the information. In these cases, the goal is to be able to look up information when you need it. Having an organized and reliable system for recording information and developing good habits for referring back to the information when needed allows you to avoid relying on your memory when possible.

Other types of information are, indeed, important to commit to memory. Remembering the name of a new neighbor who you will be seeing often can be important for social reasons. Remembering your new phone number or address can be a matter of convenience when telling people how to get in touch with you. Remembering your PIN number without writing it down can be important for security reasons. In these cases, you can use various mental strategies to boost the memory process.

Types of Memory Strategies

Generally speaking, there are two types of memory strategies: external and internal. External strategies involve using aids that are outside your body to help you remember things, whereas internal strategies are mental activities that you engage in to remember information. Both types of strategies are effective ways of learning and retaining information.

External memory strategies

These are also called "memory aids," and can take a variety of forms. The most obvious of these are calendars, diaries, lists, and notes for recording information to be remembered. These aids may be paper based, like a wall calendar or a pocket notebook, or they may be electronic, like a smart phone, personal digital assistant, or computer. Your voice mail or answering machine can be an external memory aid if you leave messages for yourself to remind you to do something at home. A timer can also be an external aid. Most of us use a stove timer to remind us when to take the cake out of the oven or the rice off the stove. Similarly, electronic calendars on computers or hand-held devices can be set to ring when you have an appointment or another task to do at a particular time of the day. Internet search engines can be used to help you with information you only partly recall. If you can't remember the name of an old movie star, but you know he was the main character in "Arsenic and Old Lace," type that into a search engine, and you will soon be reminded of Cary Grant.

The benefit of external memory aids is that, when used properly, they can be extremely reliable. If you write down an appointment in your calendar, it will be there later for your reference. Unlike human memory, physical records of information don't fade or change over time. In this sense, an external memory aid is often your best bet for information that you absolutely need to have for later. Even for situations in which it is not the most convenient way to store information—for example, learning names of your new neighbors—it can be used as a back-up source of the information. If you learn a new name but later cannot recall it, at least you can look it up and make an effort to relearn it.

Some people are hesitant to use external memory aids because, if you write something down, you don't have to rely on your brain for remembering it later. The fear is that this lack of "brain exercise" will make your memory lazy and contribute to further memory problems.

Happily, we can tell you this is not the case. To the contrary, research has shown that writing information down can be an active memory strategy that helps you remember information later, even if you do not look back at the notes you made. As such, written memory aids can be used as often as you need them without any fear that doing so is harmful to your memory in the long run.

Internal memory strategies

In contrast to external strategies, internal memory strategies rely on processes that you do inside your head. They can include mental activities such as forming a visual image of something you want to remember, repeating information over and over to yourself, or making something meaningful to you personally. Internal memory strategies are crucial for situations in which you either cannot or prefer not to refer to a written aid, such as when you will use the information repeatedly. There are a large number of these strategies that have been validated by research studies, and they are generally found to be very effective at helping people remember new information. The down side is that they also tend to require a good deal of mental effort in order to use them well. It is easy enough to write down a telephone number. It is much more difficult to find a way to make the number meaningful or to visualize the number and commit it to memory. Many people choose to use these more effortful internal strategies only for situations in which it is very important to remember the information without looking it up. In these cases, an internal memory strategy can be extremely useful.

When to Use Memory Strategies

We previously talked about the different memory processes of encoding, storage, and retrieval. These refer to the acts of getting information into your memory, holding onto the information, and getting it back out when you need it. Most strategies are best applied during encoding, when you are getting the information into memory in the first place. This helps to lay down a reliable record in your memory, which leads to better storage and easier retrieval. If you do not apply a memory strategy at encoding, there may not be much information stored in your memory when you try to retrieve it. So the best advice about using memory strategies, just like Grandma's advice, is to plan ahead. Make yourself aware of times when you need to use a strategy, and then be sure to take the time to use it. If you wait until retrieval—when you are looking at a familiar face and searching for the name, or when you are standing in front of the banking machine trying to recall your new PIN number—you may be too late.

Individual Differences

Just like many human preferences, there is considerable variability between people in their choices of memory strategies. In part, as we discussed previously, your choice of memory strategy will depend on the type of information to be remembered, such as whether you need to commit the information to memory or you can just as conveniently look it up. When it comes to choosing which particular external or internal strategy to use, however, there is room for individual preference. If you are good at creating memorable pictures in your mind's eye, you may find an imagery strategy to be useful in helping you remember names. If you are mathematically inclined, you may be able to find numerical patterns or formulas that help you remember telephone numbers. If you don't like to be bothered with creative thinking, a simple repetition strategy may be best for you.

A wide variety of memory strategies is presented in this chapter. It is unlikely that you will find all the strategies to be indispensable to you. More likely, you will find one or two that are helpful and feel natural to use, and one or two more that you could use in a pinch. The important thing is that you approach these strategies with an open mind. You never know what might work until you try it a few times.

Practice, Practice, Practice

Just like learning any new skill, it will take some practice to become good at using memory strategies. You can't expect to read a book on improving your tennis stroke or your chess game and show much improvement without practicing what you read. The same is true for learning to use memory strategies. You may find that, initially, some of the strategies discussed in this chapter seem awkward or require too much effort to bother with. However, if you put in some effort to practice the strategies, you may find they eventually become much easier to use and lead to success in remembering what you don't want to forget.

A MENU OF MEMORY STRATEGIES

Now we'll turn to a discussion of specific memory strategies. We will talk about what each one is, some of the science that tells us about its effectiveness, and the types of everyday situations in which it may be most useful. Although we will discuss each strategy separately, many of the techniques can be used together. For example, if you have a new cell phone number to learn, you may want to write it down, find a way to make the number meaningful, *and* practice retrieving the number several times. Often, using several approaches is your best bet for learning new information, particularly when you anticipate the new learning to be somewhat difficult or when knowing the information is critically important.

Memory Books

One of the most globally useful memory aids is a memory book, which is an organized combination of several different types of external memory aids. A well-designed memory book contains all the information that you need for participating in your usual activities. If you develop a good habit of using it systematically, the memory book can meet many of your needs for remembering information on a day-to-day basis. Here we will describe the important features of a memory book. Keep in mind, though, that your memory book should be personalized to best meet your own needs. It may be more or less detailed or contain different types of features than what we discuss here.

Comprehensiveness
A memory book contains all the important information that you need to be able to access readily. Of course, it is not necessary to carry

along the addresses and telephone numbers of all of your acquaintances, or calendars from the past 10 years. Instead, you should include information that is used frequently—like a calendar and a list of things to do—and information that would be needed in an emergency—like a list of your medications and important telephone numbers.

The type of information contained in a memory book will vary from person to person. You may want to include some or all of the following sections in your memory book:

1. **Calendar**. This is used to record appointments (such as doctor or dentist appointments), social engagements (celebrations, plans to meet a friend for coffee), things that need to be done on a particular date (purchase tickets for the theater on the day they go on sale), dates that need to be acknowledged (birthdays or anniversaries), due dates (for your library books or to pick up the dry cleaning), and other events occurring on particular days that one does not want to miss (a radio interview or a movie on television).

2. **List of things to do**. This section is for writing down things that you need to do, such as buying a gift, filling a prescription, or booking an appointment. It is good to get into the habit of crossing things off once they have been done, so that you don't need to remember whether you have already done them.

3. **Scratch pad**. This is for writing down information that is only needed for a short while, such as your shopping list, where you parked your car, questions you want to ask your doctor at your next appointment, or a telephone number where your daughter can be reached while she's on vacation. When the information is no longer needed, it can be crossed off or discarded to avoid unnecessary accumulation of information in your book. You could consider using sticky notes for your scratch pad, placing the note in the calendar or telephone book section while you need it, and removing it when it is no longer needed.

4. **Permanent files**. This is for information that you use frequently and want to keep permanently. It might include sections for telephone numbers and addresses, e-mail addresses, medications, passwords or code numbers (disguised if necessary for security purposes), maps or

bus numbers for places frequently visited, or addresses for Web sites used often.

A Single Tool

Ideally, your memory book will be a single tool. It is not uncommon for people to have a calendar on the wall, a pocket calendar in a purse or briefcase, a list of medications in a wallet, a list of books to be read on the dresser, and a list of things to do on a sticky note on the refrigerator. The problem with this approach is that it can be difficult to remember to check all these places, and something could easily get left behind. If you write an appointment in a pocket calendar when you are out, you have to remember to transfer it over to your wall calendar when you get home. As much as possible, it is important to put everything into a single book or device. You can create a paper-and-pencil memory book using a day timer or pocket calendar that contains an address book, blank pages for writing on, and a pad of sticky notes. If you like electronic gadgets, there are many hand-held devices like personal digital assistants (PDAs) and smart phones that are meant to be used for these purposes.

The advantage of having a single memory book is that you are more likely to carry it with you and, therefore, use it more often. Also, you will have fewer components to lose, misplace, or forget to check. You can build good habits around writing in and referring back to a memory book, and this increases its effectiveness as a memory aid.

Portability

There are many situations in which a memory book would be useful outside the home. For example, when at the doctor's office, you may need to consult your calendar in order to schedule the next appointment. You may need a friend's telephone number when you are running errands and you realize you will be late meeting your friend for lunch. A small memory book is usually better than a large one because it can fit in a purse or pocket and is more easily portable.

It is important to develop a habit of always having the memory book handy, whether inside the house or out running errands. When you are at home, you can make a point of always putting it in the same place, perhaps by your telephone or in your purse. When you are out, you take it with you. It may take some time to get into the habit of doing this, so it may be a good idea to place the book near other items that you usually take on outings such as your keys or wallet.

Some people worry that they will lose the memory book if they take it out of the house. Again, a habit needs to be developed to avoid this. You can do this by making a point of always keeping the book in your bag, your pocket, or your hand when you are not at home. While you are actively using your book, you can keep it in your hand, and when you no longer need it, you can return it to your bag or pocket. Avoid placing it on a counter while making an appointment or putting in on top of a pay telephone while making a call, because you might forget to pick it back up and take it with you.

Regular Use

The usefulness of your memory book is maximized when you refer to it regularly. To be most useful, you have to develop a habit of recording accurate information such as appointments in the first place, and you have to remember to check your calendar when you need it. If you are not already in the habit of using or checking a memory book, you may need to put some effort into developing this habit. One way of doing this is to pair checking the book with another routine that you do several times a day, such as eating a meal and preparing for bed. We talk more about habits in the next section.

Habits

You likely have a number of habits or routines built into your day that help you remember things or, just as important, allow you *not* to rely on your memory when you don't need to. Habits are the most effective strategies for remembering locations of frequently used items, like your keys or wallet, and for doing repeated tasks, like taking medication. When habits become entrenched, they happen automatically without much effort on your part. This means you don't have to spend time retracing your steps to remember where you left your keys or figuring out when you have to take your next pill. We'll talk about using habits for remembering locations of household items and for performing repeated tasks separately.

It is a fairly common experience to misplace household items. This can be frustrating when you spend a lot of time looking for things, especially when you find yourself doing the same search day after day. In this case, the saying "a place for everything and everything in its place" are good words to live by. If you have a habit of always putting your car keys in a bowl by the door, for example, then you don't have to try to remember where you put them last. You'll know exactly where they are even if you don't remember putting them there, because they are always in the same place.

The way to develop good habits regarding locations of items is to start by figuring out a *logical* place to keep each item. You are more likely to remember a logical location, like keeping your postage stamps in the same desk drawer as your stationary and envelopes, than an illogical or neutral place. As well, the logical location is also likely to be the most convenient location for using those items. After determining a logical location, the next step is to put the item in that place and then—here is the difficult part—always put it back when you are not using it. Often the reason that we lose things is because we put them down without thinking about where we are putting them. When we don't pay attention, of course we don't encode information very well, and this makes it very difficult to retrieve the information later. By making a conscious effort to return an object to a specific location, we are breaking the bad habit of putting things down without paying attention and building a good habit of using consistent, logical locations for items. With time, the habit of using the logical location will also become automatic, and acting without paying attention will help rather than hurt our ability to find things.

Another good use of memory habits is for remembering to do things that are repeated often, like taking a medication twice a day. Similar to the problem of losing common objects, we don't spend much time thinking about the things we do over and over again, and it is easy to forget to do them or forget whether we have done them. The key here is to develop a habit of doing something *at the same time* that you would normally be doing something else. With time, the one activity becomes a cue to do the other. For example, if you are already in the habit of brushing your teeth twice a day, you could keep your medication near your toothbrush and make it a habit to take your medication when you brush your teeth.

There are many other everyday situations in which habits can be used to help you remember important things to do. Some of these are listed in Box 15.1.

Developing good memory habits can be particularly difficult when it forces us to do things differently. It is hard to break old habits and to create new habits. The good news, though, is that once you have a new (good) habit, it is also hard to break. While you are developing a new habit, you may find that you slip easily into your old habit, but keep plugging away at it. Eventually, your new habit will win out and you will find that you are spending less time searching for lost objects or pondering whether you remembered to do something.

Box 15.1 When to Use Memory Habits

If you often...	Make it a habit to...
• Can't find your keys	• Keep them on a hook by the door at home and in your pocket (or purse) when you are out.
• Misplace your reading glasses	• Buy two pairs and keep them in the places you most often use them.
• Forget to take your vitamins	• Keep the bottle on the kitchen table and take them with breakfast.
• Forget to lock the door when you leave the house	• After you close the door, turn around and double-check to see if it is locked.
• Send an e-mail and forget the attachment	• Add the attachment *before* you start writing the text of the e-mail.
• Forget to check your memory book for appointments.	• Keep the memory book in a prominent place, like on the kitchen counter, and check it whenever you prepare a meal.

Paying Attention

We've talked about how failure to pay attention can result in failure to remember. If you are not paying attention to a conversation or to what you are reading, for example, it is unlikely that you will encode enough information to retrieve it later. Even things that you see over and over again may not be remembered well if you are not paying attention to the details or making a point of trying to remember them. In one well-known study, participants were asked to pick out the correct drawing of an American penny from among a group of incorrectly drawn pennies. Look at the drawings in Box 15.2 to see if you can identify the correct one. If you are like more than half the participants in the original research, you

---

Box 15.2 Memory for the Details of a Common Object

How well do you remember common objects that you see every day? Look at the drawings of pennies below, and see if you can pick out the correct drawing. After you have made your guess, compare it with a real penny to see how well you remembered the details.

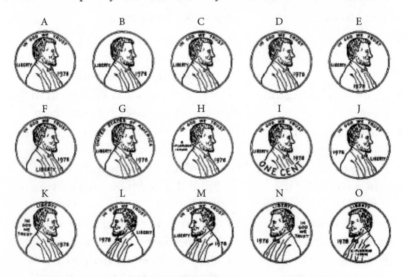

Reprinted from Cognitive Psychology, 11, R.S. Nickerson & J.J. Adams, Long-term memory for a common object, 287–307, copyright 1979, with permission from Elsevier.

will have difficulty with this seemingly simple task. How can this be? It is because with the exception of coin collectors, we don't pay attention to the details of how coins are designed. This example really drives home the point that just seeing something over and over again throughout your entire life is not good enough to get it into memory. To store information in memory, we have to pay attention, and memory strategies are one good way to force us to pay better attention.

Although failure to pay attention can result in a failure to remember, the opposite of this is also true. In other words, if you intentionally focus your attention on something, you are more likely to remember it later. One way to do this is simply to make a point of concentrating on what is happening around you. If you hear or see something that you want to remember for later, tell yourself to focus carefully, then give it your full attention. For instance, when you meet someone for the first time, make a point of paying close attention to the name. Make sure that you have heard it properly and, if not, ask for it again.

There are also specific techniques for focusing your attention on information or actions you want to remember. One particular technique is called "implementation intentions" in the scientific literature or, more simply, "see it and say it." This technique was designed to help with *prospective memory*, or remembering to do something in the future. The idea is to focus your attention on something by visualizing a picture in your mind's eye—that's the "see it" part—then stating out loud what you want to do—that's the "say it" part. Stating your intention out loud is preferable to saying it to yourself, because it will focus your attention even better. However, if you are in a situation in which it is impractical (or embarrassing) to say it out loud, saying it to yourself is second best.

As an example of when and how you might use this attention technique, imagine that you are running errands in your neighborhood and you realize that you need to stop at the corner grocery store on your way home to buy some milk. As soon as you decide this is an important thing for you to remember to do, you would use "see it and say it." You might "see it" by visualizing an image of yourself walking home, turning left off the sidewalk into the corner store, and walking over to the refrigerated compartment where the milk is kept. You might "say it" by stating out loud "I will stop at the corner store on my way home to buy some milk."

It's not difficult to come up with examples of using this technique to remember to do something in the future. If you are in the basement doing laundry and you notice that you are nearly out of laundry detergent, picture yourself walking up the stairs and writing on your grocery list in the kitchen. Then say out loud, "I need to put detergent on my shopping list." These two actions together will only take a second or two and are fairly easy to accomplish. Powerful results can come from simple actions, though. Research has shown that individuals who are instructed to use this technique are about twice as likely to complete the intended task as individuals who do not use this technique.

The see-it-and-say-it strategy can also be applied in situations in which you want to remember something that you have already done. It is especially useful for remembering actions that you might not otherwise pay attention to. Let's return to our earlier example of putting down household items like keys without thinking about where you are placing them. The best approach would be to use a good memory habit and return the keys to their preset location. If this isn't possible because, for example, you are traveling, then you could use see it and say it. Form a visual image of yourself placing your keys in the inner pocket of your briefcase and say out loud, "My keys are in my briefcase."

The technique is also useful to help you remember that you have done important things that you would otherwise worry about. You can use see it and say it when you turn off the stove after you finish cooking your supper, when you unplug your iron, or when you lock the front door on your way to bed. This will help you remember that you have done these things, so that you don't worry about it later or waste time rechecking.

Meaningfulness

Another category of memory strategy involves making information meaningful. Research has shown that it is easiest to remember new information when we think about the *semantics*, or the meaning, of that information. The levels-of-processing theory, originally proposed by Fergus Craik and Robert Lockhart in the 1970s, states that the degree to which new information is learned depends on the depth to which it was originally processed. Take as an example the task of learning a list of words. Shallow processing, such as thinking about how a word looks or what letter it starts with, leads to the poorest level of recall. Deep processing, such as thinking about what a word

---

Box 15.3 A Sample Research Study about Levels of Processing

To help us understand how people learn new names, we showed a group of research participants a list of 32 surnames, like "Mr. Dean" and "Ms. Mason." As each name was presented, we asked one of three questions to make participants focus on different aspects of the name. For some names, we drew attention to the physical look of the name by asking "What letter does it start with?" For some names, we drew attention to the sound of the name by asking "What does it rhyme with?" For other names, we drew attention to the meaning of the name by asking "What does it mean?" After seeing all the names and answering the questions, participants were given a surprise memory test for the names. The results are shown in the graph. Consistent with the levels-of-processing theory, the lowest level of recall was for names processed by physical look, and recall was only slightly better for names processed by sound. The best recall was for names processed by meaning; under some conditions, when processing names by meaning, older adults in their 60s and 70s remembered the names just as well as younger adults in their 20s! This tells us that the best way to learn and remember new names is to make the names meaningful.

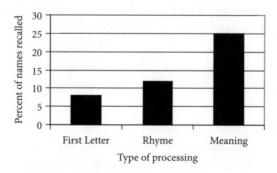

Percent of names recalled when they were processed according to their first letter, rhyme, or meaning. Troyer, Angela K. et al., Name and Face Learning in Older Adults: Effects of Level of Processing, Self-Generation, and Intention to Learn, Journals of Gerontology—Series B: Psychological Sciences and Social Sciences, 2006, 61:2, 35, adapted with permission of Oxford University Press.

means, leads to the highest level of recall. Some of our own research illustrates this effect, described in Box 15.3.

There are several ways to make information meaningful. Because this is a great strategy to use with names, we'll show you different ways to use a meaningfulness strategy for first and last names. The most obvious way to use this strategy is to think about what a name actually means. The name *April* refers to the month, *Roan* is a red color, and *Cooper* is someone who makes barrels. If you don't know the actual dictionary definition of a name, you can make it up or use a loose association. For *Graham* think of a graham cracker, and for *Barker* think of a noisy dog. You may have to ignore the spelling of the name and focus on how it sounds in order to make it meaningful. The name *Mary* could be marry or merry, *Katz* could be cats, and *Traynor* could be trainer. You may have to slightly change the sound of the name in order to find or create a meaning. *Terumi* could be true me, and *Whalen* could be whaling. If necessary, you can break the name into smaller words or syllables. *Eileen* could be I lean, and *Harrison* could be a hairy son. It may be sufficient to focus on only the first part of the name, and trust that the rest of the name will follow. Think of a tiff for *Tiffany*, land for *Landon*, and a martini for *Martinez*.

Another way to make a name meaningful is to think of other people you know with the same name. You can make associations with famous people, like Benjamin Franklin for the name *Ben*, and the actor Paul for the name *Newman*. You can also make associations with people that you know personally. The name *Zoë* may remind you of your niece, *Ellen* may be a friend from your childhood, and *Cheng* may be your neighbors' surname. It is not important how you make the name meaningful or whether it is indeed the actual meaning of the name. The important thing is that you go through the process of thinking about the name in a deep, meaningful way. When you do this, you make the name more memorable to you.

You can use a meaningfulness strategy with other types of information, as well. If you want to remember the title of a movie or book, you could try to create a mental image of the title. To remember the movie *Bicycle Thieves*, you might picture two people jumping onto bikes and furiously pedaling off into the night. To remember the book *Life of Pi*, imagine the "life" events of a blueberry pie, from picking the berries and mixing the ingredients to baking the pie and eating it for dessert.

Another use for this strategy is memorizing new numbers. If you like to play with numbers, you may be able to notice mathematical patterns in strings of digits. For the phone number 357-9281, you might notice that the first 3 numbers are ascending odd digits, and the last 4 numbers form the mathematical equation $9^2 = 81$. Some numbers may have personal or historic meaning. If your new locker combination is 16-3-45, you might think about how you learned to drive at age 16, you have 3 children, and World War II ended in Europe in 1945. For numbers that you punch into a key pad, you could look for a spatial pattern. Looking at the layout of a key pad (see Box 15.4), you can see that a PIN number 3971 uses the four corner numbers and the digits in the telephone extension 8022 are all in the same column.

Remember that the reason for making information meaningful is to help you process it at a deeper level and thus make it more meaningful to you personally. When you do this, you integrate it with your already-stored knowledge so there are more places for it to "hang onto." There are a number of ways to make something meaningful, and there are no "right" or "wrong" ways to do it. If it is meaningful to you in any way, you will remember it better.

Retrieval Practice

Another technique for learning new information is retrieval practice. As you might guess from the name, this technique involves practicing the act of retrieval, which is the final stage of the encoding-storage-retrieval process. The way to practice retrieving is simply to call to

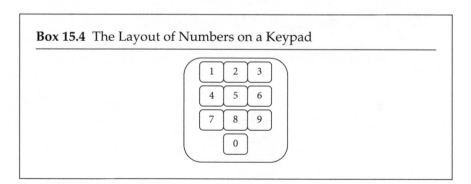

Box 15.4 The Layout of Numbers on a Keypad

mind the information that you are trying to learn over and over again. Although it involves practicing *retrieval*, you have to implement the strategy during encoding, when you are committing the information to memory in the first place.

Retrieval practice is similar to the natural memory strategy of repeating information to yourself. For example, if you are given verbal directions to a new restaurant and are told the address is "387 Northgate Avenue," you might repeat the address to yourself several times. Retrieval practice takes this natural strategy a bit further. The key to ensuring that you remember the information later is to try to recall the information over a slightly longer period, so that you find it just a bit challenging. Just as with the "see it and say it" technique, repeating the information out loud is more memorable than saying it to yourself, although the latter will do if necessary.

There are different ways to space out retrievals, and these are illustrated in Box 15.5. You can space the retrievals evenly, for example, by retrieving the information every 10 seconds. Alternatively, you can use an expanding pattern, such as retrieving after 5 seconds, 10 seconds, 20 seconds, 40 seconds, and so on. Research shows that both are effective, so you can take your pick. Either way, you want to choose intervals that are long enough that you have to put some effort into the retrieval, but not so long that you forget the information.

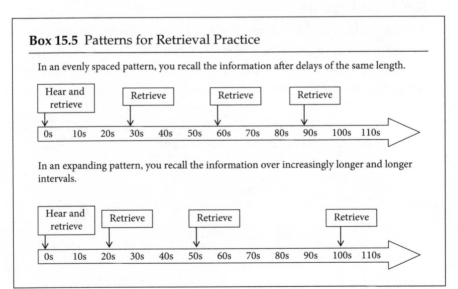

Box 15.5 Patterns for Retrieval Practice

In an evenly spaced pattern, you recall the information after delays of the same length.

In an expanding pattern, you recall the information over increasingly longer and longer intervals.

You may find that you need to adjust the timing and the number of retrieval practices depending on the difficulty of the information you are trying to learn. If you are learning a short, familiar name like *John Smith* or a 3 -digit password like *944*, it may be enough to retrieve the item 4 or 5 times after 20 second intervals. If, on the other hand, you are learning a long unfamiliar name or a 10-digit telephone number, you may need to retrieve the item 10–15 times, and start with intervals of only a few seconds. If necessary, you can break up the information and learn it in stages. For the telephone number, you could start by practicing the area code. Once you have that, you could work on the next 3 digits, then finally the last 4 digits.

Retrieval practice is a good strategy to use to hold information in your mind until you are able to write it down. For example, if you are driving in your car and the program on the radio you are listening to is reviewing a movie you think you would enjoy, you could use retrieval practice to memorize the title of the movie. If all goes well using the technique, when you arrive home 30 minutes later, you will still remember the title and can write it down in your memory book.

Retrieval practice is also a great strategy for learning a new name during conversation. When you meet someone new for the first time, you can repeat the name out loud as soon as you are introduced, for example, by saying, "Hello, Mary Jane, it's nice to meet you." Then, while you are chatting with her, you can find times to use her name that naturally fit into the conversation. Although you will be aware that you are doing this in order to learn the name, most likely, no one else will notice.

As in any of the other internal memory strategies, retrieval practice is also useful when you really need to commit something to memory without having to look it up. For example, we all know that we should not write down the PINs for our bank cards or credit cards, in case our note is lost or stolen. In this case, retrieval practice can be used to learn the number.

Research on this memory technique has shown that retrieval practice is effective for learning a variety of types of information for a variety of types of people. It is one of the better ways for students to learn rote information like spelling words or times tables. It is also useful for teaching people with serious memory problems like

Alzheimer's disease to relearn the names of their acquaintances or to learn a new routine.

Formal Mnemonics

Any chapter on memory strategies would be incomplete if it did not mention formal mnemonic strategies. You may have seen or heard about individuals with amazing memory abilities, who can memorize and spout off long lists of words immediately after hearing them. Some of these people take part in formal competitions to see who can memorize the most information—like digits, playing cards, or words—in the least amount of time. This is accomplished by learning a formal mnemonic strategy and practicing it over and over again until it becomes second nature. Two of the more common of these strategies are the method of loci and the peg-word system.

Method of Loci

This technique dates back to ancient Greece, where orators were said to have used the method of loci for memorizing their speeches. To use this technique, you first imagine a familiar place, such as your house, and several locations (or *loci*, hence the name) within that place. Then, you trace a path through the place in your mind and associate each individual item that you are memorizing, like the points you want to make in your speech, to a separate location. Later, when you want to recall the items, you retrace your path and call up the items in each location.

Let's illustrate with an example. Imagine that you are walking to the grocery store and creating your shopping list as you go. Because it is difficult to walk and write a list at the same time, you decide to use the method of loci to memorize the list of grocery items as you think of them. You decide to use your house as your location for this mnemonic. (See illustration in Box 15.6.) Your first grocery item is eggs, and the first location in your house is your front door. So, you imagine that someone has thrown eggs against your door. You see the yellow, gooey yolk sliding down the door and the broken egg shells on the ground in front of the door. The next item is apples. You imagine a giant red apple in the foyer of your house that is so big you have to squeeze past it to get into the next room. The next item is milk, and you imagine that someone has spilled a carton of milk on the carpet in the next room, your living room. Your footsteps slosh as you

Box 15.6 Using a House for the Method of Loci

To use the method of loci, take a mental walk through a familiar location like your house, and associate items to be remembered with distinct locations (or *loci*) in the house. The dotted line in the figure represents the route taken in the example in the text: front door, foyer, living room, dining room, and kitchen.

walk through the milk into the next room. The next item, spaghetti, you picture in a steaming pot of water that is sitting on the table in your dining room. The next item is ice cream, and you imagine a container of chocolate ice cream sitting on the countertop in your kitchen, melting in the heat of the day. You get the idea. Depending on how long the list is, you can keep adding items to rooms. If necessary, you can use multiple places per room, like the bed, dresser, and night table in the master bedroom. Then, when you get to the store, you take a mental walk through your house to recall each item in order. If you were forming vivid images of the items and locations as you read through this illustration, you may be able to recall the groceries now without looking back at the earlier part of this paragraph. Can you remember which item was associated with the front door, foyer, living room, dining room, and kitchen?

As with the original use of this technique, you may also find it helpful for memorizing the points that you want to make during a speech, if you do not want to refer to your notes while you are talking. You might associate the front door with your opening joke about the ape walking into a bar by imagining a miniature ape swinging around the doorknob. Your first point about overfishing of salmon could be remembered by picturing a large salmon flopping around on the floor in your foyer. You continue to do the same thing for each main point in your speech until you get to the end.

Although rooms in your house are common locations used for this technique, it is also possible to use others. You could think about the buildings on the main street in your hometown, pieces of furniture in your office at work, or players' positions on a baseball field. To make it easy, the place should be quite familiar to you, it should have a number of identifiable locations within the place, and the separate locations should be physically distinct.

Peg-Word System

This is another formal mnemonic technique that requires a bit of practice up front and, once learned, can be used to memorize long lists of items. The key with this system is memorizing an object that goes with each digit between 1 and 10. To make it easier to remember, the object names and digits rhyme, as you can see in Box 15.7. Once you have memorized the peg words, you can associate a list of items to remember with each peg word, in a similar way that we did for the method of loci. If you want to memorize your "to-dos" for the day, in order of priority, picture each one with a peg word. To remember to call your doctor to make an appointment, imagine her with *sun* shining in her face, wearing a dark pair of sunglasses. To remember to pick up your laundry from the dry cleaner, imagine a footprint from

---

Box 15.7 The Peg-Word System

One is the sun.
Two is a shoe.
Three is a tree.
Four is a door.
Five is a hive.
Six is some sticks.
Seven is heaven.
Eight is a gate.
Nine is a vine.
Ten is a hen.

a *shoe* on the coat that you will be picking up. To remember to buy your sister a birthday gift, imagine a box in wrapping paper sitting in the branch of a large *tree*. Continue with the rest of your tasks. Then, when you want to remember them later, call up the peg words in your mind along with the associated images.

We refer to these strategies as "formal" techniques because they involve some degree of initial groundwork before they can be used well. Before you can use the method of loci or peg-word system, you have to decide on and then spend some time memorizing the locations or the peg words. After you have done this initial preparation, it takes a lot of practice to use either of these techniques efficiently. As you might imagine, it takes more practice to learn these detailed strategies than simpler techniques like "see it and say it" or retrieval practice. It also takes more mental effort to apply them. In most cases, it would be easier to use an external memory aid such as making a list than using the peg-word system for memorizing a list of groceries or your list of to-dos.

In addition to the obvious effort that formal mnemonics may take, there are not a lot of day-to-day tasks for which you really need to use them for memorizing lists of objects or points in a speech. In most situations, a simple written list or note will do the trick for remembering what you need to remember. For these reasons, formal mnemonic techniques are not typically the first line of defense for everyday memory challenges. However, if you are interested in having a bit of fun and perhaps surprising people with a neat little trick, you may enjoy learning how to use these techniques.

APPLICATION OF MEMORY STRATEGIES

Now that you are familiar with a number of memory strategies, you can think about how they apply to your own everyday memory situations. In this section, we will describe some scenarios that would require a person to learn new information, and then we will discuss the strategies that could be used.

Scenario 1

Imagine that, after reading chapter 12, you have decided to increase your current level of exercise. At your local recreation center, you sign up for a fitness class that meets twice a week for 12 weeks. In the first week of the class, you notice that a good camaraderie is developing among the group members. You realize that you would like to be able to call them by their first names when you see them. You also realize that it is unrealistic to try to learn all the names at once, so you choose 2 or 3 to work on during each class. Think about which strategies you might use to help you with this.

The obvious place for starting is with focusing your attention. As you ask a group member his or her name, or when you overhear someone else using a name, be sure that you give it your full attention. Once you are sure that you have heard the name correctly, you might decide to make the name meaningful. You could think about the actual definitions of the names or other people you know with those same names. Next, you can use retrieval practice to cement the names in your memory. As you go about your fitness routine over the next hour, look around the room at the group and try to recall the 2 or 3 names you are learning that day. Repeat this several times over the course of the session, ideally at least 5 or 6 times. As soon as you can after the class is over, pull out your memory book and write down the names you learned that day. Be sure to refer back to your list of names prior to your next class.

In this scenario, we have used four memory strategies: attention, meaningfulness, retrieval practice, and external memory aids. You may think of other strategies to use or different ways to apply the ones discussed here.

Scenario 2

You are an avid reader, and you are constantly on the lookout for recommended books to read. From time to time, your friends tell you about a good book or you read a review of a book that interests you. However, when you are standing in the book store or library staring at the book shelves, none of the titles come to mind. What memory strategies could you use to help you avoid this situation in the future?

For this scenario, you could consider using an external memory aid, good habits, and, when necessary, meaningfulness and retrieval practice. You might start by designating a section of your memory book for listing the titles and authors of books you'd like to read. Next, you make a point of developing a good habit of adding to the list whenever possible. Because you always have your memory book with you, you can pull it out immediately and write down the title recommended by your friend or the newspaper review. There will be the odd time that you cannot write down the title right away, such as when you are having a conversation in the middle of your fitness class. In those cases, you can use meaningfulness to create a visual image of the title and retrieval practice to reinforce your memory of the title. As soon as you can get to your memory book, you pull it out and add the title to your list.

Scenario 3

You have had such a good experience with the fitness class that you make up your mind to further improve your healthy lifestyle by increasing your level of intellectual engagement. You decide to brush up on your Italian by taking a continuing education course. Part of your homework is to build your Italian vocabulary, and you are given a list of 20 words to learn each week. You find this rote memorization to be particularly challenging, and you look for some memory strategies to help with this.

First, you remember that writing information down helps you remember it, even if you don't look back at your notes. So, you decide to rewrite the list of words in your class notebook every week. Next, you look at each word to see if you can make it meaningful. For example, one of your words is *biblioteca*, which means library. You think of other words that start with *biblio-*, like bibliography and bibliophile, and realize these have to do with books. This helps you make the connection with library. Your final strategy is to learn a few words each day using retrieval practice. On the first day, you practice retrieving 4 words, one at a time, using an expanding pattern of retrieval, until you are confident you know them. You test yourself an hour later (a very long interval!) to make sure. The next day, you start by trying to retrieve the words from the previous day, then learn 4 more words in the same manner. You continue until you know all the words, and use the last day for a final practice.

Scenario 4

Misplacing household items is not usually a big problem for you, because you have always been in a habit of keeping things where they belong. The exception to this general rule is your umbrella. You always know where it is at home, but of course your umbrella goes out with you when it rains. You find that you often put the umbrella down somewhere when you are out and, if it's not raining when you head for home, you forget to take it with you. Six umbrellas and $120 later, you decide it is time to do something about it.

You develop a plan to come up with creative ways to use logical places when you are not at home. To avoid leaving the umbrella behind in a bus or subway, you decide to hook the umbrella strap over your wrist while you ride. You also make a point of carrying a larger purse or briefcase that a compact umbrella would fit into. You realize that a tricky scenario is when you need to put the umbrella down somewhere unusual: For example, while you visit with your neighbor, you may want to leave it on the back porch to dry. You decide that, in these cases, you will use a see-it-and-say-it strategy it to focus your attention on what you are doing. You visualize a picture of yourself placing the umbrella on the porch between the patio chairs, and you say aloud to yourself (or to your neighbor if he or she is in the room) "I'm putting my umbrella on the porch, and I'll need to remember to take it with me when I leave."

BUILDING INTO YOUR DAILY ROUTINE

As we mentioned earlier, just like any new skill, becoming good at using memory strategies takes some practice. To be most useful, memory strategies should be well rehearsed and they should be used habitually. If you decide that you would like to build this into your daily routine, be on the lookout for scenarios like those described in the previous section where memory strategies could be used. Give yourself some time at first to think about which strategies to use and—most importantly—allow yourself sufficient time to apply the strategies.

It also helps to review memory events that have happened throughout your day and think about whether you did or didn't remember the information that you wanted to remember. If you succeeded in remembering, think about what strategies you used to lead to this success and try it again the next time a similar situation arises. If you did not succeed, think about what went wrong and how you might better approach the situation next time.

To help you keep track of your experiences with memory strategies, you may find it useful to use the worksheet in Box 15.8.

A FINAL WORD

As you have read through this chapter, you may have come to the realization that successful use of memory strategies takes a bit of work. You do need to devote some time to learning strategies in the first place and, even after you have learned them, they take a bit of mental effort to apply. Like anything in life, though, what is worth doing is worth doing well. With practice, the use of memory strategies will become easier, and some strategies may even become second nature to you. Although memory strategies will not "cure" all your memory problems or lead to a perfect memory, with regular use, you should find that you are better able to remember the things that are important to you.

Box 15.8 Using Memory Strategies

Event	Strategy used	Success of strategy	Next time...
I left home and couldn't remember whether I had closed the garage door.	Routine: I held the remote control in my hand as I walked out the door and got into the car.	Didn't work. I put down the remote to find my keys and forgot to pick it back up.	I'll keep the remote in my hand until the door is closed. Also, next time I'll try "see it and say it."
I needed to memorize the number for my new bike lock.	Retrieval practice: I repeated the number 6 or 8 times over a few minutes.	Seems to be working 3 hours later. I'll need to repeat it a few more times to make sure.	I would use spaced retrieval again. Also, I'll look to see if there is an obvious pattern.

(continued)

Box 15.8 (Continued)

Event	Strategy used	Success of strategy	Next time...

Use this form to reflect on and record your progress in learning and using memory strategies for your day-to-day tasks. Think about how well the strategy worked, and whether you would change anything if a similar event occurred again. We provide a couple of samples above, to show you how to use the form.

RECOMMENDED READING

Einstein, G. O., & McDaniel, M. A. (2004). *Memory fitness: A guide for successful aging.* New Haven, CT: Yale University Press.

Epilogue

What day is Tina coming to visit? Joe thought before he headed to his desk to retrieve his calendar. He started at today's page and then flipped forward until he saw that his daughter and her husband were visiting the following weekend. There was also a note on the page for the day of their arrival saying, "See to-do list." Joe turned to the to-do section of his calendar, and found a note to take the boxes in the guest bedroom to Goodwill. "Ruth, I am going to take those boxes to Goodwill," Joe called to his wife.

Ruth smiled. *What a difference a year makes.* "Thanks honey," she said. It had been a year since Dr. Wong had told them that Joe had mild cognitive impairment. At first, both Joe and Ruth had been confused by the diagnosis. They had never heard of mild cognitive impairment, and the fact that the doctors couldn't tell them with certainty what it would lead to was frustrating. Ruth had a lot of difficulty finding any information about mild cognitive impairment, until she stumbled on some very confusing academic papers. Eventually she connected with the Alzheimer's Society in her area and received some helpful information from their staff. Gradually, she and Joe started to implement some of the recommendations made by Dr. Wong and the Alzheimer's Society.

After Joe returned home from dropping off the boxes, he sat down to pay the bills. *This system is really working.* Joe had purchased some bins to separate the bills to be paid from those already paid and to be filed. He had another bin in which he placed his keys, wallet, and calendar as soon as he came in the door.

"Lunch is ready, Joe," Ruth called. Over lunch they discussed their plans over the next 10 days before Tina and her husband arrived.

They had some shopping to do, and they wanted to buy tickets to a play they had been anxious to see.

Joe ate quickly because he had a 1:45 tee time with his former co-workers. "I'll be back by suppertime, honey," Joe said as he kissed Ruth's forehead before grabbing his keys, wallet, and calendar from the bin on his desk and heading out.

The next day was Joe's day to volunteer at the hospital. Eight months ago, Ruth and Joe discussed ways to keep Joe active. At first, Joe was reluctant to start something new. *What if people figure out I have a memory problem? What if I have trouble learning what they want me to do?*

Ruth convinced Joe that the hospital was a great choice of a place for him to volunteer. Joe had been a sales representative for health-care products, so he had been in that hospital dozens of times and knew his way around well. Ruth said she would join Joe in the placement interview and that she thought the best course of action would be to tell the volunteer coordinator about his mild cognitive impairment so that he could be placed in a volunteer role that would minimize any problems. By the end of the interview, everyone agreed that Joe would be perfect as a greeter, giving patients and visitors directions to the clinics and wards. Joe was thoroughly enjoying his weekly shift. He was getting to know some of the staff and regular patients, and knew that he was providing essential help to people who needed it.

On Thursday, Joe and Ruth attended their monthly support group. After Joe had been diagnosed with mild cognitive impairment, Ruth had searched for a support group to join. She felt it would be helpful to hear from other people going through the same thing they were and to share their experience with them. Ruth was surprised to find that there were not support groups in their city for people with mild cognitive impairment, and so she worked with her local Alzheimer's Society chapter to create one. Now, for the last six months, a group of people had been meeting along with a social worker every month in a room at the Alzheimer's Society. At first it was just three couples, but as word has spread, the group has grown to an average of 15 people coming out most months.

Most of the group sessions were open-ended. People raised problems they have run into because of mild cognitive impairment and others in the group offered what they have done to address those issues when they were in similar situations. Each month the social worker also came prepared to discuss a topic. Last month it was on estate planning and power of attorney. This month she was coming with some memory strategies that she planned to introduce to the group and get them to practice. It was obviously a desirable topic because they had the largest attendance ever! The group had quite a lot of fun generating images and associations to help improve memory for each other's names. Some of them were quite quirky, but the social worker assured them that might make the information stick in memory better.

Afterward, during the open-ended portion of the session, one woman stated, "He gets so angry with me," referring to her husband. "When I can't remember something or get stuck for a word, he just stands there looking annoyed, waiting for me to pull it out of my memory. When I ask him what the word is or what the thing is that I can't remember, he won't tell me because he says I'm just being lazy."

"Use it or lose it, as they say," said her husband.

Joe could feel his blood pressure rising. *Someone has to set this guy straight.* "When we get stuck, no amount of 'trying' is going to make it any better," Joe began. "In fact, it can make it worse because we then get anxious about not remembering, especially when someone is staring at you, waiting. Your wife has a legitimate reason why she can't remember. You can either make things worse for her, or you can support her. When she gets stuck, give her the answer, and then ask her, 'How can we help you to remember that better next time?'"

It was clear from the husband's face that he got what Joe was saying. "I was only trying to help her," he said.

"I know," said Joe, "but there are better ways. Stick with us and we'll help show you some." Joe looked across to the woman and saw her smile.

The social worker chimed in, "Some of the memory strategies we discussed today would help in situations like that, and I can see this was a favorite topic, so we can discuss and practice some more next month."

As they drove home, Ruth said to Joe, "That was a great thing you did there, Joe."

"I remember what it was like for me in the beginning," Joe said. "Mild cognitive impairment can be a scary, confusing thing, but what I have learned is that it doesn't have to be. Sure, we still don't know what the future holds for me, but now I feel in control of it. I know the kinds of things I can do for the better and to support my memory. And I am actually enjoying life more, now that I'm out doing more things. I don't know if it's the exercise, our better diets, reconnecting with the guys, my new organizational system, or what—it's probably a combination of all of that—but I feel more in control now."

"That's great, Joe. And I can see it in you. I am really proud of how you are managing this," said Ruth. *We are doing all we can and, you know what, that is the best anyone can do*, thought Ruth, as she squeezed her husband's hand.

Bibliography

Chapter 1

p. 5, "We know this because of...."

Gauthier, S., Reisberg, B., Zaudig, M., Petersen, R. C., Ritchie, K., Broice, K., Belleville, S., Brodaty, H., Bennett, D., Chertkow, H., Cummings, J. L., de Leon, M., Feldman, H., Ganguli, M., Hampel, H., Scheltens, P., Tierney, M. C., Whitehouse, P., & Winblad, B. (2006). Mild cognitive impairment. *The Lancet, 367,* 1262–1279.

p. 12, "The best way to find out...."

Ahmed, S., Mitchell, J., Arnold, R., Nestor, P. J., & Hodges, J. R. (2008). Memory complaints in mild cognitive impairment, worried well, and semantic dementia patients. *Alzheimer's Disease and Associated Disorders, 22,* 227–235.

p. 13, "MCI can be associated with...."

Greenaway, M. C., Lacritz, L. H., Binegar, D., Weiner, M. F., Lipton, A., & Cullum, C. M. (2006). Patterns of verbal memory performance in mild cognitive impairment, Alzheimer disease, and normal aging. *Cognitive and Behavioral Neurology, 19,* 79–84.

p. 15, "In this section, we'll look at...."

Perri, R., Carlesimo, G. A., Serra, L., Caltagirone, C., & the Early Diagnosis Group of the Italian Interdisciplinary Network on Alzheimer's Disease (2005). Characterization of memory profile in subjects with amnestic mild cognitive impairment. *Journal of Clinical and Experimental Neuropsychology, 27,* 1033–1055.

p. 19, "...the term *minor neurocognitive disorder*...."

American Psychiatric Association (2010). *Neurocognitive disorders: A proposal from the DSM-5 Neurocognitive disorders work group.* Downloaded from http://www.dsm5.org/Proposed Revision Attachments/APA Neurocognitive Disorders Proposal for DSM-5.pdf

p. 20, "...the National Institute on Aging and the Alzheimer's Association."

Albert, M. S., DeKosky, S. T., Dickson, D., Dubois, B., Feldman, H. H., Fox, N. C., Gamst, A., Holtzman, D. M., Jaqust, W. J., Petersen, R. C., Snyder, P. J., Carrillo, M. C., Thies, B., & Phelps, C. H. (2011). The diagnosis of mild cognitive impairment due to Alzheimer's disease: Recommendations from the National Institute on Aging and Alzheimer's Association workgroup. *Alzheimer's & Dementia, 7,* 270–279.

Chapter 2

p. 23, "The results of surveys and questionnaires...."
Reese, C. M., & Cherry, K. E. (2004). Practical memory concerns in adulthood. *International Journal of Aging and Human Development, 59,* 235–253.

p. 25, "Another way to find out what constitutes 'normal' memory change...."
Craik, F. I. M., Anderson, N. D., Kerr, S. A., & Li, K. Z. H. (1995). Memory changes in normal aging. In A. D. Baddeley, B. A. Wilson, & F. N. Watts (Eds.), *Handbook of memory disorders* (pp. 211–241). Toronto: John Wiley.

p. 27, "This indicates that aging is associated with changes in...."
Henry, J. D., MacLeod, M. S., Phillips, L. H., & Crawford, J. R. (2004). A meta-analytic review of prospective memory and aging. *Psychology and Aging, 19,* 27–39.

p. 30, "There are very specific changes...."
Raz, N. & Rodrigue, K.M. (2006). Differential aging of the brain: Patterns, cognitive correlates and modifiers. *Neuroscience and Biobehavioural Reviews, 30,* 730–748.

p. 32, "The criteria are listed in Box 2.2."
Crook, T., Bartus, R. T., Ferris, S. H., Whitehouse, P., Cohen, G. D., & Gershon, S. (1986). Age-associated memory impairment: Proposed diagnostic criteria and measures of clinical change—Report of a National Institute of Mental Health Work Group. *Developmental Neuropsychology, 2,* 261–276.

p. 32, "More recently, the term *age-related cognitive decline*...."
American Psychiatric Association (2000). *Diagnostic and Statistical Manual of Mental Disorders (DSM-IV-TR).* Arlington, VA: Author.

p. 35, "There are a number of medical and other causes...."
Van Der Werf, Y. D., Altena, E., Schoonheim, M. M., Sanz-Arigita, E. J., Vis, J. C., De Rijke, W., & Van Someren, E. J. W. (2002). Achieving and maintaining cognitive vitality with aging. *Mayo Clinic Proceedings, 77,* 681–696.

p. 37, "There is some evidence that this is because high-quality sleep...."
Van Der Werf, Y. D. et al. (2009). Sleep benefits subsequent hippocampal functioning. *Nature Neuroscience, 12,* 122–123.

p. 41, "In high doses, it inhibits the formation...."
Shors, T. J. (2009, March). Saving new brain cells. *Scientific American, 300,* 47–54.

p. 42, "Not surprisingly, when you have to do a second task...."
Anderson, N. D., Craik, F. I. M., & Naveh-Benjamin, M. (1998). The attentional demands of encoding and retrieval in younger and older adults: 1. Evidence from divided attention costs. *Psychology and Aging, 13,* 405–423.

Chapter 3

p. 49, "Worldwide estimates...."
Ferri, C. P., Prince, M., Brayne, C., Brodaty, H., Fratiglioni, L., Gangluli, M., Hall, K., Hasegawa, K., Hendrie, H., Huang, Y., Jorm, A., Mathers, C., Menezes, P. R., Rimmer, E., Scazufca, M., for Alzheimer's Disease International. (2005). Global prevalence of dementia: A Delphi concensus study. *Lancet, 366,* 2112–2117.

p. 49, "For years, professionals typically followed...."
American Psychiatric Association (2000). *Diagnostic and Statistical Manual of Mental Disorders (DSM-IV-TR).* Arlington, VA: Author.

p. 49, "In parallel, the U.S. National Institute of Aging...."

McKhann, G. M., Knopman, D. S., Chertkow, H., Hyman, B. T., Jack Jr., C. R., Kawas, C. H., Klunk, W. E., Koroshetz, W. J., Manly, J. J., Mayeux, R., Mohs, R. C., Morris, J. C., Rossor, M. N., Scheltens, P., Carrillo, M. C., Thies, B., Weintraub, S., & Phelps, C. H. (2011). The diagnosis of dementia due to Alzheimer's disease: Recommendations from the National Institute on Aging-Alzheimer's Association workgroups on diagnostic guidelines for Alzheimer's disease. *Alzheimer's & Dementia, 7,* 263–269.

p. 50, "In the remainder of this chapter...."

Welsh-Bohmer, K. A., & Warren, L. H. (2006). *Neurodegenerative dementias.* In D. K. Attix & K. A. Welsh-Bohmer (Eds.), *Geriatric neuropsychology: Assessment and intervention.* (pp. 56–88). New York: Guilford.

p. 52, "These criteria were published in 2011...."

McKhann, G. M., Knopman, D. S., Chertkow, H., Hyman, B. T., Jack Jr., C. R., Kawas, C. H., Klunk, W. E., Koroshetz, W. J., Manly, J. J., Mayeux, R., Mohs, R. C., Morris, J. C., Rossor, M. N., Scheltens, P., Carrillo, M. C., Thies, B., Weintraub, S., & Phelps, C. H. (2011). The diagnosis of dementia due to Alzheimer's disease: Recommendations from the National Institute on Aging-Alzheimer's Association workgroups on diagnostic guidelines for Alzheimer's disease. *Alzheimer's & Dementia, 7,* 263–269.

p. 54, "The Clinical Dementia Rating...."

Morris, J. C. (1993). The Clinical Dementia Rating (CDR): Current version and scoring rules. *Neurology, 43,* 2412–2414.

Chapter 4

p. 75, "Box 4.1 displays the same classifications...."

Petersen, R. C., Roberts, R. O.., Knopman, D. S., Boeve, B. F., Geda, Y. E., Ivnik, R. J., Smith, G. E., Jack, C. R. Jr. (2009). Mild cognitive impairment: Ten years later. *Archives of Neurology, 66,* 1447–1455.

p. 76, "...if there is evidence of small strokes in brain images...."

Staekenborg, S. S., Koedam, E. L. G. E., Henneman, W. J. P., Stokman, P., Barkhof, F., Scheltens, P., & van der Flier, W. M. (2009). Progression of mild cognitive impairment to dementia: Contribution of cerebrovascular disease compared with medial temporal lobe atrophy. *Stroke, 40,* 1269–1274.

p. 76, "Research studies that follow people...."

Petersen, R. C., Smith, G. E, Waring, S. C., Ivnik, R. J., Tangalos, E. G., & Kokmen, E. (1999). Mild cognitive impairment: Clinical characterization and outcome. *Archives of Neurology, 56,* 303–308.

p. 77, "...individuals with more severe cognitive impairments are more likely to develop dementia...."

Dickerson, B. C., Sperling, R. A., Hyman, B. T., Albert, M. S., & Blacker, D. (2007). Clinical prediction of Alzheimer disease dementia across the spectrum of mild cognitive impairment. *Archives of General Psychiatry, 64,* 1443–1450.

Fleisher, A. S., Sowell, B. B., Taylor, C., Gamst, A. C., Petersen, R. C., Thal, L. J., for the Alzheimer's Disease Cooperative Study. (2007). Clinical predictors of progression to Alzheimer disease in amnestic mild cognitive impairment. *Neurology, 68,* 1588–1595.

p. 77, "Along those same lines...."
Ahmed, S., Mitchell, J., Arnold, R., Nestor, P. J., & Hodges, J. R. (2008). Predicting rapid clinical progression in amnestic mild cognitive impairment. *Dementia and Geriatric Cognitive Disorders, 25*, 170–177.

p. 78, "The presence of greater atrophy or faster atrophy over time...."
Whitwell, J. L., Shiung, M. M., Przybelski, S. A., Weigand, S. D., Knopman, D. S., Boeve, B. F., Petersen, R. C., & Jack, C. R. Jr. (2008). MRI patterns of atrophy associated with progression to AD in amnestic mild cognitive impairment. *Neurology, 70*, 512–520.

p. 78, "...people who carry the ε4 allele...."
Blom, E. S., Giedraitis, V., Zetterberg, H., Fukumoto, H., Blennow, K., Hyman, B. T., Irizarry, M. C., Wahlund, L. O., Lannfelt, L., & Ingelsson, M. (2009). Rapid progression from mild cognitive impairment to Alzheimer's disease in subjects with elevated levels of tau in cerebrospinal fluid and the APOE epsilon4/epsilon4 genotype. *Dementia and Geriatric Cognitive Disorders, 27*, 458–464.

p. 78, "Discovery of high amounts of the pathological changes...."
van Rossum, I. A., Vos, S., Handels, R., & Visser, P. J. (2010). Biomarkers as predictors for conversion from mild cognitive impairment to Alzheimer-type dementia: Implications for trial design. *Journal of Alzheimer's Disease, 20*, 881–891.

p. 83, "A surprisingly high percentage of people...."
Fisk, J. D., & Rockwood, K. (2005). Outcomes of incident mild cognitive impairment in relation to case definition. *Journal of Neurology, Neurosurgery, & Psychiatry, 76*, 1175–1177.

p. 84, "...studies that include a smaller set of diagnostic tests...."
Brooks, B. L., Iverson, G. L., Holdnack, J. A., & Feldman, H. H. (2008). Potential for misclassification of mild cognitive impairment: A study of memory scores on the Wechsler Memory Scale-III in healthy older adults. *Journal of the International Neuropsychological Society, 14*, 463–478.

p. 86, "The good news, however, is that sleep apnea is treatable...."
Ferini-Strambi, L., Baietto, C., Di Gioia, M. R., Castaldi, P., Castronovo, C., Zucconi, M., & Cappa, S. F. (2003). Cognitive dysfunction in patients with obstructive sleep apnea (OSA): Partial reversibility after continuous positive airway pressure (CPAP). *Brain Research Bulletin, 61*, 87–92.

p. 87, "...some people develop other types of dementia...."
Fisher, P., Jungwirth, S., Zehetmayer, S., Weissgram, S., Hoenigschnabl, S., Gelpi, E., Krampla, W., & Tragl, K. H. (2007). Conversion from subtypes of mild cognitive impairment to Alzheimer dementia. *Neurology, 68*, 288–291.

Chapter 5

p. 92, "Rates of MCI and dementia increase with age."
Visser, P. J., Kester, A., Jolles, J., & Verhey, F. (2006). Ten-year risk of dementia in subjects with mild cognitive impairment. *Neurology, 67*, 1201–1207.
Dartigues, J. F., & Féart, C., (2011). Risk factors for Alzheimer disease: Aging beyond age? *Neurology, 77*, 206–207.

p. 92, "Prevalence rates vary widely across studies...."
Tuokko, H. A., & McDowell, I. (2006). An overview of mild cognitive impairment. In H. A. Tuokko & D. F. Hultsch (Eds.), *Mild cognitive impairment: International perspectives* (pp. 3–28). New York: Taylor & Francis.

p. 92, "Incidence rates also vary across studies...."
Luck, T., Luppa, M., Briel, S., & Riedel-Heller, S. G. (2010). Incidence of mild cognitive impairment: A systematic review. *Dementia and Geriatric Cognitive Disorder, 29,* 164–175.

p. 93, "...higher rates of MCI among men than women...."
Petersen, R. C., Roberts, R. O., Knopman, D. S., Geda, Y. E., Cha, R. H., Pankratz, V. S., Boeve, B. F., Tangalos, E. G., Ivnik, R. J., & Rocca, W. A. (2010). Prevalence of mild cognitive impairment is higher in men: The Mayo Clinic study of aging. *Neurology, 75,* 889–897.

p. 93, "Indeed, an interesting study conducted in France...."
Artero, S., Ancelin, M.-L., Portet, F., Dupuy, A., Berr, C., Dartigues, J.-F., Tzourio, C., Rouaud, O., Poncet, M., Pasquier, F., Auriacombe, S., Touchon, J., & Ritchie, K. (2008). Risk profiles for mild cognitive impairment and progression to dementia are gender specific. *Journal of Neurology, Neurosurgery, and Psychiatry, 79,* 979–984.

p. 93, "Sex does make a difference for Alzheimer's disease."
Gao, S., Hendrie, H. C., Hall, K. S., & Hui, S. (1998). The relationship between age, sex, and the incidence of dementia and Alzheimer disease: A meta-analysis. *Archives of General Psychiatry, 55,* 809–815.

p. 93, "There is also evidence that men and women have different risk factors for Alzheimer's disease."
Azad, N. A., Al Bugami, M., & Loy-English, I. (2007). Gender differences in dementia risk factors. *Gender Medicine, 4,* 120–129.

p. 93, "Estrogen helps support the growth of new *dendrites*...."
Dumitriu, D., Rapp, P. R., McEwen, B. S., & Morrison, J. H. (2010). Estrogen and the aging brain: An elixir for the weary cortical network. *Annals of the New York Academy of Sciences, 1204,* 104–112.

p. 94, "lower dementia rates in women who took hormone replacement therapy...."
Rocca, W. A., Grossardt, B. R., & Shuster, L. T. (2010). Oopherectomy, menopause, estrogen, and cognitive aging: The timing hypothesis. *Neurodegenerative Disease, 7,* 163–166.

p. 96, "The ε4 allele has been associated with an *increased* risk of developing Alzheimer's disease."
Corder, E. H., Saunders, A. M., Strittmatter, W. J., Schmechel, D. E., Gaskell, P. C., Small, G. W., Roses, A. D., Haines, J. L., & Pericak-Vance, M. A. (1993). Gene dose of apolipoprotein E type 4 allele and the risk of Alzheimer's disease in late onset families. *Science, 261,* 921–923.

p. 98, "...the link between repeated concussions acquired during sports play such as professional football and later risk of MCI and dementia."
Guskiewicz, K. M., Marshall, S. W., Bailes, J., McCrea, M., Cantu, R. C., Randolph, C. & Jordan, B. D. (2005). Association between recurrent concussion and late-life cognitive impairment in retired professional football players. *Neurosurgery, 57,* 719–726.

p. 98, "the more years of formal education...."
Luck, T., Luppa, M., Briel, S., & Riedel-Heller, S. G. (2010). Incidence of mild cognitive impairment: A systematic review. *Dementia and Geriatric Cognitive Disorder, 29,* 164–175.

p. 99, "...a downside to higher education...."
Hall, C. B., Derby, C., LeValley, A., Katz, M. J., Verghese, J., & Lipton, R. B. (2007). Education delays accelerated decline on a memory test in persons who develop dementia. *Neurology, 69,* 1657–1664.

p. 100, "One compelling piece of evidence...."
Bialystok, E., Craik, F. I. M., & Freedman, M. (2007). Bilingualism as a protection against the onset of symptoms of dementia. *Neuropsychologia, 45,* 459–464.

p. 100, "In one study, people with MCI who had more reserve...."
Solé-Padullés, C., Bartrés-Faz, D., Junqué, C., Vendrell, P., Rami, L., Clemente, I. C., Bosch, B., Villar, A., Bargalló, N., Jurado, M. A., Barrios, M., & Molinuevo, J. L. (2009). Brain structure and function related to cognitive reserve variables in normal aging, mild cognitive impairment and Alzheimer's disease. *Neurobiology of Aging, 30,* 1114–1124.

p. 100, "Two of your authors...."
Ossher, L., Bialystok, E., Craik, F. I. M., Murphy, K. J., & Troyer, A. K. (2012). The effect of bilingualism on amnestic mild cognitive impairment. *Journals of Gerontology: Psychological Sciences.* doi: 10.1093/geronb/gbs038.

p. 101, "A variety of vascular and metabolic conditions...."
Solfrizzi, V., Scafato, E., Capurso, C., D'Introno, A., Colacicco, A. M., Frisardi, V., Vendemiale, G., Baldereschi, M., Crepaldi, G., Di Carlo, A., Galluzzo, L., Gandin, C., Inzitari, D., Maggi, S., Capurso, A., & Panza, F., for the Italian Longitudinal Study on Aging Working Group. (2011). Metabolic syndrome, mild cognitive impairment, and progression to dementia: The Italian Longitudinal Study on Aging. *Neurobiology of Aging, 32,* 1932–1941.

p. 103, "Depression is a risk factor for both MCI and dementia...."
Barnes, D. E., Alexopoulos, G. S., Lopez, O. L., Williamson, J. D., & Yaffe, K. (2006). Depressive symptoms, vascular disease, and mild cognitive impairment. *Archives of General Psychiatry, 63,* 273–280.

p. 103, "Half or more of all cases of depression...." and "older adults present with different symptoms...."
Fiske, A., Loebach Wetherell, J., & Gatz, M. (2009). Depression in older adults. *Annual Review of Clinical Psychology, 5,* 363–389.

p. 104, "...major depressive disorder, and dysthymic disorder...."
American Psychiatric Association (2000). *Diagnostic and Statistical Manual of Mental Disorders (DSM-IV-TR).* Arlington, VA: Author.

p. 106, "a group *psycho-educational* program...."
Naismith, S. L., Diamond, K., Carter, P. E., Norrie, L. M., Redoblado-Hodge, M. A., Lewis, S. J., & Hickie, I. B. (2011). Enhancing memory in late-life depression: The effects of a combined psychoeducation and cognitive training program. *American Journal of Geriatric Psychiatry, 19,* 240–248.

p. 106, "among people who have both MCI and depression...."
Lu, P. H., Edland, S. D., Teng, E., Tingus, K., Petersen, R. C., Cummings, J. L., & the Alzheimer's Disease Cooperative Study Group (2009). Donepezil delays progression to AD in MCI subjects with depressive symptoms. *Neurology, 2009, 72,* 2115–2121.

Chapter 6

p. 118, "...both of which can cause memory problems...."
Etgen, T., Bickel, H., & Förstl, H. (2010). Metabolic and endocrine factors in mild cognitive impairment. *Ageing Research Reviews, 9,* 280–288.

p. 120, "...no medical tests that can definitively diagnose MCI."

Jack Jr., C. R., Albert, M. S., Knopman, D. S., McKhann, G. M., Sperling, R. A., Carrillo, M. C., Thies, B., & Phelps, C. H. (2011). Introduction to the recommendations from the National Institute on Aging and the Alzheimer's Association workgroup on diagnostic guidelines for Alzheimer's disease. *Alzheimer's & Dementia, 7,* 257–262.

p. 121, "...did not show symptoms of cognitive or functional decline...."

Riley, K. P., Snowdon, D. A., & Markesbery, W. R. (2002). Alzheimer's neurofibrillary pathology and the spectrum of cognitive function: Findings from the Nun Study. *Annals of Neurology, 51,* 567–577.

p. 128, "...due to chance factors."

Axelrod, B. N., & Wall, J. R. (2007). Expectancy of impaired neuropsychological test scores in a non-clinical sample. *International Journal of Neuroscience, 117,* 1591–1602.

p. 128, "...no medical tests that are conclusive...."

Jack Jr., C. R., Albert, M. S., Knopman, D. S., McKhann, G. M., Sperling, R. A., Carrillo, M. C., Thies, B., & Phelps, C. H. (2011). Introduction to the recommendations from the National Institute on Aging and the Alzheimer's Association workgroup on diagnostic guidelines for Alzheimer's disease. *Alzheimer's & Dementia, 7,* 257–262.

p. 131, "...falsely diagnosing people with MCI."

Brooks, B. L., Iverson, G. L., Holdnack, J. A., & Feldman, H. H. (2008). Potential for misclassification of mild cognitive impairment: A study of memory scores on the Wechsler Memory Scale-III in healthy older adults. *Journal of the International Neuropsychological Society, 14,* 463–478.

Chapter 7

p. 140, "The decision not to approve the use of the three cholinesterase inhibitors for people with MCI...."

Raschetti, R., Albanese, E., Vanacore, N., & Maggini, M. (2007). Cholinesterase inhibitors in mild cognitive impairment: A systematic review of randomised trials. *PLOS Medicine, 4,* 1818–1828.

p. 144, "Some studies find that they decrease production of the plaque pathology...."

Mangialasche, F., Solomon, A., Winblad, B., Mecocci, P., & Kevipelto, M. (2010). Alzheimer's disease: Clinical trials and drug development. *Lancet Neurology, 9,* 702–716.

p. 148, "Cholesterol lowering drugs, or *statins*...."

McGuinness, B., O'Hare, J., Craig, D., Bullock, R., Malouf, R., & Passmore, P. (2010). Statins for the treatment of dementia. *Cochrane Database of Systematic Reviews,* Issue 8.

p. 149, "Two amyloid busting drugs...."

www.Alzforum.org. Accessed June 4, 2011 for current trials in Alzheimer's disease treatment.

p. 151, "In 2008, we published...."

Troyer, A. K., Murphy, K. M., Anderson, N. D., Moscovitch, M., & Craik, F. I. M. (2008). Changing everyday memory behaviour in amnestic mild cognitive impairment: A randomised controlled trial. *Neuropsychological Rehabilitation, 18,* 65–88.

p. 154, "...there are now a handful of published studies...." for reviews see

Belleville, S. (2008). Cognitive training in persons with mild cognitive impairment. *International Psychogeriatrics, 20,* 57–66.

Martin, M., Clare, L., Altgassen, A. M., Cameron, M. H., & Zehnder, F. (2011). Cognition-based interventions for healthy older people and people with mild cognitive impairment. *Cochrane Database of Systematic Reviews,* Issue 1. Art. No.: CD006220. DOI: 10.1002/14651858.CD006220.pub2.

Mowszowski, L., Batchelor, J., & Naismith, S. L. (2010). Early intervention for cognitive decline: Can cognitive training be used as a selective prevention technique? *International Psychogeriatrics, 22,* 437–458.

p. 154, "Indeed, the 2010 Rising Tide report published by the Alzheimer Society of Canada...."

Alzheimer Society of Canada (2010). *The Rising Tide: The Impact of Dementia on Canadian Society. Retrievable from* http://www.alzheimer.ca/en/Get-involved/ Raise-your-voice/Rising-Tide.

Chapter 8

p. 160, "...there is a growing body of research...."

Savla, J., Roberto, K. A., Blieszner, R., Cox, M., & Gwazdauskas, F. (2011). Effects of daily stressors on the psychological and biological well-being of spouses of persons with mild cognitive impairment. *The Journal of Gerontology, Series B: Psychological Sciences and Social Sciences, 66,* 653–664.

p. 160, "...researchers in Massachusetts...."

Goldberg, T. E., Koppel, J., Keehlisen, L., Christen, E., Dreses-Werringloer, U., Conejero-Goldberg, C., Gordon, M. L., & Davies, P. (2010). Performance-based measures of everyday function in mild cognitive impairment. *American Journal of Psychiatry, 167,* 845–853.

p. 161, "...no serious driving impairments in people with MCI...."

Wadley, V. G., Ozioma, O., Crowe, M., Vance, D. E., Elgin, J. M., Ball, K. K., & Owsley, C. (2010). Mild cognitive impairment and everyday function: An investigation of driving performance. *Journal of Geriatric Psychiatry and Neurology, 22,* 87–94.

p. 162, "A recent *meta-analysis*...."

Apostolova, L. G., & Cummings, J. L. (2008). Neuropsychiatric manifestations in mild cognitive impairment: A systematic review of the literature. *Dementia and Geriatric Cognitive Disorders, 25,* 115–126.

p. 162, "...the prevalence of neuropsychiatric symptoms...."

Geda, Y. E., Roberts, R. O., Knopman, D. S., Petersen, R. C., Christianson, T. J.,. Pankratz, V. S., Smith, G. E., Boeve, B. F., Ivnik, R. J., Tangalos, E. G., & Rocca, W. A. (2008). Prevalence of neuropsychiatric symptoms in mild cognitive impairment and normal cognitive aging: Population-based study. *Archives of General Psychiatry, 65,* 1193–1198.

p. 162, "...mood disturbance in MCI increases the risk of progression to dementia."

Chan, W. C., Lam, L. C., Tam, C. W., Lui, W. W., Leung, G. T., Lee, A. T., Chan, S. S., Fung, A. W., Chiu, H. F., & Chan, W. M. (2011). Neuropsychiatric symptoms are associated with increased risks of progression to dementia: A 2-year prospective study of 321 Chinese older persons with mild cognitive impairment. *Age & Ageing, 40,* 30–35.

Palmer, K., Di Iulio, F., Varsi, A. E., Gianni, W., Sancesario, G., Caltagirone, C., & Spalletta, G. (2010). Neuropsychiatric predictors of progression from amnestic-mild cognitive impairment to Alzheimer's disease: The role of depression and apathy. *Journal of Alzheimer's Disease, 20,* 175–183.

Palmer, K., Berger, A. K., Monastero, R., Winblad, B., Bäckman, L., & Fratiglioni, L. (2007). Predictors of progression from mild cognitive impairment to Alzheimer disease. *Neurology, 68,* 1596–1602.

p. 163, "…we recently conducted some focus groups.…"
Parikh, P., Maoine, A., Murphy, K., & Troyer, A. (2011). The impact of memory change on everyday life in amnestic mild cognitive impairment. *Program booklet of the 26th International Conference of Alzheimer's Disease International,* p. 95.

p. 164, "…leisure activities can actually reduce dementia risk."
Verghese, J., Lipton, R. B., Katz, M. J., Hall, C. B., Derby, C. A., Kuslansky, G., Ambrose, A. F., Sliwinski, M., & Buschke, H. (2003). Leisure activities and the risk of dementia in the elderly. *New England Journal of Medicine, 348,* 2508–2516.

p. 165, "…those with hearing loss progressed to dementia more quickly.…"
Lin, F. (2011). Hearing loss and cognition among older adults in the United States. *Journal of Gerontology, 66,* 1131–1136.

p. 166, "…do poorer on tests of learning and memory.…"
McCoy, S., Tun, P., Cox, L., Colangelo, M., Steward, R., & Wingfield, A. (2005). Hearing loss and perceptual effort: Downstream effects on older adult's memory for speech. *Quarterly Journal of Experimental Psychology, 58,* 22–33.

p. 167, "…sleep changes are also evident in people with MCI.…"
Beaulieu-Bonneau, S., & Hudon, C. (2009). Sleep disturbances in older adults with mild cognitive impairment. *International Psychogeriatrics, 21,* 654–666.

p. 167, "Poor sleep can disrupt this process.…"
Walker, M. P. (2008). Cognitive consequences of sleep and sleep loss. *Sleep Medicine, 9,* S29–S34.

p. 167, "…sleep behaviour problems are not. "
Yaffe, K., Laffan, A. M., Harrison, S. L., Redline, S., Spira, A. P., Ensrud, K. E., Ancoli-Israel, S., & Stone, K. L. (2011). Sleep-disordered breathing, hypoxia, and risk of mild cognitive impairment and dementia in older women. *Journal of the American Medical Association. 306,* 613–619.

Ramakers, I. H. G. B., Visser, P. J., Aalten, P., Kester, A., Jolles, J., & Verhey, F.R.J. (2010). Affective symptoms as predictors of Alzheimer's disease in subjects with mild cognitive impairment: A 10-year follow-up study. *Psychological Medicine, 40,* 1193–1201.

p. 168, "In collaboration with others, we conducted a qualitative analysis.…"
Shaughnessy, V., Moore, T., Troyer, A. T., & Murphy, K. J. (in preparation). The psychological, physical, and social effects of mild cognitive impairment on spouses.

p. 168, "These themes were similar to those identified by other researchers.…"
Blieszner, R., & Roberto, K. A. (2010). Care partner responses to the onset of mild cognitive impairment. *The Gerontologist, 50,* 11–22.

p. 170, "…providing increased functional support to their relative with MCI."
Frank, L., Lloyd, A., Flynn, J. A., Kleinman, L., Matza, L. S., Margolis, M. K., Bowman, L., & Bullock, R. (2006). Impact of cognitive impairment on mild dementia patients and mild cognitive impairment patients and their informants. *International Psychogeriatrics, 18,* 151–162.

McIlvane, J. M., Mihaela, A. P., Robinson, B., Houseweart, K., & Haley, W. E. (2008). Perceptions of illness, coping, and well-being in persons with mild cognitive impairment and their care partners. *Alzheimer Disease and Associated Disorders, 22,* 284–292.

p. 170, "…some decline in their own cognition.…"
Mackenzie, C. S., Wiprzycka, U. J., Hasher, L., & Goldstein, D. (2009). Associations between psychological distress, learning and memory in spouse caregivers of older adults. *Journal of Gerontology: Psychological Sciences, 64B,* 742–746.

Vitaliano, P. P., Murphy, M. M, Young, H. M., Echeverria, D., & Borson, S. (2011). Does caring for a spouse with dementia promote cognitive decline? A hypothesis and proposed mechanisms. *Journal of the American Geriatrics Society, 59,* 900–908.

p. 171, "…even premature mortality."
Vitaliano, P., Zhang, J., & Scanlan, J. M. (2003). Is caregiving hazardous to one's physical health? A meta-analysis. *Psychological Bulletin, 129,* 946–972.

p. 171, "…importance of providing intervention for close family members…"
Blieszner, R. & Roberto, K. A. (2010). Care partner responses to the onset of mild cognitive impairment. *The Gerontologist, 50,* 11–22.

Ryan, K. A., Weldon, A., Huby, N. M., Persad, C., Bhaumik, A. K., Heidebrink, J. L., Barbas, N., Staffend, N., Franti, L., & Giordani, B. (2010). Caregiver support services needs for patients with mild cognitive impairment and Alzheimer disease. *Alzheimer Disease and Associated Disorders, 24,* 171–176.

van Vliet, D., de Vugt, M. E., Bakker, C., Koopmans, R. T., Pijnenburg, Y. A., Vernooij-Dassen, M. J., & Verhey, F. R. (2011). Caregivers' perspectives on the pre-diagnostic period in early onset dementia: A long and winding road. *International Psychogeriatrics, 23,* 1393–1404.

p. 172, "…positive mood outcomes for family members who participate together.…"
Joosten-Weyn Banningh, L. W., Kessels, R. P., Olde Rikkert, M. G., Geleijns-Lanting, C. E., & Kraaimaat, F. W. (2008). A cognitive behavioural group therapy for patients diagnosed with mild cognitive impairment and their significant others: Feasibility and preliminary results. *Clinical Rehabilitation, 22,* 731–740.

p. 172, "…without associated declines in the primary family caregiver's own health."
Mittelman, M. S., Haley, W. E., Clay, O. J., & Roth, D. L. (2006). Improving caregiver well-being delays nursing placement of patients with Alzheimer disease. *Neurology, 67,* 1592–1599.

Chapter 9

p. 176, "…too much cortisol also interferes.…"
Juster, R-P., McEwen, B. S., & Lupien, S. J. (2009). Allostatic load biomarkers of chronic stress and impact on health and cognition. *Neuroscience and Biobehavioral Reviews, 35,* 2–16.

p. 176, "…smaller hippocampi and do poorer on memory tests.…"
Lupien S. J., Maheu, F., Tu, M., Fiocco, A., & Schramek, T. E. (2007). The effects of stress and stress hormones on human cognition: Implications for the field of brain and cognition. *Brain and Cognition, 65,* 209–237.

p. 176, "…older adults with Alzheimer's disease have higher circulating levels of cortisol.…"
Huang, C-W, Chun-Chung Lui, C-C, Weng-Neng Changm W-N, Lu, C-H., Ya-Ling Wangc, Y-L, & Chang, C-C. (2009). Elevated basal cortisol level predicts lower hippocampal volume and cognitive decline in Alzheimer's disease. *Journal of Clinical Neuroscience, 16,* 1283–1286.

p. 176, "…people with MCI do not show this type of elevation in circulating cortisol.…"
Popp, J., Schaper, K., Kölsch, H., Cvetanovska, G., Rommel, F., Klingmüller, D., Dodel, R., Wüllner, U., & Jessen, F. (2009). CSF cortisol in Alzheimer's disease and mild cognitive impairment, *Neurobiology of Aging, 30,* 498–500.

p. 180, "…and how they can promote progression to dementia.…"
Apostolova, L. G., & Cummings, J. L. (2008). Neuropsychiatric manifestations in mild cognitive impairment: A systematic review of the literature. *Dementia and Geriatric Cognitive Disorders, 25,* 115–126.

Ramakers, I. H., Visser, P. J., Aalten, P., Kester, A., Jolles, J., & Verhey, F. R. (2010). Affective symptoms as predictors of Alzheimer's disease in subjects with mild cognitive impairment: A 10-year follow-up study. *Psychological Medicine, 40,* 1193–1201.

p. 180, "…consistent with the writings of Pelletier."
Pelletier, K.R. (1994). *Sound mind, sound body: A new model for lifelong health.* Fireside: New York, New York.

p. 180, "…benefits of a positive attitude on your cognition.…"
Wood, A. M., & Tarrier, N. (2010). Positive clinical psychology: A new vision and strategy for integrated research and practice. *Clinical Psychology Review, 30,* 819–829.

p. 181, "…having positive feelings has many health benefits.…"
Rasmussen, H. N., Scheier, M. F., & Greenhouse, J. B. (2009). Optimism and physical health: A meta-analytic review. *Annals of Behavioural Medicine, 37,* 239–256.

p. 182, "…Rush Memory and Aging Project based in Chicago.…"
Boyle, P. A,. Buchman. A. S., Barnes, L. L., &. Bennett, D. A. (2010). Effect of a purpose in life on risk of incident Alzheimer disease and mild cognitive impairment in community-dwelling older persons. *Archives of General Psychiatry, 67,* 304–310.

p. 182, "…exercise can have a tremendously beneficial impact on your mood.…"
Kramer, A. F., & Erickson, K. I. (2007). Effects of physical activity on cognition, well-being, and brain: Human interventions. *Alzheimer's & Dementia, 3,* S45–S51.

p. 184, "…a recent study using group cognitive behavior therapy for people with MCI.…"
Joosten-Weyn Banningh, L. W., Kessels, R. P., Olde Rikkert, M. G., Geleijns-Lanting, C. E., & Kraaimaat, F. W. (2008). A cognitive behavioural group therapy for patients diagnosed with mild cognitive impairment and their significant others: Feasibility and preliminary results. *Clinical Rehabilitation, 22,* 731–740.

p. 184, "In terms of treatment for depression among older adults…"
Frazer, C. J., Christensen, H., & Griffiths, K. M. (2005). Effectiveness of treatments for depression in older people. *The Medical Journal of Australia, 182*, 627–632.

p. 186, "…participants in the Baycrest MCI Program were able to learn.…"
Troyer, A. K., Murphy, K. J., Anderson, N. D., Craik, F. I. M., & Moscovitch, M. (2008). Changing everyday memory behaviour in amnestic mild cognitive impairment: A randomised controlled trial. *Neuropsychological Rehabilitation, 18*, 65–88.

p. 186, "…people with MCI can learn and use new memory skills."
Gates, N. J., Sachdev, P. S., Fiatarone Singh, M. A., & Valenzuela, M. (2011). Cognitive and memory training in adults at risk of dementia: A systematic review. *BMC Geriatrics, 11*, 55–67.

p. 187, "…power of self-efficacy to promote your success at accomplishing tasks.…"
Cervone, D. (2000). Thinking about self-efficacy. *Behaviour Modification, 24*, 30–56.

p. 188, "…was not a motivator in getting people with MCI to use cognitive strategies."
Werheid, K., Zeigler, M., Klapper, A., & Kühl, K-P. (2010). Awareness of memory failures and motivation for cognitive training in mild cognitive impairment. *Dementia & Geriatric Cognitive Disorders, 30*, 155–160.

p. 189, "…motivational interviewing…"
Rollnick, S., & Miller, W. R. (1995). What is motivational interviewing? *Behavioural and Cognitive Psychotherapy, 23*, 325–334.

Chapter 10

p. 191, "…are just not as "optimal".…"
Wadley, V. G., Ozioma, O., Crowe, M., Vance, D. E., Elgin, J. M., Ball, K. K., & Owsley, C. (2010). Mild cognitive impairment and everyday function: An investigation of driving performance. *Journal of Geriatric Psychiatry and Neurology, 22*, 87–94.

Frittelli, C., Borghetti, D., Giovanni, I., Bonanni, E., Maestri, M., Tognoni, G., Pasquali, L., & Iudice, A. (2009). Effects of Alzheimer's disease and mild cognitive impairment on driving ability: A controlled clinical study by simulated driving test. *International Journal of Geriatric Psychiatry, 24*, 232–238.

p. 192. "…differences between younger and older adults is reaction speed."
Salthouse, T.A. (2004). What and when of cognitive aging. *Current Directions in Psychological Science, 13*, 140–144.

Chapter 11

p. 216, "…reduced risk of dementia.…"
Ferland, G., Greenwood, C. E., & Shatenstein, B. (2011). Nutrition and dementia: A clinical update. *Journal of Current Clinical Care, March/April*. Retrieved from http://www.healthplexus.net/files/content/2011/April/Nutrition.pdf.

p. 217, "…reduced risk of progression from MCI to Alzheimer's.…"
Scarmeas, N., Stern, Y., Mayeux, R., Manly, J. J., Schupf, N., & Luchsinger, J. A. (2009). Mediterranean diet and mild cognitive impairment. *Archives of Neurology, 66*, 216–225.

p. 219, "…individuals with MCI and type 2 diabetes show increased risk for progression to dementia.…"

Carlsson, C. M. (2010). Type 2 diabetes mellitus, dyslipidemia, and Alzheimer's disease. *Journal of Alzhiemer's disease, 20,* 711–722.

p. 219, "…improving dietary habits in older adults with type 2 diabetes can improve cognitive performance…."
Ryan, C. M., Freed, M. I., Rood, J. A., Cobitz, A. R., Waterhouse, B. R., & Strachan, M. W. J. (2006). Improving metabolic control leads to better working memory in adults with type 2 diabetes, *Diabetes Care, 29,* 345–351.

p. 220, "…trigger the development of neurodegenerative diseases….",
Wärnberg, J. Gomez-Martinez, S., Romero, J., Diaz, L., & Marcos, A. (2009). Nutrition, inflammation, and cognitive function. *Neuroimmunomodulation: Annals of the New York Accademy of Science, 1153,* 164–175.

p. 221, "There have been a number of randomized control trials…."
Jia, X., McNeill, G., & Avenell, A. (2008). Does taking vitamin, mineral and fatty acid supplements prevent cognitive decline? A systematic review of randomized controlled trials. *Journal of Human Nutrition and Dietetics, 21,* 317–336.

p. 222, "Overall, in human and nonhuman animals, the studies find…."
Ferland, G., Greenwood, C. E., & Shatenstein, B. (2011). Nutrition and dementia: A clinical update. *Journal of Current Clinical Care, March/April.* Retrieved from http://www.healthplexus.net/files/content/2011/April/Nutrition.pdf.

p. 222, "…healthy diet and physical activity were found to independently reduce risk…."
Scarmeas, N., Luchsinger, J. A., Schupf, N., Brickman, A. M., Constentino, S., Tang, M. X., & Stern, Y. (2009). Physical activity, diet, and risk of Alzheimer's disease. *Journal of the American Medical Association, 302,* 627–637.

p. 223, "Dr. Carol Greenwood and her colleagues recently reported…."
Fiocco, A. J., Shatenstein, B., Ferland, G., Payette, H., Belleville, S., Kergoat, M. J., Morais, J. A., & Greenwood, C. E. (2012). Sodium intake and physical activity impact cognitive maintenance in older adults: The NuAge study. *Neurobiology of Aging, 33,* 829.

p. 223, "…the exercise group metabolized the fat better…."
Dekker, M. J., Graham, T. E., Ooi, T. C., & Robinson, L. E. (2010). Exercise prior to fat ingestion lowers fasting and postprandial VLDL and decreases adipose tissue IL-6 and GIP receptor mRNA in hypertriacylglycerolemic men. *Journal of Nutritional Biochemistry, 21,* 983–990.

p. 230, "Not all fats are created equal…."
Enig, M. G. (2000). *Know your fats: The complete primer for understanding the nutrition of fats, oils and cholesterol.* Bethesda Press: Maryland.

p. 230, "…Chicago Health and Aging Project…."
Morris, M. C., Evans, D. A., Tangney, C. C., Bienias, J. L., & Wilson, R. S. (2006). Associations of vegetable and fruit consumption with age-related cognitive change. *Neurology, 67,* 1370–1376.

p. 233, "…types of blood cholesterol…."
Expert Panel. (2001). Third report of the National Cholesterol Education Program. *Journal of the American Medical Association, 285,* 2486–97.

Chapter 12

p. 244, "Box 12.1 lists many activities…."
Ainsworth, B. E., Haskell, W. L., Herrmann, S. D., Meckes, N., Bassett Jr., D. R., Tudor-Locke, C., Greer, J. L., Vezina, J., Whitt-Glover, M. C., & Leon, A. S. (2011).

2011 compendium of physical activities: A second update of codes and MET values. *Medicine & Science in Sports & Exercise, 43,* 1575–1581.

p. 247, "…the Physical Activities Readiness Questionnaire…."
Retrieved November 1, 2011, from http://www.csep.ca/english/view.asp?x=698

p. 249, "Perhaps the most impressive evidence…."
Nichol, K., Deeny, S. P., Self, J., Camaklang, K., & Cotman, C. W. (2009). Exercise improves cognition and hippocampal plasticity in APOE epsilon4 mice. *Alzheimer's Dementia, 5,* 287–294.

p. 249, "Before you get too skeptical…."
Colcombe, S. J., Erickson, K. I., Raz, N., Webb, A. G., Cohen, N. J., McAuley, E., & Kramer, A. F. (2003). Aerobic fitness reduces brain tissue loss in aging humans. *Journal of Gerontology: Medical Sciences, 58A,* 176–180.

Burns, J. M., Cronk, B. B., Anderson, H. S., Donnelly, J. E., Thomas, G. P., Harsha, A., Brooks, W. M., & Swerdlow, R. H. (2008). Cardiorespiratory fitness and brain atrophy in Alzheimer disease. *Neurology, 71,* 210–216.

p. 249, "As you might suspect…."
Larson, E. B., Wang, L., Bowen, J. D., McCormick, W. C., Teri, L., Crane, P., & Kukull, W. (2006). Exercise is associated with reduced risk for incident dementia among persons 65 years of age and older. *Annals of Internal Medicine, 144,* 73–81.

Laurin, D., Verrault, R., Lindsay, J., MacPherson, K., & Rockwood, K. (2001). Physical activity and risk of cognitive impairment and dementia in elderly persons. *Archives of Neurology, 58,* 498–504.

Andel, R., Crowe, M., Pedersen, N. L., Fratiglioni, L., Johansson, B., & Gatz, M. (2008). Physical exercise at midlife and risk of dementia three decades later: A population-based study of Swedish twins. *Journal of Gerontology: Medical Sciences, 63A,* 62–66.

Middleton, L. E., Barnes, D. E., Lui, L. Y., & Yaffe, K. (2010). Physical activity over the life course and its association with cognitive performance and impairment in old age. *Journal of the American Geriatric Society, 58,* 1322–1326.

Geda, Y. E., Roberts, R. O., Knopman, D. S., Christianson, T. J., Pankratz, V. S., Ivnik, R. J., Boeve, B. F., Tangalos, E. G., Petersen, R. C., & Rocca, W. A. (2010). Physical exercise, aging, and mild cognitive impairment: A population-based study. *Archives of Neurology, 67,* 80–86.

p. 250, "…older adults who engaged in aerobic training…."
Colcombe, S. J., & Kramer, A. F. (2003). Fitness effects on the cognitive function of older adults: A meta-analytic study. *Psychological Science, 14,* 125–130.

Colcombe, S. J., Kramer, A. F., Erickson, K. I., Scalf, P., McAuley, E., Cohen, N. J., Webb, A., Jerome, G. J., Marquez, D. X., & Elavsky, S. (2004). Cardiovascular fitness, cortical plasticity, and aging. *Proceedings of the National Academy of Sciences, 101,* 3316–3321.

Colcombe, S. J., Erickson, K. I., Scalf, P. E., Kim, J. S., Prakash, R., McAuley, E., Elavsky, S., Marquez, D. X., Hu, L., & Kramer, A. F. (2006). Aerobic exercise training increases brain volume in aging humans. *Journal of Gerontology: Medical Sciences, 61A,* 1166–1170.

Erickson, K. I., Voss, M. W., Prakash, R. S., Basak, C., Szabo, A., Chaddock, L., Kim, J. S., Heo, S., Alves, H., White, S. M., Wojcicki, T. R., Mailey, E., Vieira, V. J., Martin, S. A., Pense, B. D., Woods, J. A., McAuley, E., & Kramer, A. F.

(2011). Exercise training increases size of hippocampus and improves memory. *Proceedings of the National Academy of Sciences, 108,* 3017–3022.

p. 251, "The relationship between physical fitness and cognitive ability...."
McGough, E. L., Kelly, V. E., Logsdon, R. G., McCurry, S. M., Cochrane, B. B., Engel, J. M., & Teri, L. (2011). Associations between physical performance and executive function in older adults with mild cognitive impairment: Gait speed and the timed "up & go" test. *Physical Therapy, 91,* 1198–1207.

p. 251, "Another study randomly assigned people with MCI...."
Baker, L. D., Frank, L. L., Foster-Schubert, K., Green, P. S., Wilkinson, C. W., McTiernan, A., Plymate, S. R., Fishel, M. A., Watson, G. S., Cholerton, B. A., Duncan, G. E., Mehta, P. D., & Craft, S. (2010). Effects of aerobic exercise on mild cognitive impairment: A controlled trail. *Archives of Neurology, 67,* 71–79.

p. 252, "In this section, we describe some of the many ways that the brain is changed by exercise...."
Hillman, C. H., Erickson, K. I., & Kramer, A. F. (2008). Be smart, exercise your heart: Exercise effects on brain and cognition. *Nature Reviews Neuroscience, 9,* 58–65.

p. 253, "Exercise interventions reduce rates of clinically diagnosed depression in older adults...."
Blake, H., Mo, P., Malik, S., & Thomas, S. (2009). How effective are physical activity interventions for alleviating depressive symptoms in older people? A systematic review. *Clinical Rehabilitation, 23,* 873–887.

p. 254, "The World Health Organization (WHO) recommends...."
Retrieved November 1, 2011 from http://www.who.int/dietphysicalactivity/factsheet_olderadults/en/index.html

p. 255, "A 2010 study randomized a group of older adults...."
Liu-Ambrose, T., Nagamatsu, L. S., Graf, P., Beattie, B. L., Ashe, M. C., & Handy, T. C. (2010). Resistance training and executive functions: A 12-month randomized controlled trial. *Archives of Internal Medicine, 170,* 170–178.

Chapter 13

p. 265, "These studies show two important findings."
Reviewed in Hertzog, C., Kramer, A. F., Wilson, R. S., & Lindenberger, U. (2009). Enrichment effects on adult cognitive development: Can the functional capacity of older adults be preserved and enhanced? *Psychological Science in the Public Interest, 9,* 1–65.

p. 267, "Research shows a clear association between level of formal education and cognitive abilities."
Reviewed in Katzman, R. (1993). Education and the prevalence of dementia and Alzheimer's disease. *Neurology, 43,* 13–20.

p. 268, "Recent research has shown that participation in cognitively engaging activities...."
Lachman, M. E., Agrigoroaei, S., Murphy, C., & Tun, P. A. (2010). Frequent cognitive activity compensates for education differences in episodic memory. *American Journal of Geriatric Psychiatry, 18,* 4–10.

p. 268, "Longitudinal research that has followed workers over many years...."
Schooler, C., Mulatu, M. S., & Oats, G. (1999). The continuing effects of substantively complex work on the intellectual functioning of older workers. *Psychology and Aging, 14,* 483–506.

p. 269, "Work complexity is also associated with risk of dementia."
Schooler, C., Mulatu, M. S., & Oates, G. (1999). The continuing effects of substantively complex work on the intellectual functioning of older workers. *Psychology and Aging, 14,* 483–506.

p. 269, "…by researchers at Johns Hopkins University."
Carlson, M. C., Saczynski, J. S., Rebok, G. W., Seeman, T., Glass, T. A., McGill, S., Tielsch, J., Frick, K. D., Hill, J., & Fried, L. P. (2008). Exploring the effects of an "everyday" activity program on executive function and memory in older adults: Experience Corps®. *The Gerontologist, 48,* 793–801.

p. 270, "Younger and older adults who have been bilingual most of their lives.…"
Bialystok, E., Craik, F. I. M., Klein, R., & Viswanathan, M. (2004). Bilingualism, aging, and cognitive control: Evidence from the Simon task. *Psychology and Aging, 19,* 290–303.

p. 270, "Recent research has provided even more good news.…"
Craik, F. I. M., Bialystok, E., & Freedman, M. (2010). Delaying the onset of Alzheimer disease: Bilingualism as a form of cognitive reserve. *Neurology, 75,* 1726–1729.

Ossher, L., Bialystock, E., Craik, F. I. M., Murphy, K., Troyer, A. K. (2012). The effect of bilingualism on amnestic mild cognitive impairment. Journals of Gerontology: Psychological Sciences. doi: 10.1093/geronb/gbs038.

p. 270, "There are a number of interesting differences.…"
Reviewed in Wan, C., & Schlaug, G. (2010). Music making as a tool for promoting brain plasticity across the life span. *The Neuroscientist, 16,* 566–577.

p. 271, "A recent study from Sweden showed.…"
Mårtensson, J., & Låvdén, M. (2011). Do intensive studies of a foreign language improve associative memory performance? *Frontiers in Psychology, 2,* article 12. doi: 10.3389/fpsyg.2011.00012.

p. 271, "Similarly, older adults who agreed to take piano lessons.…"
Bugos, J. A., Perlstein, W. M., McCrae, C. S., Brophy, T. S., & Bedenbaugh, P. H. (2007). Individualized piano instruction enhances executive functioning and working memory in older adults. *Aging and Mental Health, 11,* 464–471.

p. 273, "A number of recent studies that use this type of design.…"
Noice, H., Noice, T., & Staines, G. (2004). A short-term intervention to enhance cognitive and affective functioning in older adults. *Journal of Aging and Health, 16,* 562–585.

Bugos, J. A., Perlstein, W. M., McCrae, C. S., Brophy, T. S., & Bedenbaugh, P. H. (2007). Individualized piano instruction enhances executive functioning and working memory in older adults. *Aging and Mental Health, 11,* 464–471.

Carlson, M. C., Saczynski, J. S., Rebok, G. W., Seeman, T., Glass, T. A., McGill, S., Tielsch, J., Frick, K. D., Hill, J., & Fried, L. P. (2008). Exploring the effects of an "everyday" activity program on executive function and memory in older adults: Experience Corps®. *The Gerontologist, 48,* 793–801.

p. 273, "Although the studies described so far have involved older individuals with normal cognitive abilities, there is also some evidence.…"
Spector, A., Thorgrimsen, L., Woods, B., Royan, L., Davies, S., Butterworth, M., & Orrell, M. (2003). Efficacy of an evidence-based cognitive stimulation therapy programme for people with dementia. *British Journal of Psychiatry, 183,* 248–254.

p. 273, "Very early research with animals showed differences in the brains of rats...."
Volkmar, F. R., & Greenough, W. T. (1972). Rearing complexity affects branching of dendrites in the visual cortex of the rat. *Science, 176,* 1445–1447.

p. 274, "More recent research with animals has shown a role of new learning...."
Shors, T. J. (March, 2009). Saving new brain cells. *Scientific American, 300,* 47–54.

p. 277, "In a study published in the *New England Journal of Medicine*...."
Verghese, J., Lipton, R. B., Katz, M. J., Hall, C. B., Derby, C. A., Kuslansky, G., Ambrose, A. F., Sliwinski, M., & Buschke, H. (2003). Leisure activities and the risk of dementia in the elderly. *The New England Journal of Medicine, 348,* 2508–2516.

Chapter 14

p. 286, "Research on the effects of social engagement...."
Uchino, B. N. (2006). Social support and health: A review of physiological processes potentially underlying links to disease outcomes. *Journal of Behavioural Medicine, 29,* 377–387.

p. 287, "...small but growing scientific literature...."
Hertzog, C., Kramer, A. F., Wilson, R. S., & Lindenberger, U. (2009). Enrichment effects on adult cognitive development. *Psychological Science in the Public Interest, 9,* 1–65.

p. 287, "The general findings from these studies...."
Krueger, K. R., Wilson, R. S., Kamenetsky, J. M., Barnes, L. L., Bienias, J. L., & Bennett, D. (2009). Social engagement and cognitive function in old age. *Experimental Aging Research, 35,* 45–60.

p. 288, "A recent study from the University of Michigan...."
Ybarra, O., Burnstein, E., Winkielman, P., Keller, M. C., Manis, M., Chan, E., & Rodriguez, J. (2008). Mental exercising through simple socializing: Social interaction promotes general cognitive functioning. *Personality and Social Psychology Bulletin, 34,* 248–259.

p. 288, "There is accumulating evidence...."
Fratiglioni, L., Paillard-Borg, S., & Winblad, B. (2004). An active and socially integrated lifestyle in late life might protect against dementia. *Lancet Neurology, 3,* 343–353.

p. 292, "A link was recently identified...."
Bennett, D. A., Schneider, J. A., Tang, Y., Arnold, S. E., & Wilson, R. S. (2006). The effect of social networks on the relation between Alzheimer's disease pathology and level of cognitive function in old people: A longitudinal cohort study. *Lancet Neurology, 5,* 406–412.

Chapter 15

p. 303, "To the contrary, research has shown...."
Burach, O. R., & Lachman, M. E. (1996). The effects of list-making on recall in young and elderly adults. *Journal of Gerontology, 51B,* P226-P233.

p. 311, "In one well-known study...."
Nickerson, R. S., & Adams, J. J. (1979). Long-term memory for a common object. *Cognitive Psychology, 11,* 287–307.

p. 313, "Research has shown that individuals who are instructed to use this technique...."

Chasteen, A. L., Park, D. C., & Schwarz, N. (2001). Implementation intentions and facilitation of prospective memory. *Psychological Science, 12,* 457–461.

p. 313, "The levels-of-processing theory...."

Craik, F. I. M., & Lockhart, R. S. (1972). Levels of processing: A framework for memory research. *Journal of Verbal Learning & Verbal Behavior, 11,* 671–684.

p. 317, "Research shows that both are effective, so you can take your pick."

Karpicke, J. D., & Roediger III, H. L. (2008). The critical importance of retrieval for learning. *Science, 319,* 966–968.

p. 319, "...spelling words or times tables."

Landauer, T. K., & Bjork, R. A. (1978). Optimum rehearsal patterns and name learning. In M. M. Gruneberg, P. E. Morris, & R. N. Sykes (Eds.), *Practical aspects of memory* (pp. 625–632). London: Academic Press.

p. 319, "...serious memory problems like Alzheimer's disease...."

Camp, C. J., Bird, M. J., & Cherry, K. E. (2000). Retrieval strategies as a rehabilitation aid for cognitive loss in pathological aging. In R. D. Hill, L. Bäckman, & A. Stigsdoter-Neely (Eds.), *Cognitive rehabilitation in old age* (pp. 224–248). New York: Oxford.

Index

Note: *b* = boxed items

A

n-Acetylaspartate, 31
Acetylcholine, 31, 58, 140
Activities
  cognitive, recording, 295b–297b
  cognitively challenging, 262–263
  cognitively engaging, 274–275, 275b–277b
  of daily life, increasing fitness potential of,
    258b–259b
  instrumental activities of daily living or
    IADLs, 114, 116, 160–161
  leisure, 264–266, 265b, 289
  number of, cognitive engagement and,
    277–278
  personally meaningful, 181–182
  physical, 182
  for relaxation, 179–180
  that interact with other people, 182
  that provide social engagement, 284, 285b
Aerobic (endurance) exercise, 255, 256f
Age, as risk factor for MCI and dementia,
  91, 92
Age-associated memory decline or
  impairment, 20, 32, 33b
Age-consistent memory impairment, 20, 32
Age-related cognitive decline. *See* Cognition,
  age-related decline
Aging, normal
  brain changes and, 30–31
  brain size and, 57
  transition to dementia, 20
  vs. amnestic mild cognitive impairment,
    33–35, 35b
  vs. dementia, 4–5, 4b
  vs. mild cognitive impairment, 22–46,
    27, 80b
    objective memory changes, 25–30
    subjective memory changes, 23–25

"Aging in place," 197–198
Agnosia, 52
Agriculture Center for Nutrition Policy and
  Promotion, 234
Alcohol consumption, memory and, 37–38
Alleles, 95b
Alzheimer's Association
  dementia rates, 48, 48b
  diagnostic criteria for dementia, 49, 50b
  MCI due to Alzheimer's disease
    dementia, 83
Alzheimer's disease
  brain changes, 76
    pathological, 55–58
    social network size and, 292–293
  case vignette, 90b
  cognitive symptoms, 51b
  definition of, 52
  development
    bilingualism and, 270
    progression from MCI, 17, 77
  diagnosis
    criteria for, 19–20
    "possible," 52, 53b
    "probable," 52, 53b, 56b
    procedures for, 56–58
  early-onset or genetic, 54, 94
  fear of, 40
  historical background, 51
  as insidious disease, 52
  late-onset or sporadic, 54
  with Lewy body dementia, 71–72
  memory change and, 35
  prevalence, in men *vs.* women, 93
  as progressive disease, 52
  risk/risk factors, 54, 249
  symptoms
    behavioral, 54–55